Rekindling Your Spirit

*A Spiritual Journey into
Personal Change, Intimacy, and Sexuality*

Paul F. Singh, MA, LP
Psychologist, Cancer Survivor, Pastor

ISBN 1-933150-11-4

Cover design by Nick Ciske of Bethany Press. Illustrations by Scott Straw and Cheryl Smith.

About the Author

Paul F. Singh, MA, LP, has worked as a licensed psychologist specializing in marriage therapy, family therapy, and pastoral care counseling since 1989. As an adjunct professor, Singh teaches Biblical Counseling at Northwestern College in St. Paul, MN. Professor Singh integrates biblical faith and clinical counseling in a way that holistically addresses personal change, intimacy, and sexuality. He also offers a compelling blend of spiritual depth, clinical insight and personal experience in a monthly radio broadcast entitled, *The Biblical Counseling Hour with Paul Singh.*

Singh came to Christ through the ministry of the Navigators in 1979. He received a master of arts in biblical counseling from Grace Theological Seminary under Christian psychologists Dr. Larry Crabb and Dr. Dan Allender. His biblical teaching and counseling are significantly influenced by his mentor, Dr. Richard Averbeck, professor of Old Testament and Semitic Languages at Trinity Evangelical Divinity School and director of the Spiritual Formation Forum.

Singh has been a guest lecturer for the *Meet the Expert Series* at the Mayo Clinic. Singh designed an annual series called *Rekindling Your Hope: Living with New Passion, Giftedness and Purpose!* Paul offered holistic care (spirit, soul, and body) lectures to doctors, nurses, cancer patients, their families, and caregivers from the perspective of a psychologist, pastor and a cancer survivor.

Singh is the founder and president of the Institute of Biblical Education (IBE). IBE is committed to equipping the body of Christ in biblical counseling. Through his clinical training and research, private practice experience, and personal battle with cancer, Singh has pioneered an alternative approach to counseling and care giving in his Christ-centered *Twelve Stages of Your Spiritual Homecoming.* This comprehensive model is biblical, clear, and very practical.

Pastor Paul has been the teaching pastor of the "Rekindling Your Spirit" conferences and classes since 1996. Three conferences are held each year to release solid biblical truth and current clinical insight that lead to a lifestyle of authentic worship. Please visit us at www.rekindlingyourspirit.com for our current conference offerings. Pastor Paul also lectures from his new book, *Rekindling Your Spirit, A Spiritual Journey into Personal Change, Intimacy and Sexuality,* one evening per week in the Twin Cities. These classes are designed to equip people in areas of personal change, intimacy, and sexuality.

Paul loves to camp, fish, canoe, bike, and hike at Lake Superior's north shore with Beth, his wife of seventeen years, and their five children. They reside in Minneapolis, Minnesota.

Endorsements

It is with great enthusiasm that I commend to you the book *Rekindling Your Spirit, A Spiritual Journey into Personal Change, Intimacy, and Sexuality* by Paul Singh. Paul brings to his ministry a rare, but effective, blend of therapeutic excellence and theological depth.

When my wife, Bonnie, and I went to see Paul Singh for counseling and embarked on the twelve stages of spiritual homecoming, the journey led to grace, healing, repentance, and more grace.

Beyond his technical expertise, Paul brings a gentle touch that's full of grace. When we begin to honestly look at the core issues of our lives, marriages, and families, it can be quite frightening. I believe that God has given Paul a special gift, not only to touch those core issues, but then to bathe them in healing grace.

Above all, his ministry is marked by a quiet, but confident, expectation that God can touch and heal the wounded heart. I hope you will take this homecoming journey and through it come to life over and over again, as we did.

David Johnson
Senior Pastor, Church of the Open Door
Maple Grove, Minnesota

* * *

Paul Singh knows the Father Heart of God. He communicates fatherhood in his teaching, in his bearing as a pastor, and in his whole approach to healing and Christian formation. He also knows how to make the glories of Christian theology practical and accessible to people who are wounded by sin. Moreover, Paul is an encourager, a Barnabas, to both men and women who long to be more effective channels of Christ's love to others.

Valerie McIntyre
Author of *Sheep in Wolves' Clothing* (Baker Books, 1999)
Associate of Leanne Payne (Pastoral Care Ministries, 1992-2004)

Dedication

Beth Marie,
Your life is marked by sacrificial compassion and godly wisdom.
To know you is to experience life in the Spirit. You are truly a
woman of passion, giftedness, and purpose!

It is an honor to be married to you,
Paul

Table of Contents

Foreword

My wife and I have known Paul and Beth Singh for almost twenty years. We were part of their engagement process way back at Grace Theological Seminary where I was a full-time Old Testament professor in the 1980s and an intern in the Master of Counseling program. Paul was a student in the counseling program there as well. We became close friends. We both studied under Larry Crabb and Dan Allender in the field of counseling. I also had the privilege of teaching Old Testament studies to their counseling students, having already received a PhD in Old Testament and Ancient Near Eastern studies before embarking on the master's degree in counseling. Paul and I have journeyed together since that time. He calls me his mentor in counseling and biblical studies, and it is true that our relationship has had much to do with that. But we are also true friends and colleagues. And I have learned from Paul too.

I have experienced Paul as a courageously honest person, willing and often eager to deal with the struggles in his own life and soul. It has been a privilege to be involved with Paul all these years on this level. He has invited me into his heart and allowed me to be part of the work of God there, and this is no small thing. Along the way he has become a duly licensed and extremely gifted psychologist who practices what he counsels, teaches, and preaches. Many would give testimony to his effectiveness in personal and marriage counseling. His seminars and conferences have been a gift to the lives of people and, therefore, to the Kingdom of God.

Over the years we have also walked through the twelve stages of the journey into rekindling our spirits for personal change, intimacy, and sexuality that Paul writes about in this volume. This too is a gift to people and to the Kingdom of God. He cares very deeply about what happens in the lives of people and their marriages. His passion comes through in this book, as does his electrifying way of expressing himself. Paul is an artist with words as much as he is with drawings. His writing is literally and literarily filled with images. The word pictures are just as dynamic and full of impact as the illustrations that are heavily seeded throughout this book.

He uses arrows, knives, fire, and idolatrous (Baal) worship, among other images, to speak in penetrating ways about the realities that we experience as fallen people living in a fallen world with other fallen people, determined to make our way through the maze of life intact. He writes about what we do in our body, soul, and spirit to handle what we face. He knows about these things from looking deeply into Scripture, his own life, and the lives of others. There is no lack of personal experience or professional acumen and realism. This is a book about real things in the lives of real people, and he pulls no punches. This is a "no holds barred" jump into everyday reality. It is not just a reality show, but instead a show of reality.

This book, however, does not just take us into the pain of reality, but through that pain into the reality of the God who is with us in the midst of it all and ready, willing, and able to help and transform us through it, whether we know it or not. There is divine help right in the midst of the pain that we feel and that others feel because of us. It is the Father's willful intention to transform us into the image of Jesus His Son through the empowerment of the Holy Spirit:

> . . . *the Spirit* helps us in our weakness. We do not know what we ought to pray for, but **the Spirit** himself intercedes for us with groans that words cannot express. And he who searches our hearts knows the mind of **the Spirit**, because **the Spirit** intercedes for the saints in accordance with **God's** will. And we know that in all things **God** works for the good of those who love him, who have been called according to his purpose. For those **God** foreknew he also predestined to be conformed to the likeness of **his Son**, that he might be the firstborn among many brothers.
>
> (Romans 8:26-29, NIV, emphasis added).

This is what the Father, Son, and Spirit are all about, as three in one. It is a Trinitarian work of God in our lives, and it is fully available to us right now where we are. A big part of this book is about how to take this divine intent and transforming power into our lives right here and now.

So this book is about us as individuals and about God. It is also about our relationships with one another. Paul has brought all three together in a very helpful way. We cannot deal with our own selves well without God's transforming work in our lives, and our relationships with others depend on this work of God between us too. God has not designed us to live alone, but in relationship with other people. And the most core of all human relationships is the man and woman marriage bond (Genesis 2:18-25). God designed it as the first and foremost human relational institution. There is no substitute for it. A good part of this book is about taking on the challenges of this relationship in our fallen condition—the personal, relational, and sexual challenges. There are joys untold available in this man and woman bond, and Paul Singh does his best to tell about how to go after them. He is worth listening to. May the Lord bless you as you embark on the journey with him.

Richard E. Averbeck, PhD, LPC
Professor of Old Testament and Semitic Languages,
Trinity Evangelical Divinity School
        and
Director, Spiritual Formation Forum
The Eve before Crucifixion Day, April 13, 2006

Prelude to a Journey
In Search of Passion, Giftedness, and Purpose

This is a guidebook to love and intimacy. It will change your relationship with God and will change your relationships with others, especially those closest to you.

This is uncensored—a book for adults, not for children or for youth groups. It includes material your parents and teachers never taught you about human relationships, including awesome, erotic, passionate, holy sexuality.

This journey is a spiritual homecoming, a return to our Source. It is the greatest adventure of life. Indeed, it is life itself. You are an adventurer and this is your guidebook. The terrain may be difficult—there are falling rocks, steep grades, and dangerous waters ahead. But I think you are cut out for it. In fact, you were made for this journey!

Peace comes in finding our spiritual Father, but healing—transformation—comes in experiencing our Abba, our daddy. This is the name for God that Jesus cried out from the Cross. Abba implies an intimacy and closeness, a deep and trusting love, a safety and security. That intimacy with God is what empowers you to live in intimacy with others; it empowers you to live with passion, giftedness, and purpose.

How do we go there? Most of us spend all of our time on what is visible and evident—behaviors, habits, or relationships that are really just the tip of the iceberg. This journey goes below the surface, into the bone-chilling water to the greater mass below. The healing is in pressing through the pain that lies there, pressing through the emptiness and weaknesses of your spirit, to the place of your restoration, to the person you are meant to be.

The first leg of the journey is a trek across the visible part of the iceberg: grappling with your pain, with the disappointments and hurts you have experienced from others (betrayals), and looking at how your experiences have formed who you are, how they affect your reactions to life—for good or for ill. The greatest part of the journey is deep-sea diving below the waterline of the iceberg—an exploration of how you have betrayed others, how you betray yourself and, finally, how you betray God.

As with any great adventure, bring a journal. This journey is broken into twelve stages. At the end of each stage is an assignment to help you process and carry out what you've read. Pace yourself. Take time to reflect thoroughly on each stage. That will make the difference between you having an adventure or just sitting in the car at the trailhead reading about one.

And, as with the best adventures, bring some other travelers. This journey is not one to take alone. Throughout the book I will refer to an "accountability person" or your "small group" or "community." This spiritual homecoming is an intense, sometimes perilous, trip. God created us for community—to spot one another on a dangerous climb, to administer first aid, to give a victory shout when we've overcome an obstacle. God's design is for us to function together—to embrace, to listen, and to renew one another. We each need a group that will not focus only on our pain and victimization, but also on forgiveness, cleansing, healing, and the gifts of the Spirit in our lives. If you do not have such a group, start one! Use this book as your starting point.

If you are married, this journey will bring profound shifts in your sexuality and your relationship with your spouse. To be filled and empowered by God is to awaken to the mystery of authentic intimacy. To discover how to offer this to your spouse is to share in the mystery of passion!

If you are not married, this journey is for you as well. It will give you insight into how men and women need and complement each other outside of marriage in friendships and family relationships. If you plan to marry one day, it will pave the way for starting your marriage on a tender, strong foundation for healthy relating and for passionate intimacy.

Are you ready? Here is the trailhead! Take to the path! Instructions for the first climb follow in Stage One.

Praying for you and journeying with you,

Paul Singh

STAGE ONE: Defining the Journey
Recognizing the Emptiness in Your Human Spirit

In every human spirit is the need to understand and to experience a sense of belonging. A sense of belonging is to feel, in the depths of your being, intimately loved and regarded with honor and dignity.

When sense of belonging is set into a person, a sense of being develops as well. Sense of being is the ability to know and experience who you really are, to not define yourself by what others think of you. A sense of being enables you to live and laugh at life. With a healthy sense of being, you feel loved, strong, and peaceful at your core.

The road to sense of belonging and sense of being leads to a filling of your emptiness, an empowering of your spirit. That fullness and strength ignites your passion, releases your giftedness, and reveals purpose to you.

However, a lack of sense of belonging and being produces a deep ache for something more. Picture an iceberg. The visible iceberg above the water is only a small, evident part of a much greater mass below the surface. Thus, the common phrase "it's just the tip of the iceberg" when there is much more to a situation than it appears.

In the following illustration, the tip of the iceberg represents your human body—the visible part of you. The bigger heart below the waterline represents your human soul; the smaller heart represents your human spirit.

Any struggle that happens in your outer person starts with struggles in your inner person. And each affects the other. We easily consider the body and tangible elements of life because our outer selves are easily seen. In fact, we often look for solutions only in the external.

"If I could lose twenty pounds and really keep it off, it would make all of the difference." Or, "If I could win that promotion, things would really fall into place for me." Or, "Why should I put up with her nagging when everything I want in a woman is right here on this screen?" But the actions we carry out in body have their origin in the inner person—the spirit, where we hold our desires, and the soul, where we think and feel and choose.

A person who compulsively overeats is trying to fill an emptiness that is not in the stomach but in his or her aching spirit. The food addiction in the physical body does not fill the real emptiness; it only provides a momentary satisfaction and momentary distraction from the true issue.

The same is the case for someone who spends all of his or her time at the office, at the expense of family and relationships, often at the expense of rest and exercise and good nutrition as well. He or she may be vying for some recognition, or the next promotion, or a few thousand dollars more that would "make things fall into place." The overworking doesn't fill the emptiness; it only provides a momentary sense of worth and momentary busyness to distract from the real problem.

Likewise, the desire to view sexually stimulating material represents an ache to be genuinely loved and held in true, authentic intimacy—not the counterfeit, anonymous, voyeur experience. That false intimacy only provides momentary satisfaction and momentary distraction from the real need.

In fact, in each of these scenarios, the false remedy creates a greater ache and emptiness, a greater demand that we usually try to fill with more of what is false, creating a greater ache. With the greater ache brews anger—an anger of revenge that demands: Who can I find to blame for this? In emptiness and anger, more of the false remedy is applied, increasing the ache again. Do you see the makings of addiction? Addiction can happen on any front. It doesn't have to be alcoholism or crack addiction or nymphomania. It can be any "socially acceptable" activity that ends up pushing away life and keeping us from addressing fundamental needs within.

For the purposes of this book, I will call anything that you do that no longer feels like a choice to you, addiction. It could be overeating or under-eating, it could be pornography or masturbation, it could be smoking seven cigarettes a day or drinking seven colas a day. I want to shift your paradigm of addiction to help you to realize that anything you use to fill the emptiness within you, other than what was meant to fill it, is keeping you from becoming whole, keeping you from being satisfied, keeping you weak, not making you strong. Perhaps keeping you trapped in addiction.

This doesn't happen only in our "habits"; it happens in our relationships as well. Sometimes we try to fill our emptiness with a person, with the need to be needed. We crave unconditional love, genuine acceptance, and true intimacy, and don't know where to find it. But we do know how to become indispensable to someone else, to solve all of their problems, to wear ourselves out on their behalf. And to take pleasure in playing the martyr—living in self-pity that all we do is never fully acknowledged or appreciated. Our apparent self-sacrifice doesn't fill the craving. It only provides momentary satisfaction and momentary distraction from the real need. For the purposes of this book, I will call this co-addiction. Co-addiction is an addiction to a person—often, to another addict. Co-addiction is another word for co-dependency.

Defining the Emptiness
A lack of sense of belonging and being may show itself in two ways of relating. I'll call them a chameleon or a king cobra.

A chameleon changes who he or she is according to circumstances. In order to answer the question, "Who am I?" a chameleon asks, "Who do people want me to be?" If you exhibit a chameleon relational style, you struggle with setting healthy boundaries in your life. That troubled thinking is driven by persistent pain regarding a sense of belonging and being.

On the other hand, a king cobra believes he or she is really the king of the jungle. He or she feeds on other snakes and keeps others away from his or her territory through fear. A king cobra doesn't care what others think and is not concerned about a lack of being because it seems an unproductive waste of time. The king cobra, however, has boundless needs. He or she loves to be around chameleons, who need to be needed. To the king cobra, this is a marriage made in heaven. To the chameleon, it is an exhausting nightmare. Tragically, king cobras eventually consume and push away the very ones who serve them.

King cobras are usually so driven that they are not able to slow down and identify the core spiritual pain that fuels their task-oriented lifestyle (and, as mentioned, usually do not think it is important to do so). For this type of person, to take a break is laziness. If others do so, they risk the king cobra's wrath.

4

You saw in the iceberg diagram that your soul is your inner self, below the waterline, invisible. Your mind, emotions, and will are there—your thinking, feeling, and choosing. At the core of your soul is your spirit, the essence of you, the place your desires reside, the place in which you are capable of connecting with God.

The emptiness we experience is an emptiness in the spirit—the very core of us. A gaping hole was torn there when humanity disconnected from God. An ancient story that you may know is the first stop on our journey[1]:

Hole in Your Human Spirit

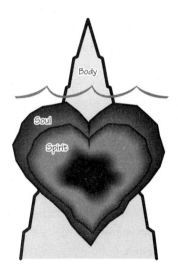

Regardless of your background,
something is missing...

It is leaving
a hole in your spirit.

The Perfect Honeymoon

There was a time when humanity was perfectly filled by God's love and perfectly empowered by God's strength. Man and Woman experienced being perfectly loved and perfectly loved each other. It was a world with no pain, no betrayal. Man and Woman had a whole, unbroken sense of belonging to God and each other. They knew perfect sense of being—perfectly loved at the core, perfectly strong at the core, and perfectly peaceful at the core.

Read the ancient story that still greatly affects your life today:

The serpent was clever, more clever than any wild animal GOD had made. He spoke to the Woman: "Do I understand that God told you not to eat from any tree in the garden?"

The Woman said to the serpent, "Not at all. We can eat from the trees in the garden. It's only about the tree in the middle of the garden that God said, 'Don't eat from it; don't even touch it or you'll die.'"

The serpent told the Woman, "You won't die. God knows that the moment you eat from that tree, you'll see what's really going on. You'll be just like God, knowing everything, ranging all the way from good to evil."

(Genesis 3:1–5, MSG)

The Tragic Divorce

And she bought it. So did her man. They ate fruit from the tree. And they could see what was really going on—the serpent was right in that. They could see their betrayal, they could see their shame, they could feel fear, they could plan deceit. It was indeed a whole new world. Paradise lost. In the midst of the new revelation, they heard the real Voice of Conviction—God was calling to them in garden.

GOD called to the Man: "Where are you?"

He said, "I heard you in the garden and I was afraid because I was naked. And I hid."

GOD said, "Who told you you were naked? Did you eat from that tree I told you not to eat from?"

The Man said, "The Woman you gave me as a companion, she gave me fruit from the tree, and, yes, I ate it."

GOD said to the Woman, "What is this that you've done?"

"The serpent seduced me," she said, "and I ate."
(Genesis 3:9–13, MSG)

Do you notice how everyone found someone to blame? God was angry. He cursed the serpent to ever crawl on its belly and be an enemy to humanity; He cursed the woman to have pain in childbirth; He cursed the man to have pain in his toil; and He cursed humanity with death. Man and Woman would age and die. But God loved them; He clothed their nakedness and sent them away from the garden so they could not eat from the Tree of Life, as well, and remain in their broken state forever.

In God's tender love and strength and utter holiness, He gave humankind the gift of freedom to choose whether to stay in fellowship with Him through obedience or to separate from Him by choosing a different way.

Man and Woman were filled with sadness—their sense of belonging and being was ripped from them, leaving a hole in their spirits, a sense of emptiness and weakness—a lack of empowerment in the human spirit. Intimacy was lost, the fire of passion was extinguished, and peace was replaced by fear and pain. Separated from God, humankind was no longer constantly filled with God's love. The joy of life departed, and the dread of living with the enemy became the painful reality.

All of humanity has inherited this relationship that was broken in the garden—for all generations, but not for all time. True inner healing of your spirit comes from receiving the tender, intimate love and strength of God through new relationship with Him. A relationship that God readily grants when we ask Him, and an intimacy and filling with love that He restores when we pilgrimage home.

This relationship with God can start in an instant—you may have a relationship with God already. But the journey, this spiritual homecoming, is not only about knowing Him, but about learning how to allow Him to fill you, to heal you, to truly bring you into the person He created you to be. To find God is to find your sense of belonging and being and to experience God.

Restoring Sense of Belonging and Being

God's love is infinite, of limitless dimension. I describe three facets of it that are instrumental to your spiritual homecoming:

- *Tenderness of love allows you to feel safe, desired, and valued for who you are and not for what you can do.*
- *Strength of love emboldens you to live out your passion, your giftedness, and your purpose.*
- *Peace of love is the weaving of the two; it enables you to live without fear and anxiety.*

God's tenderness of love filling your heart is what restores your sense of belonging and creates a foundation to receive His strength of love; strength of love is what restores your sense of being.

God's design was to impart these to you first through your parents and then through Him. Your first experience with tenderness of love was intended to be in the womb of your mother and, later, in the embrace of your mother's arms and your father's arms. This tenderness of love provides the nurture and security you need to grow and know that you have value. Your first experience with strength of love was intended to be from your father—providing the protection and affirmation to enable you to confidently do all that you were created to do. When these are present, they weave together to create a profound sense of peace and intimacy in the spirit of a child.

The tenderness of a mother and the strength of a father invite a child's spirit to cry out for the ultimate tenderness and strength: God's peace of love. When this happens, whether you are a child or an adult, when you cry out to God to receive from Him, He fills you with His tenderness of love and strength of love, filling your emptiness and empowering your spirit.

Clinically, if a child does not bond with his or her mother in the womb, or with both mother and father in the first three years of life, an attachment disorder occurs. If you have an attachment disorder with a parent, you will have pain in your spirit regarding sense of belonging—you will feel rejection, inadequacy, and anxiety deep within you.

As a psychologist and pastor, I have seen that the biggest threat to well-being in the soul is the spirit of fear. When you lack love and strength in the core of your being, a spirit of fear controls you. Then, when you are disappointed or relationally hurt, your natural, fearful, response is "fight or flight"—self-protection. Some forms of self-protection are healthy; however, self-protection that is driven by fear will flood your spirit, soul, and, in some cases, your body with paralysis. The spirit of fear thrives in an environment of emptiness and disempowerment. Fear wants to devour your human spirit. Only the love of God can release you from the spirit of fear.

The Spirit of Fear

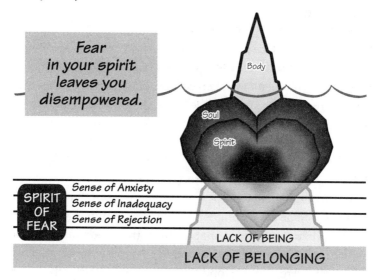

9

None of us have experienced perfect love from our parents or from others in our lives; each of us must address the resulting pain of life and the gaping hole within us, however great or small. The journey of life is to go to the place we can release our pain and fear in order to be filled and strengthened. That empowers us to not only be loved but also to love others, to live out the rich lives of passion, giftedness, and purpose for which we were intended.

Identifying the Pain

You must acknowledge the emptiness inside of you before God can fill you. Emptiness that is so familiar, it seems normal. Doesn't everyone live this way—with an indefinable ache? A quiet (or not-so-quiet) dissatisfaction?

How have you experienced your emptiness so far? Have you realized that when you try to fill it, it becomes greater, more unwieldy, not less? Have you noticed that emptiness in your spirit translates to rage in your soul? Rage that is an anger of revenge. A desire to betray those who have betrayed you. Are you so angry about your life that you resort to blaming others, yourself, or God for why life does not work?

Those who are most ready for this journey are those who are tired of "normal" *and* tired of revenge. Tired of all of the pursuits that turn out to be momentary satisfaction and momentary distraction from the real need. Tired of the increasing sense of emptiness that follows, that disempowers the will—renders it weak and impotent—in the inner person and leaves the outer person powerless in its struggle.

When you are filled and empowered in your spirit, the change in your inner person also changes how you live in your outer person. You can experience transformation from the inside out! Do you want it? Or are you more comfortable keeping your momentary satisfactions? Are you too fond of the gratification that the anger of revenge gives?

The reason it is hard to let go is that your pain is legitimate. The betrayals in your life are real—the way others have let you down or hurt you or violated you. In one sense, you are justified to be angry. In fact, betrayal is the root of all anger, and anger is behind all addictions and co-addictions. But a time does come when enough is enough. Emptiness begets emptiness, and anger begets anger, and you do not want to live the endless cycle of it anymore. That determination is your fuel for the journey of your spiritual homecoming.

The Soul's Self-Protection Plan

Most psychology focuses on the Soul, your "thinker, feeler, and chooser." From our thinking flow our images of others, ourselves, and God. From our feelings, whether we can identify them or not, flows a sense of well-being (or lack of it). From our choices, our goals and strategies are evident. Some of us have the goal to avoid pain at all costs and are more interested in a life of self-protection than a life of love. To love is to risk betrayal, and therefore, pain. When betrayal damages your spirit, your natural reaction is to fear and to deflect the pain with some type of anger.

All of these functions of the soul affect outward behavior. If, in your spirit, you have unresolved relational pain, you may not feel it. It may be numb—frozen. To love risks thawing those emotional nerve endings, causing you to reexperience the pain. Because of this, many people avoid relational intimacy. They substitute it with false intimacy, which falsely promises safety.

For example, making love to a pornographic image does not carry the risk of disappointment that can occur when two real people make love. If a man is committed in his thinking not to feel pain again, he will use whatever form of relational protection it takes to avoid such pain.

In another example, a woman struggling with anorexia nervosa will have a self-image that she is fat. This often comes from being betrayed by someone close to her who (intentionally or unintentionally) judged her by her weight at one point in her life.

Denying herself food becomes her false security in this instance—vowing that no one will ever judge her negatively because of her weight again.

Fear Forges a False Self

The way you relate to other people develops over time into a true self or a false self in your soul. Love forms the true self—the self filled with God's love and connected to who you were created to be in your passion, giftedness, and purpose. However, the spirit of fear forges a false self—the self that is disconnected, self-protective, and relates out of unresolved pain. The false self is you operating out of your core emptiness and disempowerment, out of the pain of lack of sense of belonging and sense of being.

The false self relates to others in numerous ways. In graduate school, Dr. Dan Allender coined six specific styles that men and women use. Most people have a primary relational style and a secondary relational style—someone may be a tough boy or tough girl "king cobra" at work but a totally checked-out and helpless little boy or little girl adult at home. All of these styles are your soul's attempt at self-protection.

Six Relational Styles of Men and Women[2]

The little boy or little girl adult and the tough boy or tough girl are on opposite ends of the spectrum. The other styles fall somewhere in between.

Little Boy or Little Girl

Little boy and little girl adults are usually victims in the midst of crisis, utterly dependent on others, weak and unable to do what a situation requires. Unwilling to accomplish their own goals, they manipulate others to be their strength. They show gratitude but not tenderness and have contempt for those who show them pity. Their relationships are highly enmeshed to the point that no one believes they could survive on their own. Little boy and little girl adults are full of self-contempt for their own weaknesses.

Good Boy or Good Girl

Good boys and good girls are unwilling to be strong to help themselves but instead give their strength to others in order to please them. Other people find them kind and self-sacrificing. Good boys and good girls define love as "being needed" and think others will love them for their acts of service. Their goal is to keep relationships nice, pleasant, safe, and superficial. They avoid conflict and rejection, authenticity and true intimacy. They fear that if people really knew them, their falseness would be found out. They only give in a relationship in order to garner attention, gratitude, friendship, or love.

Religious Boy or Religious Girl*

Religious boys and religious girls are driven by the law, duty, and an intellectual concept of God. They use their strength to "be good"—to follow the rules, be moral and righteous, and fix any defects in themselves or others. In the name of "faith," they run from deep issues of the heart: guilt, shame, fear, and anger. They are harsh and demanding with others, and feel contempt for those who fail to strive as they do. They are more concerned about right doctrine than about loving others. They earn love by good deeds rather than unconditionally offering love or receiving it.

Party Boy or Party Girl

Party boys and party girls want to avoid responsibility, commitment, and dealing with pain—their own or that of others. They just want to have a good time. Relationally, they are extremely superficial. To become vulnerable and admit having needs feels dangerous and even life-threatening. They have difficulty sustaining long-term relationships that require depth and intimacy. In fact, they escape intimacy by inviting others to join in "just having a good time." They refuse authentic tenderness and strength.

---

* The religious boy/girl is a new relational style that has been adapted from Dr. Dan Allender's original work.

Driven Boy or Driven Girl

Driven boys and driven girls exude power, control, and competence. They are task-oriented and use strength to achieve, succeed, and accomplish. All they really want is admiration—forget tenderness! They may consider feelings and relationships a nuisance and offer others practical advice or instruction rather than empathy or intimacy. They live in a whirl of perpetual busyness and refuse to take the time to feel or reflect. Their relentless pursuit of competing and completing isolates them from others.

Tough Boy or Tough Girl

Tough boys and tough girls are domineering and controlling. They are demanding in relationships, business-like, rarely tender. They are distrusting because of past experiences, and therefore unwilling to show feelings—or to feel at all. They keep control in their lives by utter self-sufficiency—seldom asking a favor or accepting help. They control relationships and work situations with anger and intimidation. They blame others when things go wrong, to the point of verbal or physical abuse, and have only contempt for the people they control.

Do you see yourself in one of these relational styles? Your parents? Your children? What traits of relating have been passed on to you, and what traits are you passing on?

Men and Women: Empty and Disempowered

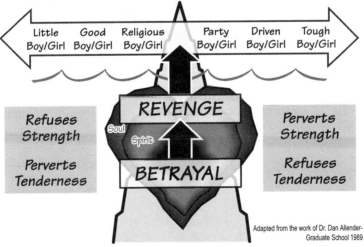

Adapted from the work of Dr. Dan Allender-
Graduate School 1989

Each style of the false self is a product of anger in the soul. Anger is a legitimate emotion—when used properly, it can keep

boundaries and relationships healthy. When used improperly, it worsens the pain in the spirit and destroys relationships.

> *Do not hate your brother in your heart. Rebuke your neighbor frankly so you will not share in his guilt. Do not seek revenge or bear a grudge against one of your people, but love your neighbor as yourself. I am the* LORD.

> (*Leviticus 19:17-18,* NIV)

Healthy anger comes out in the form of gracious confrontation. It identifies the truth of a painful situation and confronts the other person with tender honesty, respect, and God-given mercy and grace. However, many times we use anger inappropriately to strike back at others. Some people do this passively, afraid to express anger because they have been taught that it is inappropriate. This only causes them more anger, which shows itself through lying, undermining, and backstabbing. Others express anger aggressively. They blow up, spew foul words, and sometimes lash out physically—throwing objects or assaulting people or things.

When your spirit is betrayed and you deflect your pain with anger, confusion disempowers your thinking. That leads to a lack of well-being that can manifest itself in anxiety, depression, despair, or simply feeling lifeless and "checked out." All of these are aspects of the false self.

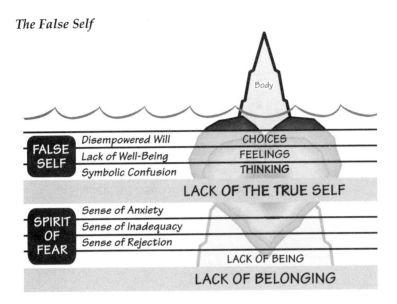

FALSE SELF	Disempowered Will	CHOICES
	Lack of Well-Being	FEELINGS
	Symbolic Confusion	THINKING

LACK OF THE TRUE SELF

SPIRIT OF FEAR	Sense of Anxiety	
	Sense of Inadequacy	
	Sense of Rejection	
		LACK OF BEING

LACK OF BELONGING

People who have unresolved betrayal in their spirits not only struggle with a lack of true self, but ultimately with a lack of purpose. When you have a lack of well-being, your will becomes disabled by helplessness and hopelessness and you feel weak and ineffective—disempowered. These are the central dynamics in the soul that cause people to lose hope and end up with a life of addictions and/or co-addictions for a very long, or, sometimes tragically short, life journey.

When you begin to break your addictions or co-addictions, the anger in your soul will start to surface. Everyone who has experienced betrayal deflects his or her betrayal pain in the spirit with anger in the soul. If you are alive, you have experienced some level of pain and some level of anger. Those people who humble themselves and are honest are the people who change.

Numbing the Pain with Addiction
If you struggle with addiction or co-addiction, you use addictions (objects) and co-addictions (people) to keep yourself numb to the pain. In the 1990 movie *Awakenings,* based on a true story, a ward of patients left catatonic for decades by encephalitis were given an experimental drug that "awakened" them. The patients all

began to come alive with passion! It is a perfect picture of how our addictions and co-addictions keep us numb and internally dead.

A Life of Idolatry

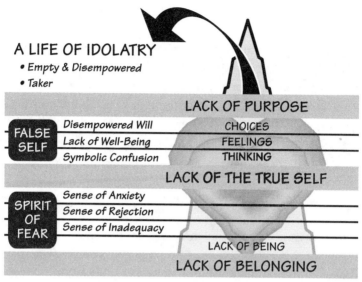

With an addiction/co-addiction you constantly do two things:
1. Disconnect from a painful reality in your spirit and soul.
2. Reconnect to a pleasurable unreality in your body.

Ask yourself whether you are using the relief of addiction to disconnect from your pain:
- Do you overeat and it no longer feels like a choice? And do you keep gaining weight? (Food Addiction)
- Do you struggle with pornography, masturbation, or illicit sex? (Sexual Addiction)
- Do you work more than fifty hours per week at the expense of building relationships with your spouse and children? (Work Addiction)
- Are schedules, tasks, appearances, and performance more important to you than relationships? (Perfectionism)
- Do you drink, smoke, or use recreational drugs, and it no longer feels like a choice? (Substance Addiction)

- Do you surf the Internet, hunt, fish, garden, or watch TV at the expense of your family relationships? (Hobby Addiction)

Also ask yourself whether you are using the relief of co-addictions to disconnect from your pain:
- Are you unable to say "No" to certain people?
- Are you in controlling relationships?
- Are you emotionally dependent on someone?
- Are you in an enmeshed relationship, where you don't know where the other person leaves off and you begin?
- Do you have blurred boundaries in your relationships?
- Are you exhausted from playing the role of the "martyr"?
- Do you try to rescue people from feeling their pain?

If you run from addressing these issues, the spirit of fear will continue to drive your thoughts, feelings, and choices. The twins of fear—emptiness and disempowerment—will continue to foster your false self. And your body will keep settling for an escape to a false intimacy when it craves authenticity.

Sexual Addiction
Many of the men I counsel struggle with the sexual addiction of pornography and masturbation. After a client hits bottom and is willing to talk about it, he starts to see that having sex with himself (masturbation) is self-centered and lonely and does not fill his human spirit at the core. His core emptiness is so painful that he is desperate to do something. But to disconnect from the painful reality and run to sex, work, sports, computers, hunting, or other activities to mask his pain is cowardly.

Food Addiction
Many clients also struggle with addictive eating disorders. The food addiction of overeating is common to both genders. With a food addiction, the more you overeat, the emptier you feel, since food will never meet the real need in your spirit. The deeper level of emptiness intensifies the helplessness and hopelessness in the

spirit, so the addict wants even more to disconnect from the pain in the inner person, reconnecting to a temporary pleasure in the outer person—overeating. However, overeating leaves the addict ashamed of his or her body and, therefore, craving more food to compensate for the guilt and shame in the spirit.

Co-Addiction

The struggle for co-addicts is similar. The co-addict sees being needed as a way to fill him or herself up. An addict is a good target for a co-addict, because the addict always has a need. The co-addict's giving is not out of love (which is other-centered), but out of need to receive (which is self-centered). When the addict does not show appreciation or affirmation, the co-addict's rage exposes his or her agenda.

Both the addict and the co-addict live in perpetual emptiness and disempowerment. They never reach their destinations in life.

An Addict	A Co-Addict
✔ Is empty	✔ Is empty
✔ Always has a need	✔ Needs to be needed
✔ Feels great about him or herself to the point of selfishness and disregard for others (ego-maniac)	✔ Feels bad about him or herself (self-hatred)
✔ Feels entitled to everything	✔ Feels undeserving of everything
✔ Is disempowered	✔ Is disempowered
✔ Struggles with anger and denial	✔ Struggles with anxiety and depression
✔ Lives in the pleasure of the moment; returns to the life of the living dead	✔ Lives in the past or the future
✔ Is enamored with him or herself (classic narcissism)	✔ Is self-deprecating (reverse narcissism)

Addicts and co-addicts are merely medicating the pain of betrayal in their spirits and the anger of revenge in their souls. But addiction and co-addiction are just blockades to what they really want and need: to be filled and empowered.

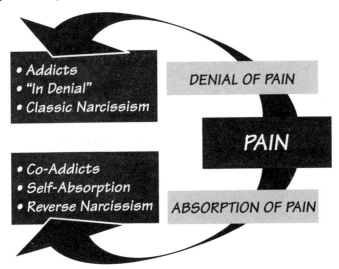

- Addicts
- "In Denial"
- Classic Narcissism

DENIAL OF PAIN

PAIN

- Co-Addicts
- Self-Absorption
- Reverse Narcissism

ABSORPTION OF PAIN

There is life beyond addiction and co-addiction. The way to experience the mystery of passion, giftedness, and purpose can be found as you enter into the hole within your spirit. The One who awaits you longs to fill and empower you with all He has to offer. This journey back home, into His arms, is the path to experiencing the authentic love of God and the empowerment of His strength.

The journey is painful and requires courage, yet it is the only way to true recovery and healing within the human spirit. God's tenderness of love can restore your sense of belonging and being as you discover how to let Him fill your emptiness. His strength of love can empower you, casting out the twins of fear—emptiness and disempowerment—and releasing your passion, giftedness, and purpose.

God's love can restore your sense of being, which will redefine your sense of doing. Imagine what it would it be like to feel loved, strong, and peaceful at your core—to be free of addictions and co-addictions. Out of that restoration naturally flows your love for God and others.

You likely have done above-the-waterline "body work"; some of you have even taken the time to do "soul work"—identifying how you think, feel, and make choices in life. My invitation to you is to do the "spirit work," identifying the emptiness and disempowerment in your spirit and facing the betrayals in your life that have led to your patterns of revenge and false relief.

Your Father God is waiting for you, ready to hold you in tenderness of love, strength of love, and peace of love, more than you have ever known or experienced! The choice to take this journey is yours alone.

Personal Journaling and Small Group Questions
Spiritual Homecoming Assignment One

Personal Journaling Questions

1. List the betrayals you have experienced in life. Be complete—list 50 to 100.
2. List the issues that have given you the most anger or desire for revenge in life. Again, be complete—list everything.
3. List the top 12 things you do that no longer feel like a choice (addictions).
4. List the top 12 people to whom you cannot say no (co-addictions).
5. Do you feel you have a sense of belonging and sense of being? Or do you have pain in these areas?
6. At work, is your relational style that of the chameleon or the king cobra?
7. At home, is your relational style that of the chameleon or the king cobra?

Small Group Questions

1. What… are the key truths that stood out to you in this stage?
2. Why… do you need to know these truths?
3. How… do you apply these truths to your life?
4. Your pain… What pain does this stage reveal in your life?
5. Your sin… What are you doing with your pain?
6. Repentance… What do you need to do differently?
7. Prayer… What do you need to ask God for help with?

STAGE TWO: Telling Your Story
Making Sense of Your Pain and Its Impact

How have you been betrayed on this journey of life? What is your pain? Humanity's deepest longing is for intimacy. When your longings, hungers, and thirsts are not met, you feel pain.

Three Levels of Desire

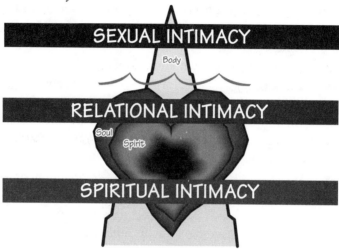

Have you longed for sexual intimacy? Relational intimacy? Spiritual intimacy? What pain have you experienced in those realms?

Betrayal Number One

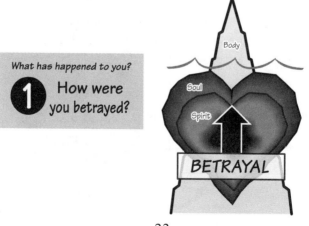

Picture an emotional "onion" of pain. The outer layers are the pain you've experienced from others, and the middle layers are the pain you've experienced from your parents. The core of the onion is your emptiness and disempowerment—your pain of being disconnected from God. To go to that core pain, you start by facing the outer layers, your experiences of betrayal.

There are seven categories of painful experiences in life spawned by humankind's ancient betrayal of God in the Garden of Eden. These are seven arrows of betrayal that continue to pierce the heart of humankind:

- Arrow of Neglect—emotional or physical abandonment.
- Arrow of Emotional Betrayal—violent emotions targeted at you or affecting you.
- Arrow of Physical Betrayal—violent physical contact.
- Arrow of Sexual Betrayal—touches, looks, or attitudes that are inappropriately sexual.
- Arrow of Psychological Betrayal—humiliation or intimidation that causes you mental anguish.
- Arrow of Church Betrayal—behaviors, expectations, or teachings that wrongly use the authority of the church to control or harm you.
- Arrow of Spiritual Betrayal—behaviors, expectations, or teachings from someone in spiritual authority over you that wrongly control or harm you.

What Is Your Pain?

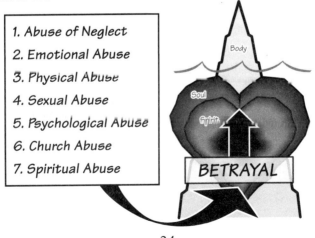

1. Abuse of Neglect
2. Emotional Abuse
3. Physical Abuse
4. Sexual Abuse
5. Psychological Abuse
6. Church Abuse
7. Spiritual Abuse

Body

Soul

Spirit

BETRAYAL

The Effects of Betrayal

The pain you have experienced in life has profound repercussions in your human spirit. We all want a sense of belonging and being in our spirits, but, in our pain, we experience the opposite of what we want—rejection, inadequacy, anxiety, shame.

Whether you have experienced sexual abuse, physical abuse, or other betrayal, the impact is the same on your spirit. At the moment of betrayal, we are filled with a horrible shame. We believe we have become defective and have to hide it from everyone. In fact, we might rather die than let someone look into the most humiliated parts of who we are or what we have done.

Shame is the feast upon which the twins of fear—emptiness and disempowerment—thrive in your spirit. The more you hide your shame, the more fodder for their feast. Emptiness and disempowerment want to block three levels of intimacy forever in your life: relational intimacy with others, sexual intimacy with your spouse, and spiritual intimacy with God.

Shame and fear keep you alone and hiding, preventing you from experiencing the levels of intimacy for which you long. Whether you are single or married, God wants to restore the gift of intimacy to you. Your courageous first step toward His restoration is acknowledging the shame you bear from the arrows of betrayal. At the end of this stage are homework assignments that will help you do this.

In order to experience release from your shame, it is important to name the things that have haunted you your whole life. It is helpful to do this with someone else; find someone to whom you can talk about your shame, someone you trust. Go before God together and pray through the betrayals and resulting shame you have experienced. Don't let shame keep you alone and hiding. Let that person support you as you admit to him or her, and to God, the shame you bear.

When you have identified the betrayals of others in your life, the outer layers of the onion, the next layer is the pain from your family—your parents or those who raised you, and siblings. The purpose of looking at this pain is not to blame your parents; it is simply to understand the source of your pain and how it influences your adult choices—and adult mistakes (about which you are probably angry).

Every person needs the tenderness of love that flows from a mother and the strength of love that flows from a father. If you experienced one, or many, of the arrows of betrayal in your family, you lack the internal peace that comes from knowing you are loved—you lack a complete sense of belonging and a sense of being. As children, we develop our images of God based on our relationships with our parents. So, understanding what kind of home you came from can help you understand your image of God and your core pain as an adult. What was your home like growing up?

The ideal environment is a home of tenderness and strength, one in which parents are physically, emotionally, and spiritually present. Love is the basis for their discipline and guides their morals, values, and choices. The children witness the love and obedience their parents give to God and mirror that love in their hearts and actions. With the strength of their father's love, and the tenderness of their mother's love, they are at peace and can be filled with God's love. They are empowered to freely love others. They have an authentic view of God as both love and strength that results in deep inner peace.

How did the home you grew up in form your concept of God? Arc you willing to let God change your mind about who He is? If you did not bond with your parents, if you felt physically or emotionally abandoned, the place for recovering and healing from those primary wounds in the spirit is to connect with the parental heart of God. It is very possible to have your sense of belonging and sense of being restored. You need to be willing to let God define to you who He is, not be trapped in your assumptions of Him.

The Mother Wound

> For as the woman originates from the man, so
> man has his birth through the woman; and u..
> originate from God.
>
> *(1 Corinthians 11:12, NASB)*

The symptoms of addiction and co-addiction are usually a cry from the human spirit to be loved, held, desired, and protected. A mother nurtures and protects her child—within her womb where life begins, and in her arms after the baby is delivered.

> *Yet You are He who brought me forth from the womb;*
> *You made me trust when upon my mother's breasts.*
>
> *(Psalm 22:9, NASB)*

A sense of belonging and a sense of being are established within the first three years of a child's life. Craig Lockwood writes about this in his book, *Falling Forward:*

> *A "sense of being," a term coined by Frank Lake and popularized by Leanne Payne, could be described as a core sense of warmth that is connected to the baby's ability to peacefully exist, without feeling a need to earn his [her] acceptability. It is a primary, psychological base of trust; this sense of being assures him [her] that he [she] is not in danger of losing love or significance, even though he [she] is doing nothing to earn that significance... In the first year of life, relationship with the mother is the primary experience of the child. Successful bonding causes trust to be formed between mother and baby. She conveys acceptance and love through her eyes, her touch, her breasts, her cooing, talking and singing... As all of his [her] needs are met in the milieu of love, the baby receives a sense of well-being, peace, safety and rest during early stages of attachment.[3]*

27

Husbands and wives who struggled with bonding with their mothers and fathers also struggle in bonding with each other. Deep down in their spirits, they cannot give what they did not receive themselves. Marriage and family force a couple to look at why they struggle with intimacy issues.

You were parented in an imperfect way, but the issue is no longer about how you were parented. It is about how you are responding to life now, and, if you have children, how you are parenting now. When you deny your own betrayals of the past, you actually reproduce those betrayals in your children.

As a psychologist, I have seen many adult men and women suffer a wound from a lack of belonging or a lack of being. In the field of psychology, these wounds are referred to as attachment disorders. Biblically, we know that they pass as a generational curse from parents to children, to children's children.

> You shall have no other gods before Me. You shall not make for yourself an idol, or any likeness of what is in heaven above or on the earth beneath or in the water under the earth. You shall not worship them or serve them; for I, the LORD your God, am a jealous God, visiting the iniquity of the fathers on the children, and on the third and the fourth generations of those who hate Me, but showing lovingkindness to thousands, to those who love Me and keep My commandments.
> (Deuteronomy 5:7–10, NASB)

The Deuteronomy passage refers to idols and making physical idols, but the following passage in Colossians is clear about idolatry in the heart:

> Put to death, therefore, whatever belongs to your earthly nature: sexual immorality, impurity, lust, evil desires and greed, which is idolatry.
> (Colossians 3:5, NIV)

However long the history of "visiting the iniquity of the fathers on the children" in your family, these wounds can be healed through inner healing of the human spirit. If you did not receive the tenderness of love you needed from your mother, you can ask God to "restore the years the locusts have eaten" (Joel 2:25, NIV). In the time of Joel, God had sent plagues of locusts on the people to gain their attention and turn their hearts back to Him. When they did return to Him, He promised full restoration to prosperous life, in spite of the damage the locusts had done. That kind of restoration is possible for you when you turn back to God, no matter what kind of harm you have experienced.

In order to allow God to do this restoration, it is helpful to understand what type of mother you experienced. Did your mother struggle with being present for you during the foundational years of your life? From the relational styles of the false self that we discussed earlier, what was your mother's primary way of relating?

- Little Girl
- Good Girl
- Religious Girl
- Party Girl
- Driven Girl
- Tough Girl

How Did Your Mother Fail to Love You?

Did your mother have a tenderness of love that flowed with passion, giftedness, and purpose? Or did she distort strength by refusing to be strong or refusing to be tender? Was she critical, controlling, or harsh? Did she love with her hands, but not her emotions? Was she co-dependent, enmeshed with you? Did she use her children to meet emotional needs that her husband could not? Was she a worrier, busy with tasks and not relationally present? Was she depressed, or struggling with addictions? What did you see modeled? Who did you become or vow you would never become as a result of your mother?

The Father Wound

The mother is not solely responsible for a sense of belonging and a sense of being. These are intuitively felt by the baby through both the mother's and father's love. For the mother to bond with the baby, she needs to be at rest in spirit, soul, and body. If she has a husband who gives her relational strength and takes care of things around the house while she is pregnant, then she can rest and bond with the baby.

However, if the mother is in a marriage crisis and does not feel the strength of love of her husband, she has to be the strong one and is not free for resting and relaxing, which help her bond with the baby in the womb. A baby's little human spirit can perceive the pain in the mother's spirit. If the father is not available to the mother's needs, the baby can feel the stress within the fragility of his or her first home—the womb. The roots of core anxiety are formed in the baby's uncertainty about what is going on in the world.

Looking at what type of father you experienced can help you seek from God what you did not receive in strength of tenderness. Was your father present to your mother and, therefore, you, during the foundational years of your life? From the relational styles of the false self that we discussed earlier, what was your father's primary way of relating?

- Little Boy
- Good Boy
- Religious Boy
- Party Boy
- Driven Boy
- Tough Boy

Forming an emotional and spiritual connection with a baby is difficult and confusing for most fathers. In reality, the father's most important role is simple: to pray for his children. As he develops his relationship with God, he passes it on to them. However, a father who puts business, work, or ministry before his wife and children abandons them—he has very little emotional energy left for them when he is at home.

Many fathers are excellent providers and protectors, as they have been trained to be by their fathers. But men can have a huge separation between their heads and their hearts. If a man's father was disconnected from his heart, he has passed that on to his son. If a man had a mother who was disconnected from her heart as well, he doesn't know how to connect his head and his heart even if he wants to.

A father was designed to relationally love his children—to show interest in them, to affirm them, to value their talents and individual personalities.

> *A father has a unique ability to "name" his children, establishing both their value and identity as individuals. He communicates their value through his emotional and spiritual connection with them.*[4]

Unfortunately, many fathers have little relational tolerance for their children. The father who sees his child as an interruption to his work or relaxation goals will primarily relate to his children in anger.

> *Fathers, do not provoke your children to anger, but bring them up in the discipline and instruction of the Lord.*
>
> (Ephesians 6:4, NASB)

Did your father have strength of love that flowed with passion, giftedness, and purpose? Or did he distort strength by refusing to be strong or refusing to be tender? Was he a workaholic, emotionally detached, or too busy? Was he absent, or unreliable, or dishonest? An addict? Did he abandon his family? Was he judgmental and self-absorbed or depressed? What did you see modeled? Who did you become or vow you would never become as a result of your father?

How Did Your Father Fail to Love You?

Regardless of how you were fathered or how you are fathering, you can choose today to father with a strength of love that you have never known if you seek the One who can fill you and empower you. Your past family pain can be the door to new faith, new hope, and new love.

Many times, the betrayal you experienced from others distracts you from looking at your primary pain with your parents and your core pain with God. But you must face all three levels of your pain with someone you trust, and—most importantly—with God, in order to overcome them. Whatever your level of betrayal pain, ignoring it or running from it doesn't make it go away; it only festers. Facing it enables you to enter in to the tenderness, strength, and peace of love that God has for you.

Facing Your Own Story

> *More than anything in the world, the shamed person*
> *wants to be invisible or small so that the focus will be*
> *removed, the hemorrhage of the soul stopped.*[5]

The result of betrayal is shame. Have you noticed that someone who is experiencing shame has a hard time looking others in the eye? Someone experiencing shame wants to hide from others and hide from God—as Adam and Eve did in the Garden of Eden.

When the seven arrows of betrayal pierce your human spirit, the pain of shame defiles the dignity that God placed in you in the womb. Out of your shame, you will make vows to try to protect yourself, but in the process you will harm yourself.

Think about a painful time in your life when you thought, *I will NEVER....* The "I will never" vows are words said out of pain with your parents or others. Sometimes they are thoughts that your mind forgets but remain embedded in your spirit and continue to affect the thoughts, feelings, and choices of your soul—and the actions of your body.

Clinically, when someone betrays you, you are being objectified—violated. As a psychologist, I help my clients to see this as victimization. However, as a pastor and lecturer, I help my clients see that victimizing someone—betraying them—is, at its core, sinning against them. If you do not acknowledge the pain in your spirit—you probably do not recognize the sin against you. When a person does not acknowledge a betrayal, he or she can swirl around in a depressive funk for years without reprieve. And, as we will discuss later, that betrayal is not always from someone else. We also have to deal with how we betray ourselves.

It is essential to identify how you have been sinned against, by whom, and the resulting inner vows you made in an effort to protect yourself from further relational betrayal. Craig Lockwood says that inner vows are like "policies by which our lives are governed." We must consciously choose to break them.

To take this part of the journey, you need to ask yourself three critical questions:

- What has happened to me on the journey?
- Who betrayed me? How was I betrayed?
- What is my shame or relational pain?

Our spirits are like houses with many rooms. When something painful in life happens in one room, we immediately run out of the room, slam the door shut, and vow never to go back there again. That is how the shame from pain becomes locked and buried deep within the human spirit.

The twins of fear—emptiness and disempowerment—gloat. You are now imprisoned in shame in your very own spirit. They applaud your sense of feeling unloved by your betrayer, for binding yourself with the vow you just created. The twins of fear celebrate your hopelessness.

> Do not eat the bread of a selfish man, or desire his delicacies; for as he thinks within himself, so he is. He says to you, "Eat and drink!" but his heart is not with you.
>
> (Proverbs 23:6-7, NASB)

The spirit of fear that is rooted in betrayal affects your thinking, feelings, and choices. When your human spirit is paralyzed with fear, the propensity to be a taker rather than a giver develops. You become confused in your thinking about yourself, others, and God. Your beliefs produce a lack of well-being in your soul. When people do not feel loved, they do not feel strong. Thus, they are rendered impotent to a life of addictions and co-addictions.

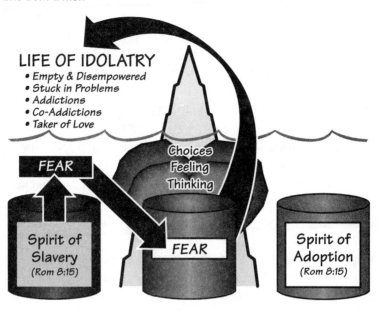

One of my clients has shared her story at a number of my conferences. She had struggled with anorexia for most of her childhood and into her marriage. I will refer to her as Ann—not her real name. One day when she was a little girl, she had reached to take a brownie from a pan that her mother had taken out of the oven. Her father slapped her hand and said, "Ann, you do not need that!" From that moment, she vowed within her spirit never to be fat because she feared being shamed by the most powerful man in her life—her father.

Fathers have the profound ability to name us—to call us out into our own, to put a voice to a mother's nurture, telling us we are desirable and have what it takes. At that moment, in Ann's mind she was labeled fat, ugly and disgusting. Her spirit was ripped by betrayal. The voice of shame hourly distorted her self-image and whispered to her that she was fat. In her spirit, Ann longed for her daddy's love and approval. She committed to doing whatever it would take, which ultimately played out in putting her own life at risk through starvation.

She thought that if she did not have a body like a Barbie® doll, then she would be judged as overweight and undesirable. Her sense of well-being died the day her father made that comment. As she grew up, she felt trapped, helpless, hopeless, and depressed about having a body that never could reflect the waistline, thighs, legs, and breasts of Barbie®. How could she ever become Daddy's little doll that he could show off to his buddies?

Over time, Ann adopted a new relational goal: to never be betrayed by her body again. Strategically, she watched everything she ate and became her own worst critic, judging her body and slapping her own hand daily. Even though she was trained and worked as a nurse, she was trapped in an addiction.

When a woman falls 15 percent below her normal weight, she enters physical starvation and needs to be hospitalized. Anorexia also threatens a woman's ability to have monthly periods or become pregnant. At this point, Ann and her husband came to me for therapy. Ann had already been hospitalized multiple times due to the effects of starvation. As a physician, her husband knew he was at risk of losing his wife to this addiction. Later on you will read how Ann started to connect what was going on in her inner person with what she was doing with her outer person.

The Choice to Change

The purpose of the second stage has been to help you enter into the deep sadness of shame in your spirit. Several assignments follow for you to complete before continuing to Stage Three. The critical question to ask is "How were you betrayed?" This can be horrible to revisit; however, choosing to reflect and face this will take you down the path of recovery, healing, and restoration.

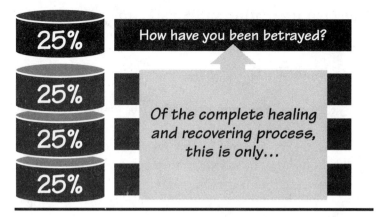

25% = How You Were betrayed.

Be courageously honest with how your heart has been treated on the journey, and you will discover the keys to the shame buried in your spirit. Your shame drives the contempt and anger you have toward yourself, others, and God. And your anger compels you to numb yourself with addictions and co-addictions.

I encourage you to press on. Don't allow the spirit of fear to paralyze you. Move ahead on the fuel of being fed up with living this way any longer. Don't forgo the freedom of being released of your shame. You do not have to take it with you to the grave. Instead, you can experience personal change, authentic intimacy, and restored sexuality. Take this journey to connect with the One who can release you from your shame and restore the years that the locusts have eaten.

Personal Journaling and Small Group Questions
Spiritual Homecoming Assignment Two

Personal Journaling Questions

1. Refer to the different home environments described in this stage. Which one or two describe your home growing up?
2. List the top 12 ways your mother betrayed you.
3. List the top 12 ways your father betrayed you.
4. List the top 12 ways your abuser betrayed you.
5. List the top 12 ways you were disappointed or betrayed by your spouse.
6. List the top 12 ways you were disappointed or betrayed by your church.
7. List the top 12 ways you were disappointed or betrayed by your workplace.
8. List the top 12 ways you were disappointed or betrayed by any others.
9. What are the corresponding images you have of women, men, spiritual mentors, and leaders as a result?
10. List the top 24 things that have given you the most shame in life.

Small Group Questions

1. What... are the key truths that stood out to you in this stage?
2. Why... do you need to know these truths?
3. How... do you apply these truths to your life?
4. Your pain... What pain does this stage reveal in your life?
5. Your sin... What are you doing with your pain?
6. Repentance... What do you need to do differently?
7. Prayer... What do you need to ask God for help with?

STAGE THREE: Your Story Unfolded
Facing How You Betray Others, Yourself, and God

People invest thousands of dollars in the recovery process and never get to the healing process. The current professional culture of psychologists is trained to look at your victimization—how you were betrayed. However, to continually and exclusively stir up that pain of betrayal causes you to be re-victimized. You must move past how you were victimized, or sinned against, to what you are now doing with your pain. What most of us do with betrayal is to betray in return. We betray others. We betray ourselves. We betray God.

The critical question in Stage Two was, How have you been betrayed? Now, the critical question for your next stage is, How do you betray?

> *Search me, O God, and know my heart; try me and know my anxious thoughts; and see if there be any hurtful way in me, and lead me in the everlasting way.*
>
> *(Psalm 139:23, NASB)*

Betrayal Number Two

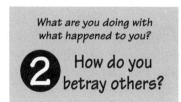

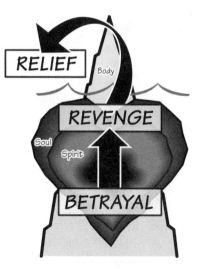

The living God gives hope. You can do nothing about how you were betrayed. You can do everything about no longer betraying others, yourself, and God. You can do something deep within your spirit, soul and, ultimately, your body. The twins of fear want to keep you trapped in denial,

I have not been betrayed!

self-absorption,

I have been betrayed, and it is all that matters and all I will look at!

and arrogance,

I would never betray someone else! (But if I do, they deserve it.)

If the twins of fear—emptiness and disempowerment—can keep you avoiding the hole in your spirit, you will never taste what the twins of faith—fullness and empowerment—can offer you. Fullness can offer you the authentic inner love of God, and empowerment can offer you the authentic inner strength of God. To enter into the hole in your spirit and see the goodness of God, you must shift from a pain focus (How was I betrayed?) to a sin focus (How do I betray others and God?) This enables your heart to admit your need for God. If the journey toward personal change, intimacy, and sexuality means only facing the shame of pain, then all you need is a good therapist. However, if the core issue is facing what you are doing with your pain, that is different. When we betray others, we are lashing out in anger, and as a result, we experience guilt. Then, the issue is no longer core shame but core guilt. To face core guilt, you do not need a therapist, you need a Savior!

When the twins of fear are replaced by the twins of faith, you will have the hope of being filled and empowered to gratefully, freely, exuberantly love God and others.

The one who does not love does not know God, for God is love.
(1 John 4:8, NASB)

Betrayal is the failure to love. When you experience betrayal pain, you feel unloved. The call of this life journey is to love in spite of how we ourselves have been betrayed. When a scribe asked Jesus which commandment was the greatest, Jesus said:

*The foremost is, "HEAR, O ISRAEL! THE LORD
OUR GOD IS ONE LORD; AND YOU SHALL
LOVE THE LORD YOUR GOD WITH ALL YOUR
HEART, AND WITH ALL YOUR SOUL, AND
WITH ALL YOUR MIND, AND WITH ALL YOUR
STRENGTH." The second is this, "YOU SHALL
LOVE YOUR NEIGHBOR AS YOURSELF." There
is no other commandment greater than these.*

(Mark 12:29-31, NASB)

Facing How You Betray Others

It takes incredible courage to name the guilt of how we betray
others.

*You have heard that the ancients were told, "YOU
SHALL NOT COMMIT MURDER" and "Whoever
commits murder shall be liable to the court." But I say
to you that everyone who is angry with his brother
shall be guilty before the court.*

(Matthew 5:21-22, NASB)

Jesus was not giving a new law in this passage; He was referring
to Leviticus 19:17-18, which deals with the issue of hatred. He
makes it clear that anger is a form of murder in your soul. We
try to use anger to counter the shame of betrayal in the spirit.
Unresolved anger is the ugly and deadly passion of revenge that
unconsciously says, *You hurt me; now you will pay—I will hurt you
back and for all eternity!;* It doesn't counter or reduce our shame; it
only adds guilt to the emptiness.

41

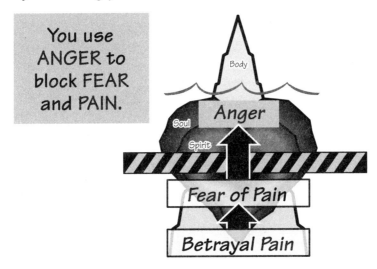

We all try to use the deadly knives of betrayal against the relational pain we have in ourselves, with others, and with God. In the process of stabbing our perceived sources of pain, we gash open further the holes in our spirits, causing more core emptiness—fueling addictive, co-addictive and depressive lifestyles.

Why You Get Depressed

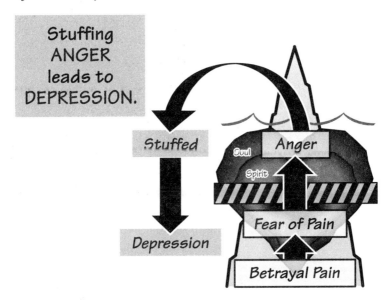

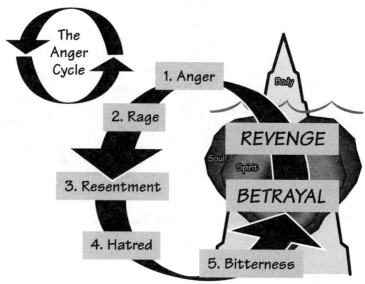

The Knife of Contempt

We have a human pull deep in our spirits to blame someone when life goes wrong. Therefore, the knife of contempt offers three more ways to kill the sense of shame in your spirit. When Adam had his guilt and shame exposed, he was the first to blame everyone else for his problems. He had the audacity to say: "The woman You gave me, she made me take the apple!" And so the tradition of blame travels through the generations.

The knife of contempt makes three kinds of cuts: the gash of self-contempt, the gash of other-contempt, the gash of God-contempt. Dr. Dan Allender has said that self-contempt is a dagger turned inward, as if self-hatred could kill the shame. Self-contempt ranges from being unable to receive a compliment, to cutting yourself down, to harming yourself—such as cutting or burning—to the extreme self-contempt of suicide.

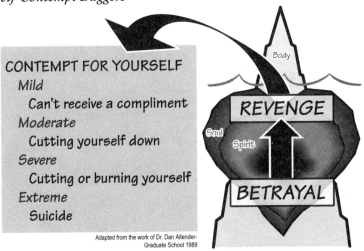

CONTEMPT FOR YOURSELF
Mild
   Can't receive a compliment
Moderate
   Cutting yourself down
Severe
   Cutting or burning yourself
Extreme
   Suicide

Adapted from the work of Dr. Dan Allender-
Graduate School 1989

The knife of other-contempt lacerates anyone who is perceived as a source of disappointment. You attack verbally, emotionally, physically, sexually, psychologically, or spiritually. Whatever it takes is fair in the world of shame. You express contempt for others by degrading them with your words, your eyes, your demeanor, and your actions. How you express your contempt depends on your personality and relational style—whether couched in a hateful attack or veiled in a warm smile and gentle rebuke. Contempt for others ranges from critical looks, abusive words, and abusive actions to the extreme of homicide.

Other-Contempt Daggers

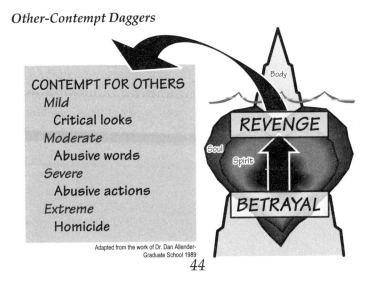

CONTEMPT FOR OTHERS
Mild
   Critical looks
Moderate
   Abusive words
Severe
   Abusive actions
Extreme
   Homicide

Adapted from the work of Dr. Dan Allender-
Graduate School 1989

The third kind of contempt is to blame God, your Creator, for whatever stains your spirit, soul, or body. Contempt for God ranges from swearing—taking His name in vain—to scoffing at the name of God, to blaming God for the evil in the world and even for your own choices, to the extreme contempt for God of removing His honor from the culture.

God-Contempt Daggers

CONTEMPT FOR GOD
Mild
  Using God's name in vain
Moderate
  Scoffing at God
Severe
  Kicking God out of culture
Extreme
  Blaming God for evil

REVENGE

BETRAYAL

Body
Soul
Spirit

Contempt poisons your thinking, feelings, and choices. The betrayals you commit seek to kill the spirits of the very ones you love. Do you see the destructive dynamics of this unresolved anger in your soul? When your spirit is shamed, you lash out with murderous intent. Your lashing out only makes your wounds fester, and weakness and disempowerment prevail in your soul. You become susceptible to the waters of addiction and co-addiction, but those waters can never wash away your core shame or drown your core guilt.

Another issue that blocks your ability to address your emptiness and disempowerment is transference.

The Knife of Transference

Transference occurs when a similar event or pattern in your present relationship unlocks your past betrayal and revenge.

You unconsciously transfer, or project, those intense feelings from a past relationship onto the present person. We all struggle with some level of transference because we all have unresolved relational pain or relational sin buried in our human spirits.

The knife of transference destroys many marriages and families. It damages your sexuality and any hope for experiencing intimacy. It causes employees and CEOs alike to lose their jobs. It causes churches, parishes, and synagogues to split. The knife of transference has murdered innocent school children in school shootings and has divided the races for generations.

If you ignore transference, you will remain stuck in life, no matter how much therapy and medication you have. Transference is a spiritual issue. To deal with it you have to understand the ugly passion for murder within the soul. Yet, understanding transference only at a soul level will leave you disheartened and even angrier. You will be caught in a perpetual loop of "same song, different verse" with every person you meet. The roots of the soul's transference lie in the unresolved betrayal pain in the human spirit. Knowing this will give you hope of passing through its emotional labyrinth.

Transference shows itself in different contexts: in marriage, in race relations, with authority figures, with peers, and other contexts.

Transference in Marriage
If a woman had a workaholic, angry, and very hypocritical father, she might default to seeing the same traits in her husband because something he does triggers her unresolved pain and unresolved sin from her relationship with her own father. She can interpret those traits to be her husband's, even though they are not. She may transfer her father's betrayals onto her husband, and blame him for her father's wrongdoing.

She may have also made internal vows that she would never marry a man like her father. That judgment embedded in her spirit would then distort how she viewed men. She may also make vows regarding God for allowing such pain to come into her life, judging that God was absent, critical, and controlling, like her father. The painful vows cemented to the foundation of her human spirit would not only keep her out of the one relationship that could heal her—her relationship with God—but also drive her to false comforts—overeating, perfectionism, or overworking.

A typical outcome of such transference onto her husband would be for her to gossip about him, demonize his name in the community and church, or be emasculating and critical of him in person.

A husband in this scenario might very well have a similar trait to the offending father. He might also be a workaholic. However, the amount of blame that his wife transfers onto him is not for his own failings, but for her father's failings. It doesn't deal with the real issues between man and wife, but brings in outside baggage that both exacerbates and blocks the real problems.

Often a person in transference will suddenly exhibit an intense inner rage that eclipses the present relationship. The other person in the relationship will wonder what hit him or her. That person may even realize he or she did something wrong, but will also wonder, "Did I deserve this?"

For those who have children, the transference can be even more broadly damaging. One parent in transference may turn the children against the other parent, robbing the children of a relationship critical to their sense of belonging and being. Children turned against their fathers lose the taste for strength of love that primarily a father can offer—however small or great his ability to offer it. They lose their respect for their father and, therefore, for authority, and often will eventually turn on their mother as well.

As you were betrayed, so you betray others. Some of your anger in your current relationships may be appropriate; however, the majority of deep rage that you have for others is not. Have you developed a harsh, critical, or controlling false relational style toward someone? Do you attempt to control his or her life and reputation through gossip?

47

Facing your own transference is not easy. Many people cannot bear to have the light shine on the unresolved pain of betrayal in their spirits, the unresolved anger of revenge in their souls, and the illegitimate ways they find relief through addiction and co-addiction. It is too risky to let their longings for tenderness, strength, and peace come alive. They would rather have their longings remain frozen by fear than risk the pain of thawing and coming alive. That is the control the spirit of fear exercises over their lives: feeling dead inside and being paralyzed with fear in addiction and co-addiction. The momentary difficulty of facing your transference is worth the lifetime of freedom, healing, and restoration it can bring.

Transference in Race Relations

Other contexts of transference happen similarly. In racial transference, generally a painful, or perceived-painful, racial offense has occurred. It may happen when one has been betrayed by someone of another race, or it can be a parent interjecting a hateful racial attitude into a child's soul. Parents condition their children to betray others through their example.

Racist people self-protect by avoiding or rejecting people of other races. You may not engage in overtly racist words or deeds, but what are your thoughts regarding someone of another race? If you have a prejudice in your past, when you meet someone of a different race in the present, those past feelings of betrayal are unlocked and released on the present person. You might treat him or her with aggressive hate or defensive body language, or smile sweetly but with an internal rage.

The only way to break the generational stronghold of racism is to cast off your fears of another race and come to know people of that race. As you experience their love for you, it will begin to displace your prejudice. Certainly, all races have bad apples. However, to generalize that all other ethnicities are less than yours is an attempt to kill their passion, giftedness, and purpose.

Transference with Authority Figures

Likewise, many times a boss or a spiritual authority such as a pastor, priest, or rabbi can remind us of our fathers or mothers. They might trigger unresolved issues of betrayal as well. I have watched many corporate and spiritual leaders become the target of another person's vile transference, to the point of corporations crumbling and religious communities splitting.

Transference with Peers

School violence, specifically school shootings, are a tragic example of transference with peers. When a child has experienced tremendous rejection from family, peers, community, or the culture, his or her human spirit floods with embarrassment and shame. To survive without hope, that child must keep his or her emotions frozen as much as possible through addictions. As we have discussed, the natural pull in the soul is to use the anger of revenge to murder the pain of shame in the human spirit. Eventually, a student whose pain is frozen experiences a new form of rejection in the present—not being accepted to a college, being turned down for a date, being picked on by a bully, or other triggers. Instantly his or her frozen shame thaws—that young lifetime of raw pain and shame can feel like he or she is dying all by him or herself. We have seen young students faced with this pain, who do not see hope for the future, determine to take as many others as possible down with them in last desperate acts. To kill the feeling of their own shame, they kill any perceived sources of that shame as well.

Children not only need a supernatural healing of their sense of belonging and sense of being wounds, but they need to have their true selves called forth by the passion of God and the people of God. When children experience in their hearts what they know about God's love in their heads, they are transformed and adopt a new relational style. When a teenager is filled with the living love of God, he or she has a fighting chance to be empowered by the living strength of God.

49

At that time the disciples came to Jesus and said, "Who then is greatest in the kingdom of heaven?" And He called a child to Himself and set him before them, and said, "Truly I say to you, unless you are converted and become like children, you will not enter the kingdom of heaven. Whoever then humbles himself as this child, he is the greatest in the kingdom of heaven. And whoever receives one such child in My name receives Me; but whoever causes one of these little ones who believe in Me to stumble, it would be better for him to have a heavy millstone hung around his neck, and to be drowned in the depth of the sea.
(Matthew 18:1-6, NASB)

As you journey on your spiritual homecoming, help involve the children in your life in their faith as well, bringing them back to health in spirit, soul, and body. Many children are dying inside for lack of healing in their lives for lack of being "named"—called forth to be who they are.

On a final note about transference, sometimes people who want to avoid responsibility for what they are doing with their own pain will accuse another of transference. They will misuse their power to deflect their own issues and sin by making everything about transference. This is a form of self-protection that perverts the truth of transference into a weapon to destroy others. Everyone has unresolved pain and sin. Everyone transfers at some level. Do not use the card of transference as a way to evade facing your own sin, and do not buy into this with others.

The way out of transference, and out of contempt, is to go to the roots of the anger of revenge in your soul. You cannot do anything about your pain (though God can), but you can do something about what you are doing with your pain. Be brutally honest as you ponder what you have done with your betrayal pain. It takes courage and humility to do this type of rock climbing, but seeing the summit is worth every intentional step.

If you can come to terms with not just your story, but what you have done with your story, you are well into your spiritual homecoming. Regardless of the shame you have identified in Stage Two or the guilt you are identifying in Stage Three, there is One who accepts your human struggles and is welcoming you home just the same. To come back home to "Abba (Papa) God," you must be honest about what you have experienced in life and what you are doing with it. God sees all of it and knew it long ago; you don't need to save face with Him.

The deep unresolved guilt and shame in your spirit affect how you eventually betray yourself with the illegitimate relief of addictions in your body and co-addictions in your relationships. The clinical dynamics of betrayal, revenge, and relief are the three fronts of the daily battle that have to be identified and worked through if you want to experience lasting change.

Facing How You Betray Yourself
If the first betrayal was how you yourself have been betrayed, and the second is how you betray others, the third betrayal is how you betray yourself. You do this through any attempts to fill your core emptiness in your spirit with anything and everything but the love and strength of God, illegitimately filling yourself with objects (addictions) or people (co-addictions). We can lust in thought, word, or deed. We all try to cope with the pain in life by murder in the soul and lust in the body.

> You have heard that it was said, "Do not commit adultery." But I tell you that anyone who looks at a woman lustfully has already committed adultery with her in his heart.
>
> —Jesus (Matthew 5:27-28, NIV)

Both addictions and co-addictions betray you because they do not do what they promise. Addictive habits and co-dependent relationships never fill you deeply enough. They steal life from you and leave you emptier than before.

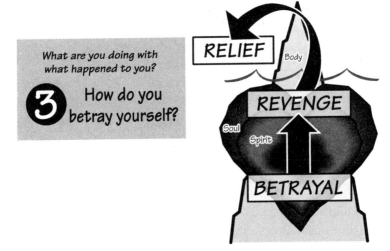

Addictions and co-addictions involve three phases:
- Daily disconnecting from the painful reality of not having sense of belonging or sense of being.
- Daily disconnecting from the angry reality of having a false self and no purpose in life.
- Daily reconnecting to a pleasurable unreality that tries to numb the painful and angry realities of life.

All addictions and co-dependent relationships are difficult to overcome. But if you can identify how you daily disconnect from reality and daily connect to unreality, you can make your way out of the jungle.

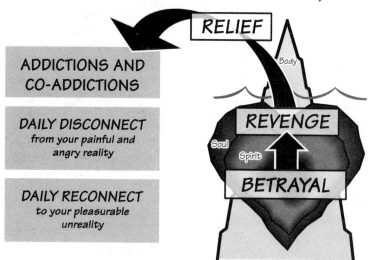

For instance, a man struggling with a pornography addiction needs to understand two central principles:

- His struggles with pornography in his outer person (his body) directly correlate to his struggles of emptiness and disempowerment in his inner person (his spirit and soul).
- His struggles with emptiness and disempowerment—not being filled with God's love and strength—in his inner person directly affect his struggles with pornography in his outer person.

Though his head may cognitively know that God loves him, his heart cannot seem to experience and feel it. Core emptiness results in a deprivation neurosis within the masculine spirit. If the masculine soul does not experience the strength of love from God, he tries to work hard to feel loved. He shifts from desiring to be loved to demanding to be loved. Work, athletics, or hobbies tend to be the places where a man finds recognition and feels loved from sources outside of himself. However, to feel love within is the cry of every human spirit.

When a man feels empty of love at his core, he will be driven to find love from others. Hence, most men are "doers" with little emphasis on taking the time in "being." However, a man must have a little space to daily receive the essential elements that give his "doing" purpose and efficacy in order to heal the deprivation neurosis within his masculine spirit. Constant "doing" leaves a man feeling empty, inadequate, and angry that what he does is never enough.

It is very difficult to get out of the quicksand of spiritual disempowerment if you know the love of God in your head but cannot experience the love of God in your heart. Men can pierce through chaos and confusion and complete a job or solve a problem. However, to feel the love of God, men need to also become good at "being"—stopping to take the time to receive. When a man daily receives the authentic love of God, a sword is released to him to fight powerfully to the glory of the One who is filling him with this love and strength.

Likewise, if the masculine soul does not experience the tenderness of love from God, he feels weak, unloved, and anxious. Many times these issues are masked by strong denial. To see a problem he cannot fix himself leaves a man feeling inadequate and like a failure. His machismo refuses to look at the painful reality of living in this broken world. (However, a wife or significant other, frustrated by her husband's relational avoidance, will easily bust his delusions that everything is fine!)

Then, when the seven arrows of betrayal penetrate this man's human spirit, the pain of shame starts to destroy the dignity and strength of masculinity that God put into that man at birth. Many men start to struggle with sexual addiction to pornography and masturbating as a lifestyle, or other addictions. And many confess that their struggle with pornography and masturbation started in their early teenage years.

Do you not know that your bodies are members of Christ? Shall I then take away the members of Christ and make them members of a prostitute? May it never be! Or do you not know that the one who joins himself to a prostitute is one body with her? For He says, "THE TWO SHALL BECOME ONE FLESH." But the one who joins himself to the Lord is one spirit with Him. Flee immorality. Every other sin that a man commits is outside the body, but the immoral man sins against his own body. Or do you not know that your body is a temple of the Holy Spirit who is in you, whom you have from God, and that you are not your own? For you have been bought with a price: therefore glorify God in your body.

(1 Corinthians 6:15-20, NASB)

Addiction Cycles

ADDICTION	Sexual	Perfectionist	Work
Disconnection from Core Pain	Then intensified by any parental pain, then exacerbated by any abuse pain.		
Resulting Sense of Fear	Emptiness and inadequacy in human spirit.		
Attempt to Deflect Pain with Anger	Directed toward others, oneself or God, which then causes a drive to find relief.	Directed toward anyone who brings chaos to the inner or outer world (others, oneself or God), which then causes a drive to find relief.	Directed toward others, oneself or God, which then causes a drive to find relief.
Pursuit of Short-term Comfort	Whether pornography, masturbation, illicit sex, or other sexual intrigue, the pursuit only exacerbates the emptiness. This realization produces more pain of guilt and shame and the feeling of being more cut off from God's love and emptier than before.	Driven to have a perfect-looking outer world to cover up the imperfect inner world. This is exhausting and only gives short-term relief of shame.	Lack of love, inadequacy and anger drive to excessive work so that someone will notice importance and significance. Compliments only last so long and do not fill the emptiness.
Compounding Pain	The cycle produces more pain of guilt and shame, and feelings of being more cut off from God's love and emptier than before.	Lack of deep rest in the spirit cuts off receptivity to God's love, which could disrupt the shame; and God's strength, which could put the inner and outer worlds in order. The result is greater emptiness than before.	The workaholic is angered by the need to work for love and significance. This rage in the soul further alienates from being open to God's love and is intensified if not feeling loved by spouse or significant other.
The Addiction Cycle Continues	The added pain pushes to find more comfort from sexual intrigue, and the sexual addiction cycle goes on.	The added pain pushes to find more comfort in order, and the perfection addiction cycle goes on.	When disapproval is sensed or feeling insignificant, the added pain pushes to find more comfort in work and accomplishment, and the workaholic addicition cycle goes on.

56

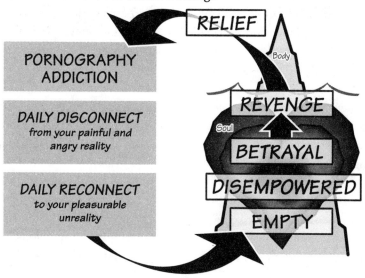

The good news is that when a man finally learns how to first let the love and strength of God fill his human spirit, the strength of tenderness is released in his masculine spirit and he can start to give and experience authentic intimacy.

How You Get Stuck in Other Bondages

The same principles apply to other addictions. Few people who struggle with an overeating addiction would ever argue that the overeating never fills the core emptiness inside. They see how they are trying to comfort an emptiness of their spirits and the anger of their souls by eating.

> *All things are lawful for me, but not all things are profitable. All things are lawful for me, but I will not be mastered by anything. Food is for the stomach and the stomach is for food, but God will do away with both of them. Yet the body is not for immorality, but for the Lord, and the Lord is for the body. Now God has not only raised the Lord, but will also raise us up through His power.*
>
> (1 Corinthians 6:12-14, NASB)

Most overeating addicts have already concluded that whatever they do, they will never be able to lose the weight or keep it off long term. However, since the food addiction never works, it actually increases a sense of emptiness because of the seductive promise that it was supposed to fill them.

When the overeating addict starts to be filled by the love of God and empowered by the strength of God in the inner person, the weight not only starts to come off, but the person also has a fighting chance to keep the weight off.

We often do not think of "socially acceptable" sin as addiction; in fact, we tend to reward or admire high achievers like perfectionists or workaholics. But, these addictions are just as insidious in feeding the emptiness and disempowerment in the human spirit.

A perfectionist does not feel God's love and, therefore, the world seems insecure and out of control. He or she may know of God's love in his or her head, but cannot feel it in the heart. The opposite of feeling love is feeling shame. Hence, a perfectionist's inner world is full of shame and disorder.

Similarly, a workaholic searches for his or her value or significance in work and accomplishment. He or she does not feel God's love or a deep sense of significance at his or her core. Therefore, a workaholic tries to work harder in order to feel loved and significant. He or she may know of God's love in his or her head, but cannot feel it in the heart. A workaholic craves verbal affirmation from others, hoping it will touch the deep void of not feeling loved or significant in his or her human spirit. It's a predicament that works perfectly for the corporate world. Like a hungry dog, a workaholic will keep working and working for the scraps, hoping there is more.

Living this way is wretched! If you are married, you made your vows and promised to be faithful "until death do us part!" To put work or hobbies before your spouse and/or children is to betray them with the knife of neglect, which says, *What I want comes first over your welfare and well-being.* The betrayal of neglect will never give love to those for whom you are providing through your workaholism.

Co-addiction works the same way as these addictions. Co-addicts "give to get" in most relationships. They try to fill their own empty cups by filling the empty cups of other people. But an empty cup cannot fill another empty cup. Since co-dependent relationships do not fill core emptiness, the emptiness grows and the corruption of manipulating others continues.

Facing How You Betray God

The first betrayal asked, "How were you betrayed?" The key word is **"betrayal."** The second betrayal asked, "How do you betray others?" The key word is **"murder."** The third betrayal asked, "How do you betray yourself?" The key word is **"lust"** (longing for the forbidden—a picture of addictions and co-addictions). The fourth betrayal asks, "How do you betray God?" The key word for this betrayal is **"idolatry."**

Betrayal Number Four

The opposite of loving God is betraying God. How could a human possibly violate God? We do it every day by a lifestyle of replacing God, which is the same thing as idolatry. Addiction is idolatry—

giving deference to a false god, trying to fill the hole in your human spirit with something other than the true living God.

What do you do when your world is collapsing or you are under a lot of stress? Do you reach for Häagen Dazs®, or surf x-rated websites, or reach for a cigarette or a drink? Whatever you do when your world collapses reveals your idolatry.

> *For My people have committed two evils:*
> *They have forsaken Me,*
> *The fountain of living waters,*
> *To hew for themselves cisterns,*
> *Broken cisterns*
> *That can hold no water.*
>
> *(Jeremiah 2:13, NASB)*

We abandon God, the fountain of living waters, and substitute Him for a lifestyle of addictions and co-addictions. There are five elements of worshiping addictive and co-addictive false gods:

- Pain in your spirit regarding a lack of belonging
- Pain in your spirit regarding a lack of being
- A lack of the true self in your soul
- A lack of purpose in your soul
- A life of idolatry in your body and relationships

> *The idols of the nations are but silver and gold,*
> *The work of man's hands.*
> *They have mouths, but they do not speak;*
> *They have eyes, but they do not see;*
> *They have ears, but they do not hear,*
> *Nor is there any breath at all in their mouths.*
> *Those who make them will be like them,*
> *Yes, everyone who trusts in them.*
>
> *(Psalm 135:15-18, NASB)*

Though this passage talks about idols that are crafted, not merely idols of the heart, the principle is that idols are dead and fail to fulfill us.

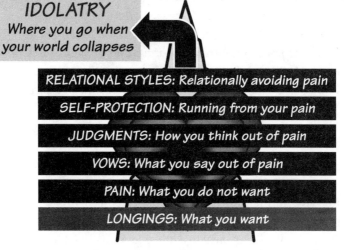

Idols cannot do anything except distract us from the God who can do something extraordinary in our lives. The most common idols I have seen in the Christian church are food, sex, money, power, pleasure, and co-dependency (co-addiction). As a Christian psychologist, I see the cycle of idolatry as rampant in Christians as in those who do not know the living God. The building blocks of addictions and co-addictions are:

- Longings: what you want
- Pain: what you do not want
- Fear: what you do not want to face
- Vows: what you say out of pain
- Judgments: how you think out of pain
- Self-protection: running from your pain
- Idolatry: where you go when your world collapses

We also ignore God. Christians who profess to be followers of Christ, yet only think about God when they are in church, are one example. The rest of the week, instead of being in awe of how great the loving God is, those people worship themselves through their own agendas. They have no regard for what God wants to tell them or have them do each day of their journey on earth.

This is the message we have heard from Him and announce to you, that God is Light, and in Him there is no darkness at all. If we say that we have fellowship with Him and yet walk in the darkness, we lie and do not practice the truth; but if we walk in the Light as He Himself is in the Light, we have fellowship with one another, and the blood of Jesus His Son cleanses us from all sin.

(1 John 1:5-7, NASB)

When others betray you, your human spirit fills with deep sadness. But when you live a life of betraying others and yourself, it fills your human spirit with deeper grief. When you live a life of betraying God, you will have profound sorrow until you learn to shift from a life of betrayal to a life of love. This is what Rekindling Your Spirit is all about. Regardless of what you have done (your guilt) or what you have become (your shame), the living God is able and willing to fill you with His love and strength.

Personal Journaling and Small Group Questions
Spiritual Homecoming Assignment Three

Personal Journaling Questions

1. List the top 24 people you have betrayed or are betraying.
2. List the top 12 ways you betray(ed) your mother in thought, word, or deed.
3. List the top 12 ways you betray(ed) your father in thought, word, or deed.
4. List the top 12 ways you betray(ed) your abuser(s) in thought, word, or deed.
5. List the top 12 ways you betray(ed) your spouse(s) in thought, word, or deed.
6. List the top 12 ways you betray(ed) friends or others in thought, word, or deed.
7. List the top 12 ways you betray(ed) your church(es) in thought, word, or deed.
8. List the top 12 ways you betray yourself, including:
   - Addictions
   - Co-addictions
   - Self-contempt
9. List the top 24 things you feel most guilty about.
10. List the top 12 ways you betray God in thought, word, or deed.

Small Group Questions

1. What... are the key truths that stood out to you in this stage?
2. Why... do you need to know these truths?
3. How... do you apply these truths to your life?
4. Your pain... What pain does this stage reveal in your life?
5. Your sin... What are you doing with your pain?
6. Repentance... What do you need to do differently?
7. Prayer... What do you need to ask God for help with?

STAGE FOUR: Waging War
Three Spiritual Attacks in the Daily Battle

How do you face your core spiritual pain? At this part of your homecoming you may be a little weary. This will probably be the step in your journey that takes you right into "life." Begin this stage by praying this brief prayer:

> *Investigate my life, O God, find out everything about me; cross-examine and test me, get a clear picture of what I'm about; see for yourself whether I've done anything wrong — then guide me on the road to eternal life.*
>
> (Psalm 139:23–24, MSG)

I also regularly claim the following promise in prayer. God is true to keep His promises to all who will take Him up on them. Pray this verse and ask Him to help you make the connections between your painful images of your father, the painful images of your mother, and your painful images of God.

> *Call to Me and I will answer you, and I will tell you great and mighty things, which you do not know.*
>
> (Jeremiah 33:3, NASB)

Do you see any correlation between the painful images of your father and mother and your painful images of God?

We ask this question at our "Rekindling Your Spirit" weekend conferences, and the majority of the people who take the courage to share make the correlation between their father pain, their mother pain, and their perceived God pain. It is critical to understand that while the father and mother pain can be real, the God pain is only projected from our perceptions of our earthly father and mother onto God. This is your core pain in your human spirit.

Spiritual Projection

Uncovering the core pain in your spirit starts by realizing that you live in an imperfect world with imperfect parents. There is no perfect marriage, perfect parents, or perfect home. If you say you had a perfect home and a perfect life, as a psychologist, I would call that clinical denial. We live in an imperfect world.

The way to discern how you project your father and mother pain onto God is to identify the painful images of your parents, as you have already done. You may have had a:

- Busy father or mother
- Distant or absent father or mother
- Critical father or mother
- Judgmental father or mother
- Controlling father or mother

These events or patterns fill your human spirit with the shame of feeling ignored or attacked, even if it was unintentional on the part of your parent. However, your perceptions of God become infected in the process of not receiving your parents' tenderness, strength, and peace.

You may start to think, *Maybe God does not want to spend time with me either.* Or, *Maybe God will attack me like my parents did in their unpredictable moods.* Whatever opinion you have of God, it is usually rooted in what you experienced or did not experience with your parents. Unfortunately, your view then becomes your spiritual reality.

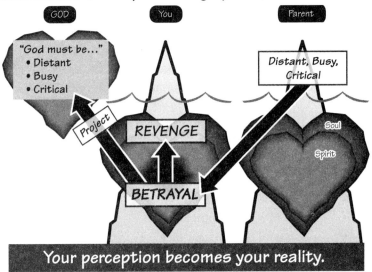

Your perception becomes your reality.

However, our distortions of God are not true. To blame God for what He is not is to stereotype Him—to be prejudiced against Him. We say without knowing, "God, this is who You are!"

Your view of God is not only projected by who you perceived your parents to be, but is also shaped by how your father and mother view God; how your pastor, priest, or rabbi views God; even how Hollywood views God. As we read in Stage One: the sins of parents will visit the next generations (Exodus 34:7).

As long as distorted thinking about God remains in your soul, you will continue to run from the very One who can actually offer what you need to be filled and empowered in your human spirit. God is the One who can release the passion He put within you. God is the One who can release the giftedness He has put within you. God is the One who can release the purpose He has put within you. What will it mean for you to take time and finally get to know God?

The Genesis of the Hole in Your Spirit[6]
In Stage One, you read part of the story of Adam and Eve—a picture of the intimate and passionate honeymoon humanity had

with God, at first. The Man and Woman were perfectly filled by God's love and perfectly empowered by God's strength. Man and Woman perfectly loved God and perfectly loved each other.

For one moment, we were in paradise, filled by the Almighty's tender love and holy strength that gave us a peaceful and quiet sense of belonging and a sense of being beyond human comprehension. Then, the choice to listen to one lie removed us from our Creator.

The perfect honeymoon was followed by the tragic divorce. The loss of belonging and being filled Man and Woman with deep sadness. An emptiness entered the deep spirit of humankind, a hole ripped there by the choice to separate from God and go a different way.

With the hole in the human spirit came weakness, lack of empowerment. The joy of life left. Man and Woman became subject to pain and struggle. Their betrayal of God gave root to weeds in the garden of life—heavy guilt and shame that would try to choke the very breath out of humankind.

The Impact of Your Spiritual Pain

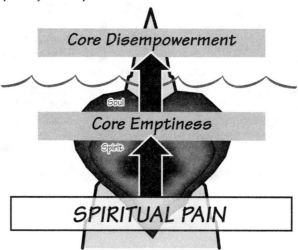

Ever since the Garden of Eden, humanity has been trying to cover up its core shame with the leaves of addiction and co-addiction—

our idolatry. We are deceived to believe that we can hide our spiritual nakedness from the One who created us and calls us by name!

Waging War on Three Fronts
We are all engaged in a war for our spirits, our souls, and our bodies. This entire stage flows out of my twenty-year relationship with my mentor from graduate school, Dr. Richard Averbeck. All of my thoughts from the book of Genesis is an adaptation of Dr. Averbeck's work.

The War in Your Spirit
We are in an all-out war on our spirits. This is a picture of spiritual cancer. The strongholds of fear in our spirits can overtake us in our life of addictions and co-addictions. For spiritual pain, you need to seek a competent, Christ-centered third party who is trained to help you with spiritual pain to experience long-term, lasting, personal change.

The Enemy's First Attack and Your Response

The War in Your Soul
The fear in our spirits gives us a natural inclination to worship

ourselves and become a "taker" of love rather than a "giver" of love. As you have seen, the lack of a true self will lead to a lack of true purpose in life. This is why the greatest commandments are to "love the Lord your God with all your heart, soul, mind, and strength, and to love your neighbor as yourself" (Mark 12:30-31).

You have a natural pull to love yourself by taking care of your own needs first. Consequently, you fail to love God and others. In the process of not loving God and others, you betray God and others. We are in an all-out war on our souls as well as our spirits.

The Enemy's Second Attack and Your Response

Disconnected from God, we lost our sense of our true self and our sense of purpose. We shifted from loving God and one another to betraying God and one another, giving the twins of fear—emptiness and disempowerment—a foothold.

This is a picture of the relational cancer of the soul and of how the stronghold of anger can paralyze us with a lack of purpose in a life of the false self. The strongholds of revenge are housed in the human soul. For relational pain, you may need a holistic approach (spirit, soul and body) for your healing process.

The War in Your Body

How do emptiness and disempowerment work from the soul into the human body? Without a sense of belonging or a sense of being, we desperately try to fill our emptiness—the hole in our human spirits—with an object or a relationship. This is addiction and co-addiction—idolatry.

Only God can fill that hole with His love, strength, and peace. Your other attempts are unsuccessful, yet always seem to promise more. So you live desperately trying to fill the hole in your human spirit, worshiping the addiction or co-addiction—the "demon" inside of you. The body yearns to be filled by whatever will distract from the emptiness. The flesh of the body is driven by revenge and lust, waging war against your body, your soul, and your spirit.

Ironically, the addictions and co-addictions that you think will give you more, will turn and possess you. The spiritual bondage of addictions and co-addictions stain and damage those closest to you. Your emptiness and disempowerment spread into their lives.

The Enemy's Third Attack and Your Response

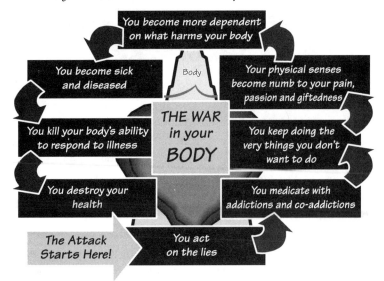

The strongholds of erotic and non-erotic lusts are housed in your human body and your relationships; they can paralyze you in a life of addictions and co-addictions. For physical pain and sexual pain, you may need a holistic approach (spirit, soul, and body) for your healing process.

Cycles of Addiction
Sexual Addiction Cycle, Genesis 3:1–12
- Listen to the father of lies.
- Doubt the truth of God.
- See an erotic image.
- Desire and lust after it.
- Take what is forbidden.
- Hide guilt and shame.
- Fear the consequences.
- Blame the woman or man and God.

Both men and women struggle with sexual addiction, though it is more common for men. It is with his eyes that a man can violate a woman's privacy and dignity by looking at her nakedness with his searching, lusting eyes to fill up his core emptiness. He will secretly use his eyes to betray her by taking off her clothes in public, or by looking at naked images of women in pornography.

For him, to secretly look at what he should not is a form of voyeurism. We have adopted this practice culturally as we watch love scenes in movies, choose styles of dress that are provocative and revealing, look into the private lives of others through "reality" TV—as though we are standing outside their window and looking in at what we should not be seeing.

Pornography is a form of cannibalism. A man consumes a woman's nakedness to satisfy his appetite that is driven by his starvation—his core emptiness. However, one meal is never enough. In the process, women feel prostituted, robbed, used and discarded.

Masturbation is then the practice of having lonely orgasms with just yourself. Self-stimulation is a desperate cry for the authentic touch of the lover of your dreams. The stark reality is that you are alone and starving for relational intimacy—avoiding the real by choosing the counterfeit. Forgoing the courageous for the cowardly.

Self-sex is blatantly taking, not giving. Clinically, this will corrupt and condition a man to be driven by a sexual libido that fulfills itself through taking and not giving. This forges a foundation for narcissistic sex that is most concerned with self-gratification. The man has little concern to fight for the woman and honor her with tender patience and surrender to the dreams of her heart. Instead, he lives for himself, distorting the passion of the marriage bed, discarding her and her relational longings.

This false intimacy of pornography, masturbation, or narcissistic sex does not satisfy and drives the hunt for more. Struggling with lust in the body is directly related to struggle within your soul and spirit.

In Stage One you read the story of Adam and Eve's betrayal of God in the Garden of Eden—the reason for the hole in the human spirit. This same story has the first account of misogyny. It is the first time a woman was violated and dishonored by blame. She was abandoned by a self-serving, disloyal love.

God found Adam hiding from Him and asked him if he'd eaten from the forbidden tree.

> *The man said, "The woman whom You gave to be with*
> *me, she gave me from the tree, and I ate.*
> *(Genesis 3:12, NASB)*

When Adam was confronted with his failure to love God by keeping His commandments, he didn't take responsibility for his own sin; he blamed his wife. That sin has been passed on through generations. Women have, for centuries, been degraded by both the church and the marketplace devaluing their giftedness and purpose. This stems from the curse of Adam.

Out of misogyny has flowed misandry. Misandry is the disrespect and dishonoring of men. Because of misogyny, misandry has become a culturally acceptable response—to emasculate men with anger.

Dear men and women, the dishonor of betraying each other never works! Both misogyny and misandry are the deep, ugly work of the twins of fear. If you practice misogyny, you will not be filled, for the true feminine teaches the relational art of receptivity and sense of being. If you practice misandry, you will not have strength to do what you want to because the true masculine teaches us the art of empowerment and doing. Men need both the true masculine and the true feminine to be filled; women need both the true feminine and the true masculine to be filled.

Food Addiction Cycle, Genesis 3:1–12

The same story in Genesis applies to all addictions and false ways of filling our emptiness. In a food addiction cycle, as an addict you:

- Listen to the father of lies in how to be filled.
- Doubt the truth that only God's love can fill and empower.
- See a delicious image.
- Desire and lust for that food.
- Take what is forbidden.
- Hide the guilt and shame with baggy clothes.
- Fear the consequences of judgment, rejection, and poor health.
- Blame others and God for his or her empty, out-of-control, and disordered life.

Both misogyny and misandry keep all addicts and co-addicts empty through lack of love and lack of strength. The bondage of fear in your human spirit flushes your human soul with murder and your human body with lust.

- Your spirit experiences pain of betrayal.
- Your soul is filled with the anger of revenge.
- Your body seeks relief in addictions and co-addictions.

The tragic divorce keeps us separated from the love of God and the strength of God. We continue to live out of a lack of receptivity and a lack of empowerment. The pain and betrayal of life leaves many of us hopeless. Trapped by the spirit of fear, we remain lost to the beauty and strength of the power of God. In the trance of the father of lies, we blindly grope to eat and drink of our false gods but are, instead, eaten by our addictions and sucked dry by co-addictions.

Waiting for Heaven
We all deeply ache for a place where there is no more pain—where no more betrayal occurs. There is a future place where you will be perfectly filled and perfectly empowered; there is a place where God's perfect love will cast out all fear forever and ever.

Aching for Something More

Pre-Fall Gen 1-2	Fall Gen 3:1-6	Post-Fall Gen 3:7 - Rev	Heaven Currently waiting
Honeymoon with God	Tragic Divorce	Hole in Your Spirit	Ache for Something More
• Perfectly loved by God • Perfectly love God and each other • No betrayal • No pain	• Separated from God • Cut off from receptivity and empowerment • Betrayal • Pain	NON-BELIEVER • Apart from God—life of Idolatry BELIEVER • Sealed by Holy Spirit • Flesh wars with Holy Spirit to fill the hole • Sometimes choose life of obedience to Spirit—worship • Sometimes choose life of disobedience in self—idolatry	• Hungering for paradise again • Hungering for perfect love again • No more betrayal • No more pain

There, you will taste and experience tenderness, strength, and eternal peace. You will be able to rest and not strive. This is the place of great food, drink, music, company, and celebration. This is the eternal stress-free vacation! This is where you will be perfectly loved and will love perfectly. You know that this perfect place for which we all hunger and thirst is called Heaven.

However, there is also a place we all dread. Second by second, minute by minute, this place is filled with eternal pain. It is a place of eternal betrayal where the dead will violate you—a place devoid of any kind of tenderness, strength, or peace. The place where the presence of fear haunts, a place for the enemies of God to anguish forever. The eternal place of spiritual bondage—Hell.

Spiritual Bondage

When our intimacy with God is disrupted, we live in spiritual bondage and idolatry. To return to God and have our intimacy with Him restored is our path to freedom and worship and a life with Him in heaven. In order to have intimacy with God, the life of idolatry must be disrupted.

Remember the woman who struggled with anorexia nervosa? Do you see that the spirit of fear was filling her spirit and flushing her soul and body with the paralysis of fear, which left her stuck in an eating disorder for decades?

When she started to see the stronghold in her life was core emptiness and disempowerment in her spirit, she was able to see a new vision for filling and empowering her spirit. She could identify the primary stronghold in her soul of how her thinking, feelings, and choices were fear-based. However, this clinical insight alone did not produce any change.

Finally, she saw how the secondary stronghold of anorexia nervosa in her body was literally destroying her body and possibly her life.

This woman in her thirties desperately wanted to become pregnant and have another child. However, with anorexia, a woman often loses her ability to have her monthly period and, therefore, cannot become pregnant. Furthermore, 15 percent of women who suffer with this disease die of complications related to it. She had been unsuccessfully hospitalized for starvation more than once. Her husband, who was a physician, and I took her problem very seriously. She needed a new vision and treatment plan for authentic freedom and healing in her spirit, soul, and body. Gloriously, this woman decided to pursue her spiritual homecoming with the hope of tasting the impossible—becoming pregnant.

She needed a holistic plan to her caregiving that addressed the strongholds in her spirit, soul, and body. At this point in her journey, she had only worked on the soul and body strongholds in her life. She lacked a sense of belonging and a sense of being and was entrenched in her false self. The eating disorder was an attempt to control her outer world by desperately trying to control her inner world.

During her therapy, friends joined her weekly sessions to support and pray for her. She had a passive personality, so she had stuffed her anger for her entire life. She was struggling with depression and passive suicidal thinking when she first saw me. She was not going to actively take her life; however, she was not going to prevent herself from being killed either.

The process for this woman was long and exhausting, but she became free of fear in her spirit, soul, and body. She also healed in spirit, soul, and body as she was filled by the healing love of God and empowered to live as her passion, giftedness, and purpose was unlocked.

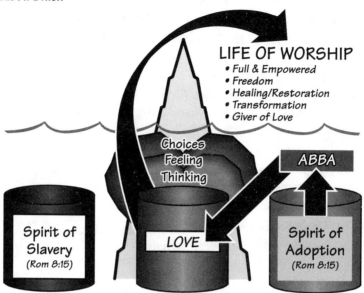

The spirit of adoption flushed out the spirit of fear, which was flooding her spirit, soul, and body.

> *For you have not received a spirit of slavery leading to*
> *fear again, but you have received a spirit of adoption as*
> *sons by which we cry out, "Abba! Father!"*
> *(Romans 8:15, NASB)*

Her body healed as she made her spiritual homecoming. Nine months after she graduated from her therapy, her period came back and she became pregnant. She had a blonde little boy nine months later!

The key to mastering the spirit of fear is found in the Bible:

> *There is no fear in love; but perfect love casts out fear.*
> *(1 John 4:18, NASB)*

Being filled with the love of God casts the spirit of fear out of your life. If you have found God, seek to experience His tender and strong love for you!

∗ ∗ ∗ ∗ ∗ ∗ ∗

Personal Journaling and Small Group Questions
Spiritual Homecoming Assignment Four

Personal Journaling Questions

Take a few minutes to say this prayer:

"Investigate my life, O God, find out everything about me; cross-examine and test me, get a clear picture of what I'm about; see for yourself whether I've done anything wrong—then guide me on the road to eternal life."[7] I claim your promise: "Call to Me and I will answer you, and I will tell you great and mighty things, which you do not know."[8] God, would you tell me great and unsearchable things I do not know about how I see my father and mother and how I have projected those unfair images onto You? I ask these things in Jesus' name. Amen.

1. List the top 12 most painful images of your mother.
2. List the vows and judgments you made out of fear from your mother pain.
3. List the top 12 most painful images of your father.
4. List the vows and judgments you made out of fear from your father pain.
5. List your top most painful images of God.
6. List the vows and judgments you made out of fear against God.
7. How does the list of painful images of your mother and father relate to your perceived painful images of God?
8. List the ways in which you ignore God.
9. List the ways in which you do not stand up for God.
10. List the top 12 things you worship (addiction, idols) instead of the living God. (List your addictions again, but now with a deeper realization of what addiction is.)
11. List the top 12 relationships you worship (co-addiction idols) instead of the living God. (Who do you "bow to" by not being able to say no to them?)

Spend time in prayer breaking the vows and judgments you have made against God and others. Ask God's forgiveness for the characteristics of your parents that you have projected onto God. Ask forgiveness for the ways you have ignored God and have not stood up for Him. Spend time in prayer acknowledging your idolatry, item by item, and confessing, renouncing and repenting.

Breaking Your Vows and Judgments

Small Group Questions

1. What… are the key truths that stood out to you in this stage?
2. Why… do you need to know these truths?
3. How… do you apply these truths to your life?
4. Your pain… What pain does this stage reveal in your life?
5. Your sin… What are you doing with your pain?
6. Repentance… What do you need to do differently?
7. Prayer… What do you need to ask God for help with?

Interlude: Spiritual Homecoming Is at Hand!

In the first part of this book, I spoke to you as a Christian psychologist addressing two issues:

> ***What are you struggling with?*** *(What are your addictions and co-addictions?)*

> ***Why are you struggling with it?*** *(How have you been betrayed?)*

In the second half of the book, I will speak to you as a Christian pastor addressing one issue:

> ***Where do you go from here? How to make the spiritual homecoming journey that will fill you, empower you, and release your passion, giftedness, and purpose.***

At this point of your spiritual homecoming, you are facing four critical spiritual homecoming questions:

How were you betrayed? Facing what has happened to you, your story, your relational pain or relational shame, is 25 percent of the spiritual homecoming journey.

Are You Stuck in Your Pain?

25% How have you been betrayed?

ARE YOU STUCK HERE?

25% OF YOUR PROCESS...

How do you betray others, yourself, and God? Facing what you are doing with your story, your relational sin or relational guilt, is 75 percent of the spiritual homecoming journey.

Are You Ready to Move Through Your Process?

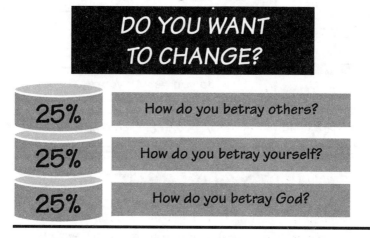

75% OF YOUR PROCESS...

If you are stuck looking at your shame, your victimization, how you were betrayed—the first 25 percent of the journey—this will re-victimize you and keep you victimized!

If you look at how you betray others, yourself, and God—you will move through the complete 100 percent of your spiritual homecoming. Repenting of your relational sin will deeply heal your relational pain because your sin can come up and out of you. You can shift from betraying God and others to loving God and others.

100% OF THE HEALING AND RECOVERY PROCESS

25%	How have you been betrayed?
25%	How do you betray others?
25%	How do you betray yourself?
25%	How do you betray God?

100% OF YOUR PROCESS...

If you remove the 75 percent of how you are protecting your pain, your pain that has been protecting your sin is going to come up and out of you, and that is when you will genuinely deal with your pain.

The pain in your spirit, the pain in your soul, and the pain in your body and your relationships will come up and out of you. You will truly heal from the inside out! This will bring you into actual freedom and healing in your spirit, soul, and body. Your freedom, healing, and restoration will come as you find your way to the sacred Cross.

Finding Your Way to the Cross

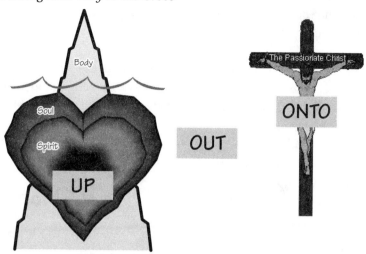

How do you release your relational guilt and shame at the Cross? And how do you receive God's relational forgiveness and cleansing at the Cross?

The Art of Releasing and Receiving at the Cross

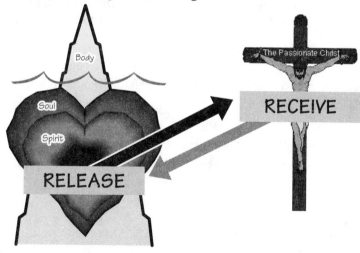

To acknowledge your guilt at the Cross is an experience of sacred release of your guilt. It will bring you deep forgiveness and cleansing. To acknowledge your shame at the Cross is an experience of sacred release of your shame. It will bring you into deep freedom and healing.

We will always struggle with the flesh and the spirit (outer person and inner person) through betrayal, revenge, and lust. The question is, how do you want to struggle? Well? Moderately? Poorly? Not at all?

The Hope of Deliverance, Healing, and Restoration

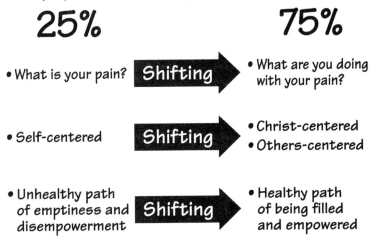

If you want to struggle well, you want to find your way to the sacred Cross. To do this, you need to find the answers to five critical questions:

- What is your relational sin?
- What is your relational pain?
- What is the relational Cross?
- How do you take up your Cross daily?
- How do you follow Christ?

Entering into the hole in your spirit, rather than running from it, will allow you to face your core emptiness. As you enter into the hole in your spirit, you will find new tenderness, new strength, and new peace. You will find the God of the universe.

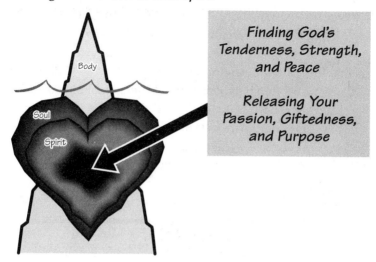

Body

Soul

Spirit

Finding God's
Tenderness, Strength,
and Peace

Releasing Your
Passion, Giftedness,
and Purpose

> *One thing God has spoken, two things have I heard:*
> *That you, O God are strong, and that you, O Lord,*
> *are loving.*
>
> (Psalm 62:11-12, NIV)

As you experience the love and strength of the living God, your sense of belonging and sense of being will be birthed and healed. When your core emptiness starts to be filled and empowered, your passion, giftedness, and purpose will come forth!

You will shift from a lack of belonging to a sense of belonging, from a lack of being to a sense of being, from the false self to the true self, from a lack of purpose to a sense of purpose. These shifts will fill you with a sense of awe for who God is, and you will shift from a life of taking (idolatry and worshiping false gods) to a life of giving (worshiping the true God) and a new sense of gratitude for what God has personally done for you!

Your spiritual homecoming is at hand. The choice to continue is yours!

* * * * * * *

Personal Journaling or Small Group Questions
Spiritual Homecoming Assignment—Interlude

Personal Journaling Questions
1. What is your relational pain or relational shame—how have you been betrayed?
2. What is your relational sin or relational guilt—
   - How do you betray others?
   - How do you betray yourself?
   - How do you betray God?
3. What sin and pain do you need to release at the Cross?
4. What do you need to receive at the Cross?
   - Forgiveness
   - Cleansing
   - Healing
   - Gifts of the Holy Spirit (Empowerment)
5. What are some areas in which you need to die to your own will and surrender to God's will? Bring those before Him in prayer and ask Him to empower you to surrender to His will. Have your small group or community pray this with you.

Small Group Questions
1. What... are the key truths that stood out to you in this stage?
2. Why... do you need to know these truths?
3. How... do you apply these truths to your life?
4. Your pain... What pain does this stage reveal in your life?
5. Your sin... What are you doing with your pain?
6. Repentance... What do you need to do differently?
7. Prayer... What do you need to ask God for help with?

STAGE FIVE: Opening Your Heart to God
Finding Your Way to Your Abba Father

The miracle of receptivity takes place when you choose to receive God's tenderness of love and strength of love. This sacred miracle does not automatically occur just because you have experienced a religious rite of passage such as being a church member, or being baptized, or being confirmed. You can experience one or all of those wonderful religious traditions and still be empty and disempowered at your core. However, the miracle of receptivity can occur in the hearts of all who seek it.

When the living Christ enters the house of your spirit, Jesus will take you, in spirit, to His Father. When you connect to the Father God in your human spirit, the Father can fill and empower you with the gifts of the Holy Spirit. The Holy Spirit will enable you to express your true self with passion, giftedness, and purpose. That is the miracle of receptivity—your openness to God's filling and empowering, to Him enabling you to express your true self.

The Journey to New Faith

Growing up as the son of a Lutheran minister, I thought I was automatically a Christian. I really never gave it much thought until one of my friends in high school became a "Jesus freak," and I vowed that I would never do that!

In college, I encountered my first personal crisis in life. My parents announced that they were divorcing. I was close to both of my parents, and, as I heard the news, I felt the knife of betrayal cutting me in half and the tenderness and strength of love being ripped apart in my spirit.

As a freshman, I was attending a small state university north of Minneapolis. Both my girlfriend and my parents lived in Minneapolis, so I wondered if I should move back when I heard the news. I happened to have my dusty old confirmation Bible on the bookshelf in my dorm room. I thought, *Maybe it is time to finally open it.* So I took the book, closed my eyes and said,

"God, if you truly speak to your people through the Bible, then speak to me!"

With my eyes closed, I blindly opened the pages and the very first thing I read was:

> "Ho, ho, flee from the land of the north, says the LORD."
> (*Zechariah 2:6, RSV*)

I was absolutely shocked! I thought, *This works! God does speak to His people through the Bible.* Well, today I have graduated from seminary, and I would not interpret the Scriptures like that. However, it did eventually influence my own spiritual homecoming.

I attended my second year at a university in the Twin Cities. I did not know a soul on campus and sensed it would be good to plug into a Christian group. I met a man by the name of Jerry in his late twenties from a Christian organization. He struck me as very kind, yet very strong, and he seemed to have an authentic relationship with God. That summer I attended a seven-week leadership training program with the organization. The first night, my team of seven men gathered, and each shared how he became a Christian. They all seemed to have a time, a place, and a date when they had opened the doors of their hearts and had accepted Christ.

I was extremely nervous and a little embarrassed because I could not recall specifically inviting Christ to come into my life. The last man to share his story before me quoted this verse from the last book of the Bible:

> Behold, I stand at the door and knock; if anyone hears
> My voice and opens the door, I will come in to him and
> will dine with him, and he with Me.
> (*Revelation 3:20, NASB*)

When I heard that verse, I was not sure if I had ever done that in my life. But, I knew I wanted to. When it was my time to share my story, I said that I was the son of a Lutheran minister, and I was a Christian. This was not a pushy group. They accepted my story, and we called it a night. However, I went to bed sweating.

I said, "Lord, I want to make sure I have opened the door of my heart and have officially invited You in, if I never have before. However, if the rapture was scheduled for tonight, could you hold it off for just one day?"

I did not want to make the most important decision of my life in a smelly bunk room with six other sweaty guys!

So the next day, on the bank of the Mississippi River, I bowed before the Creator of the universe.

At that moment, I said, "Jesus, I believe you are the Son of God. I want to make you Lord of my life by listening to you and obeying you. I am not sure if I have ever done this or not. Therefore, Jesus, I hear you knocking at the door of my heart, and, today, I officially invite you to come in and be my Lord and Savior. Amen."

After I prayed, I did not hear any bells or whistles. I was not really expecting anything. But a peace did come over me as I returned to work.

That summer surprised me; it changed my life and my life message forever. All of a sudden, the Bible came alive in me and the words made sense to me. Prior to that, it was just a good religious book. I was amazed! How could this book that I had owned for years suddenly come alive and make so much sense?

I did not realize at the time that Jesus must reign in your heart in order for His Word, the Scripture, to dance there also. That summer was the first time I listened to the voice of God through the Spirit of His Son Jesus.

*Why do you call Me, "Lord, Lord," and do not do what
I say?*

(Luke 6:46, NASB)

I may have called Jesus my Lord before, but that summer I was really hearing Him and doing what He said. For the first time in my life I was challenged to do the very things God's Spirit impressed me to do. A community of other students, who also took the time to daily listen and obey the voice of God, made this radical way of living a little more palatable.

They were there for me when I went through a time of really doubting my security as a Christian. At one point, one friend asked me if I was struggling with guilt. I said no, but as I thought about that question, I came to realize that I really was. I did not understand then how to release my guilt at the Cross. A verse that helped me was 1 John 5:11-12.

*And the testimony is this, that God has given us
eternal life, and this life is in His Son. He who has the
Son has the life; he who does not have the Son of God
does not have the life.*

(1 John 5:11-12, NASB)

I realized I did have the Son of God living in me; therefore, I did have eternal life. The power of the truth of God just shattered all of the fears of my guilt.

I took the lordship of Christ seriously, and God took me down the path of personal change to a new level of intimacy with Him. God was building a foundation in me for a long-term relationship with Him.

For the next fifteen years, my sense of belonging to Christ matured, and my sense of being came forth in natural ways that surprised those who knew me. I felt the emptiness in my spirit dissipating, and I was empowered by new tenderness, strength, and peace from Christ living in me.

However, to be really honest, I did not experience the empowerment of the Holy Spirit that I suspected was available to a Christian. I felt like God was filling me, but empowerment was not tangible. At times I felt stuck and sensed that my struggle with life was really no different than a non-Christian's. The leadership staff asked me to join them, but I felt my life was too hypocritical to become a Christian leader, so I sadly declined.

My Spiritual Homecoming

I was single during this time and had been praying a very simple but obscure verse concerning my future wife:

> *If you are willing and obedient, you will eat the best from the land.*
>
> (Isaiah 1:19, NIV)

I knew it would only be by God's grace that I could be willing and therefore obedient. So I asked God, by His grace, to make me willing and obedient so that He could also give me the best wife in the land for me.

One Saturday evening, as I was leading a singles group at a large evangelical church, a beautiful, green-eyed, German blonde named Beth walked into the gathering. I was so struck by the beauty, compassion, and spirit of worship that flowed through her that I immediately lost my place in the lesson. The whole group just roared! It was obvious to everyone that I had just been smitten by the visible competence, giftedness, and softness of this woman!

After our first date, we both knew we were going to marry each other! A turning point in my spiritual homecoming journey occurred while I was dating Beth.

One morning, a pastor at church spoke of how he had gone through deliverance from generational bondage that had changed his life forever. He shared a verse that addressed how the sins of parents will visit the future generations (Exodus 34:7). I knew that

I needed to experience this healing prayer, though I was afraid of what it would mean to be set free from any bondage that kept me disempowered in life. I trusted him, so I shared all of the sources of guilt and shame in my life. I also shared what I knew of my father and mother's struggles and their parents' struggles.

The prayer took about two hours, and like my conversion to Christ, I did not experience any bells or whistles. I simply experienced a deep peace beyond my human understanding. But that night my destiny changed forever. I experienced what the apostle Paul prayed for the church of Ephesus:

> That the God of our Lord Jesus Christ, the Father
> of glory, may give to you a spirit of wisdom and of
> revelation in the knowledge of him. I pray that the eyes
> of your heart may be enlightened.
> (Ephesians 1:17-18, NASB)

The eyes of my heart were opened for the first time. With new vision, I saw the sacrifice made for me—Jesus Christ hanging on the Cross. Then what I witnessed disrupted all of my cognitive, intelligence-based understanding of faith. In my vision, Jesus came off the Cross and met me. I was stunned by the reality that Jesus Christ was actually alive and well. Wow! Why had I not realized this before?

Like most people, I had a schism (disconnect) between my head and my heart. This separation relegated the love and strength of God to my head only. Until this moment of my spiritual homecoming, I had never been able to access this experience in my heart.

I was so overwhelmed by His love for me that I shouted, "Jesus Christ is alive and well! I am not going to follow denominations; I am going to follow Jesus!" All I wanted to do was follow Christ.

With that came an empowerment of my human spirit that filled me with strength from above that I had never known—I experienced the miracle of receptivity and empowerment! This amazing filling of God's love and strength has never left me. Even in the times that I wander away from this spiritual reality, Jesus always meets me. When I turn back and look to Him again, He has been loyal to me, even within the desert experiences of life.

After these substantial experiences with Christ, my denominational judgments were disrupted and broken, which was a defining moment in my global perspective of faith. I no longer cared if someone was Protestant or Catholic, evangelical or charismatic. What mattered was whether they encountered Jesus at the Cross and were willing and obedient to follow Him.

That day of deliverance from my generational strongholds was truly a picture of amazing grace. I had been spiritually blind for fifteen years, even as a sincere follower of Christ, but now I could see.

As a Lutheran baby, I had already been baptized by the sprinkling of water on my head. But now I wanted to have a "believer's baptism." When you are baptized as a believer, you publicly state:

- I am a sinner and have betrayed God and others.
- Jesus died and was buried, in substitution for my own spiritual death and burial.
- Jesus rose from the dead, empowering my own spiritual resurrection.

I was impassioned to publicly identify with the death, burial, and resurrection of Jesus Christ, so I asked the pastor who took me through the deliverance to baptize me as a believer in Christ. Later that month, my family and friends gathered one Sunday afternoon at a lake where, for the first time, I publicly shared my decision, fifteen years earlier, to follow Christ and what had happened to me as I gained freedom from generational strongholds. Unknown to me, my decision the summer of 1979 to become a Christian was just the start of my spiritual homecoming, which ultimately saved my life in more ways than one.

I asked Beth's father for his blessing to marry his daughter, which he granted. Within our first year of marriage, we flew to Anaheim to attend an inner healing conference. During one workshop, the leader invited participants to share a painful memory with the large group and then ask Jesus to reveal Himself in that memory. Of course, I was too self-conscious to do that publicly. Also, as a therapist I did not want to drop my professional demeanor and be vulnerable with a group of strangers. But on the last day of the conference, God cornered me. Someone with a prophetic ministry asked me, "Is that your wife?" as she pointed to a crowd of multiple blondes. As I confirmed it, she said, "Something quick is going to happen to you. I am not sure what it is, but whatever it is, do not become bitter." Then she left.

I tried to dismiss the whole thing. But, somehow I knew that if she was right, I would become bitter. Why? Because I knew in my heart that I did not trust God. Since I did not trust God, I was susceptible to bitterness.

Prior to attending this inner healing conference, I had written a letter to my father that I had no intention of mailing. I just needed to put my thoughts on paper. I read the letter aloud to a trusted co-worker. My friend wept; I did not shed a tear.

I thought, *Wow, I am really disconnected from my pain with my father. How can this person weep for me when I am the one who experienced it?*

So I made a deal with God. I offered, "God, I will share this painful memory this afternoon in the workshop if nobody else volunteers. However, I just ask that no one laugh at me when I share this memory."

You will find out later what happened. You will also see that those prophetic words came into being one decade later. By that point in my life, I am glad that I had already been taught how to be filled through the miracle of receptivity and strengthened through the miracle of empowerment.

Experiencing the Miracle of Receptivity

To experience the miracle of receptivity, ask yourself two questions:

Have I come to the point in my spiritual life where I know for sure that, if I died tonight, I would go to Heaven?[9]

If I died tonight and stood before God, and He asked me, "Why should I let you into my Heaven?" what would I say to Him?[10]

The first question is one that everyone needs to answer before they die. The rest of this stage will help you to do that. The answer to the second question is in the following verses:

> For I delivered to you as of first importance what I also received, that Christ died for our sins according to the Scriptures, and that He was buried, and that He was raised on the third day according to the Scriptures.
> (1 Corinthians 15:3-4, NASB)

> But as many as received Him, to them He gave the right to become children of God, even to those who believe in His name, who were born, not of blood nor of the will of the flesh nor of the will of man, but of God.
> (John 1:12-13, NASB)

You need to know that:
- Jesus is the Son of God.
- Jesus died for your sins.
- Jesus was buried and raised back to life on the third day.

To experience the miracle of receptivity, you need to:
- Believe in Jesus as the Son of God and in Jesus as your Lord, which automatically leads to believing in Jesus as your Savior.
- Repent.
- Daily confess your sin when you betray God and others.

- Daily renounce your sin when you betray God and others.
- Daily change the way you are living.
- Follow Jesus as your Lord, daily listening to Him, daily obeying Him.

Here I am! I stand at the door and knock. If anyone hears my voice and opens the door, I will come in and eat with him, and he with me.

—Jesus (Revelation 3:20, NIV)

Opening the Door of Your Spirit

At the point of opening the door of your spirit and asking Jesus to come in, you will experience a sacred release and sacred receptivity simultaneously. In sacred release, with the eyes of your heart (Eph. 1:17, 18), you symbolically stretch out your hands to the cross and release your sin (guilt) and pain (shame). In sacred receptivity, with the eyes of your heart (1 John 1:19), you symbolically receive God's forgiveness, cleansing and healing.

Why do you call me, "Lord, Lord," and do not do what I say?

—Jesus (Luke 6:46, NIV)

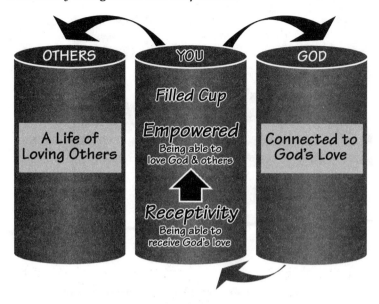

As you make Jesus your Lord, He is also your Savior. At that moment of sacred release, you will experience the sacred receptivity of being filled with a holy love. At that moment you will also be filled with a sacred empowerment of a holy strength that will inundate your spirit, soul and body with the peace of Christ.

From that moment, you have daily access to the Cross of Christ to be filled and empowered. You will also be able to release your sin (guilt) and your pain (shame). As you do this daily, you will have increasing measures of freedom and healing.

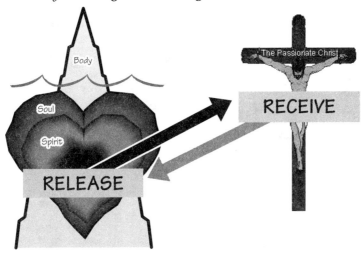

If you are not sure that you have ever made Jesus your Lord, invite Him to come in.

> *Behold, I stand at the door and knock; if anyone hears*
> *My voice and opens the door, I will come in to him and*
> *will dine with him, and he with Me.*
>
> *(Revelation 3:20, NASB)*

When you are His follower, you should sense His daily desire to be with you, His knocking at the door of your heart. These are the dynamics that bring you into sacred intimacy. Great rest comes in experiencing in your heart what you know in your head about God's great tenderness of love and strength of love. This will release a sacred peace within you that surpasses all understanding and comes directly from the Father.

> *Jesus said to him, "I am the way, and the truth, and the*
> *life; no one comes to the Father but through Me.*
>
> *(John 14:6, NASB)*

Only by receiving Jesus into your life can you have access to the Father.

- Jesus takes you to the Father.
- The Father releases the Holy Spirit within you.
- The Holy Spirit is the One who fills you and empowers you.

If you want to follow Jesus Christ, you will need to shift your focus from your relational pain to your relational sin, which will bring you to the relational Cross.

> *If anyone would come after me, he must deny himself*
> *and take up his cross daily and follow me.*
>
> *(Luke 9:23, NIV)*

When you have a relationship with God through Jesus' death on the Cross, you can come to the Cross daily to receive the mystery of God's goodness. As you have your sense of belonging and your sense of being restored through your journey of intimacy with God, your true self will experience passion, giftedness, and purpose.

Receiving Your Sense of Belonging and Being

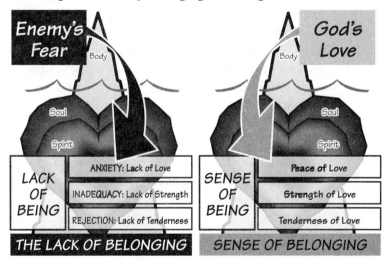

This is a critical moment in your spiritual homecoming journey. To be filled and empowered is to have your spirit filled with the love of Jesus and empowered with the strength of Jesus. What will your response be? Here are three simple steps to inviting Jesus Christ to fill and empower you.

The Step of Believing

- Believe that Jesus Christ is the Son of God.
- Believe that Jesus died on the Cross for your betrayals (sins).
- Believe that God raised Him from the dead.

> *But as many as received Him, to them He gave the right to become children of God, even to those who believe in His name, who were born, not of blood nor of the will of the flesh nor of the will of man, but of God.*
>
> *(John 1:12-13, NASB)*

The Step of Confessing

- Confess that you are a sinner (a betrayer), asking general forgiveness for the sins you are not yet fully aware you have committed.
- Confess that you have betrayed God.
- Confess that you have betrayed others.
- Daily confess your specific sins, as the Holy Spirit enables you to see them, whether they are from the past or present. As you draw closer to Him, who is light, you will be able to see things as He sees them with increasing clarity.

> *If we confess our sins, He is faithful and righteous to forgive us our sins and to cleanse us from all unrighteousness. If we say that we have not sinned, we make Him a liar and His word is not in us.*
>
> *(1 John 1:9-10, NASB)*

The Step of Receiving

- Open the door of your heart and ask Jesus to come in.

- Choose to make Him the Lord and Savior of your life by daily confessing your betrayals and moment-by-moment turning from them, receiving His forgiveness and strength to live differently.

Here I am! I stand at the door and knock. If anyone hears my voice and opens the door, I will come in and eat with him, and he with me.
—Jesus (Revelation 3:20, NIV)

Truly, truly, I say to you, he who hears My word, and believes Him who sent Me, has eternal life, and does not come into judgment, but has passed out of death into life.
—Jesus (John 5:24, NASB)

This is a simple prayer to say to God, opening the door of your spirit to Jesus Christ:

Dear Father-God:

I confess to You that I am a sinner.
I have betrayed You, God, by failing to love You.
I have betrayed others by failing to love them.
I believe that Jesus Christ is the Son of God.
I believe that Jesus died on the Cross for my sins (betrayals).
I believe that You, God, raised Him from the dead.
I now open the door of my spirit to Jesus.

Jesus, I ask you to come in and be my Lord and Savior.
I choose to daily confess and turn from betraying You and others.
I choose to live a life of honoring You and giving thanks to You.
I choose to love You by learning how to listen and obey You.
I thank You, God, my heavenly Father, for giving me Your Holy Spirit to fill me each day with new power, new love, and the ability to follow You.

I pray this in the powerful name of my Lord Jesus.
Amen.

The Assurance of Eternal Life with God

If you have believed in Jesus Christ as the Son of God, confessed your betrayals, and opened the door of your heart to Jesus Christ,

He will live in your heart forever. When your body dies, your spirit, which is united with His Spirit, will enter into eternal paradise.

> And the testimony is this, that God has given us *eternal life, and this life is in His Son. **He who has the Son has the life; he who does not have the Son of God does not have the life.** These things I have written to you who believe in the name of the Son of God, so that you may know that you have eternal life.*
> *(1 John 5:11-13, NASB, emphasis added)*

This verse answers both questions one and two:

Have I come to the point in my spiritual life where I know for sure that, if I died tonight, I would go to Heaven?

Yes! You can be certain that you have eternal life with God. God promises that if you believe in the name of the Son of God, you have eternal life.

If I died tonight and stood before God, and He asked me, "Why should I let you into my Heaven?" what would I say to Him?

If you believe in Jesus Christ as your Lord and Savior, you have been adopted as a child of God; He has given you the right to live in Heaven with Him

When you make Jesus Lord of your life, He is your Savior from sin and death. Your spiritual homecoming really just starts here. Living out your decision to follow Christ will release your passion, giftedness, and purpose as you make your journey home.

Daily Practices for Your Homecoming Journey:

- Ask the Lord to reveal what is true about His heart and character through His Word.
- Ask the Lord to strengthen your faith in what He says is true.
- Worship God the Father each day. This means to honor Him and thank Him for who He is and for His blessings.
- Choose to love Jesus each day by listening to His Holy Spirit and obeying what He says.
- Ask God to fill you daily with His power, love, and self-discipline through His Holy Spirit living in you.

The Foundation of Receptivity and Empowerment

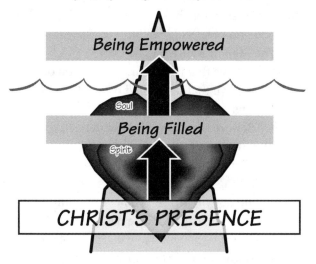

The next stages of your spiritual homecoming journey will help you to understand the daily art of receptivity and the daily art of empowerment.

* * * * * * *

Personal Journaling and Small Group Questions
Spiritual Homecoming Assignment Five

Personal Journaling Questions

1. Have you come to the point in your spiritual life where you know for certain that, if you died tonight, you would go to Heaven?

    If you died tonight and stood before God and He asked you, "Why should I let you into my Heaven?" what would you say to Him?

2. Have you taken the three steps to invite Jesus Christ to fill you and empower you?

    ### The Step of Believing
    *   Believe that Jesus Christ is the Son of God.
    *   Believe that Jesus died on the Cross for your sins (betrayals).
    *   Believe that God raised Him from the dead.

    ### The Step of Confessing
    *   Confess that you are a sinner (betrayer), asking general forgiveness for the sins you are not yet aware you have committed.
    *   Confess that you have betrayed God.
    *   Confess that you have betrayed others.
    *   Daily confess your specific sins, as the Holy Spirit enables you to see them, whether they are from the past or present. As you draw closer to Him, who is light, you will be able to see things as He sees them with increasing clarity.

    ### The Step of Receiving
    *   Open the door of your heart and ask Jesus to come in.
    *   Choose to make Him the Lord and Savior of your life by daily repenting of your sins—betrayals.

Do you want to make Jesus Lord and Savior of your life?
If so, pray the prayer you read earlier, or one similar in your own words, to open the door of your spirit to Jesus Christ:

Small Group Questions

1. What... are the key truths that stood out to you in this stage?
2. Why... do you need to know these truths?
3. How... do you apply these truths to your life?
4. Your pain... What pain does this stage reveal in your life?
5. Your sin... What are you doing with your pain?
6. Repentance... What do you need to do differently?
7. Prayer... What do you need to ask God for help with?

STAGE SIX: Lasting Personal Change
Three Spiritual Tools for the Journey

If you have made it this far through the book, you have a framework for personal change, authentic intimacy, and restored sexuality. The last part of this book will equip you with tools for the rest of your spiritual homecoming journey. The three spiritual tools in this stage are adapted from my time with Leanne Payne. I commend to you her books *Healing Presence* and *Listening Prayer*.

This stage can be described by the word "maturity." How do you grow up in faith? How do you experience being daily filled and daily empowered by God?

> *Because of the sacrifice of the Messiah, his blood poured out on the altar of the Cross, we're a free people—free of penalties and punishments chalked up by all our misdeeds. And not just barely free, either. Abundantly free! He thought of everything, provided for everything we could possibly need, letting us in on the plans he took such delight in making. He set it all out before us in Christ, a long-range plan in which everything would be brought together and summed up in him, everything in deepest heaven, everything on planet earth.*
>
> *It's in Christ that we find out who we are and what we are living for. Long before we first heard of Christ and got our hopes up, he had his eye on us, had designs on us for glorious living, part of the overall purpose he is working out in everything and everyone.*
>
> *It's in Christ that you, once you heard the truth and believed it (this Message of your salvation), found yourselves home free— signed, sealed, and delivered by the Holy Spirit. This signet from God is the first installment on what's coming, a reminder that we'll get everything God has planned for us, a praising and glorious life.*
>
> (Ephesians 1:7-14, MSG)

To grow up in your faith you must eat the bread of life and drink the water of life—"being" (resting in God) will help you grow into "doing." When you try to "do" in the Christian life before you have spent time simply "being," you become spiritually malnourished and stunted.

When you know the living God and have a relationship with Him, there are three primary arts to being receptive to His love and empowering, by His strength.
- The Art of Embracing God's Presence
- The Art of Listening Prayer
- The Art of Renewing Your Spiritual Vows

The Art of Embracing God's Presence
Embracing God's presence means taking time to reflect on who lives within you.

Daily Embracing the Presence of God

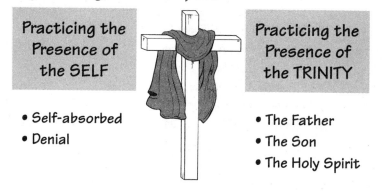

Practicing the Presence of the SELF
- Self-absorbed
- Denial

Practicing the Presence of the TRINITY
- The Father
- The Son
- The Holy Spirit

The apostle Paul explains this to the community of Galatians, saying:

> *I am crucified with Christ: nevertheless I live; yet not I, but Christ liveth in me: and the life which I now live in the flesh I live by the faith of the Son of God, who loved me, and gave himself for me.*
> (Galatians 2:20, KJV, emphasis added)

If you have opened the door of your spirit to Jesus Christ and asked Him to come in as your Lord and Savior, then His Holy Spirit lives in you! However, many people do not think about that spiritual reality. Most Christians "practice their own presence" or are "checked out" in their addictive and co-addictive worlds. When you are "practicing the presence of self," you are absorbed in your own feelings; denying that you even have feelings about certain issues; and you constantly analyze your actions, attitudes, and other people's reactions to you.

Practicing the Presence of God (the Trinity)

> *On that day you will realize that I am in my Father,*
> *and you are in me, and I am in you.*
> *—Jesus (John 14:20, NIV)*

Most people think that God is very distant and lives somewhere in the galaxy. However, the truth is that Jesus lives in the Father. When you ask Jesus to come into your spirit, you also come into Jesus' spirit. So if you live in Jesus, and Jesus lives in the Father, then you spiritually live in the Father, too. If you have invited Jesus into your spirit as Lord and Savior, the Father is only a breath away. (Marie Barnett wrote a song about this spiritual phenomenon called "Breathe," sung by Michael W. Smith. It is a song worth playing each morning as you reflect on Who lives in you!)

Reflect daily on the reality of Galatians 2:20 above. When you belong to God, your sense of being will come forth by the Spirit of God.

Declare daily, "Father, I belong to you." This rivets your spiritual foundation to the love and strength of God.

I often play a worship song that speaks of the living presence of God within me. I light a candle to symbolize the living fire of the Trinity of God living in me. I light this candle with my family as we seek to take the first moments of our day to be filled and empowered by God. Then, when we "do" for God, it is not out of our emptiness or disempowerment, but out of His resources within us. Each day we go as a family before God and invite the Holy Spirit to continue to fill us and empower us with His healing and anointing. My five children know that as believers in Christ they are sealed in God with the Holy Spirit who lives within them. Yet they also know that living out their faith means a daily decision to spend time with Him and submit to Him. The impact of a child filled and empowered by the love and strength of God is incredible, especially in the adolescent years.

For a child to take the time to embrace the living presence of Christ, he or she must witness Dad and Mom spending this time with God regularly. When you spend time this way, the Lord will show you how to embrace His presence with such fluidity that you will think about Him consistently. This is vital as you make family, personal, and business decisions quickly through each day. Knowing and expecting that the Father will empower you brings passionate faith to life!

This prayer declares the living presence of Christ within you:
> *Christ be with me, Christ within me,*
> *Christ behind me, Christ before me,*
> *Christ beside me, Christ to win me,*
> *Christ to comfort and restore me.*
> *Christ beneath me, Christ above me,*
> *Christ in quiet, Christ in danger,*
> *Christ in hearts of all that love me,*
> *Christ in mouth of friend and stranger.*[11]

Christ is with you! This is, in part, how you are daily filled and empowered to shift from a life of idolatry to a life of worship. Embracing God's presence is the first way to experience the art of receptivity. As you reflect upon the spiritual reality that the Trinity lives in you, and the Father pours out the gifts of the Holy Spirit into your very being, you will start to experience the connection of your head with your heart, your intellect with your emotions.

The Holy Spirit connects what you know about the love and strength of God with the holy presence of God. When you experience the holy presence of the Almighty, the space within you is filled with the most majestic presence of the universe. Such an incredible peace will touch you in these moments that your heart will naturally respond with love for the One who is filling you with the very essence of His Heart.

> *Meanwhile, the moment we get tired in the waiting, God's Spirit is right alongside helping us along. If we don't know how or what to pray, it doesn't matter. He does our praying in and for us, making prayer out of our wordless sighs, our aching groans. He knows us far better than we know ourselves...and keeps us present before God. That's why we can be so sure that every detail in our lives of love for God is worked into something good.*
>
> (Romans 8:26-28, MSG)

The Father, Son, and Holy Spirit are constantly discussing your welfare as you make this dusty journey; let that knowledge give you new faith, new hope, and new love.

Prayer of Embracing God's Presence

> *Jesus, thank you for living in me. Thank You for taking me to the Father. Father, thank You for releasing the gifts of the Holy Spirit in me. Please fill me with Your love and empower me with Your strength. With awe and gratitude, I pray. Amen.*

The Art of Listening Prayer

The art of listening prayer literally saved my life. Remember the prophetic word I had received? "Something quick is going to happen and, whatever it is, don't get bitter!"

One summer day, when I was in my early forties, during my listening prayer time I sensed that I should go see a urologist. I was very perplexed at this. Of all doctors, I did not want to see a urologist. And, like most men, I wanted to put it off by being too busy at work. My choice was to procrastinate or to obey the living Lord God Almighty.

Reluctantly, I saw the urologist and he checked my medical records. After a few brief minutes, he said very kindly and gently, "Paul, do you know that your PSA levels have been misdiagnosed for four years?" At that moment the fear of God filled me like I had never experienced before. He went on to say that there was a high probability that I had prostate cancer and that I would need a biopsy immediately. That was one of the hardest days of my spiritual journey.

My brother Dr. Errol Singh is a urological surgeon, and, since I had lost confidence in the medical community with four years of misdiagnosis, I asked him to complete the biopsy. The biopsy was positive for prostate cancer. I was near the third stage of cancer with a grade four out of five tumor. That day, the frailty of life became clear as I realized the balance of my life was in the Lord's hands—and always had been, even though I had not recognized it.

Later, my Mayo Clinic surgeon found it remarkable that a man like me in his early forties with no history of cancer in either side of the family would have requested a biopsy. He said that the biopsy saved my life.

I am grateful for the three urologists who gave me the medical care I needed to survive the cancer. I am grateful that God uses medical professionals to give us the physical care we need. But, the biopsy did not save my life. It was the living Lord God who prompted me to see the urologist. That is Who saved my life.

> *This is eternal life, that they may know You, the only true God, and Jesus Christ whom You have sent.*
>
> (*John 17:3, NASB*)

Eternal life is knowing God forever. To know God is to listen to Him and to talk to Him. Christians often do a good job of talking to God in prayer, but do we develop good listening skills that recognize and honor His heart, asking Him to direct our hearts, our decisions, and our paths?

I want to teach you a very simple but profound method of prayer that can bring new depth and intimacy to your relationship with God. I have adapted five steps to listening prayer: Seek, Reflect, Respond, Listen, and Obey.

Daily Listening Prayer and Listening Obedience

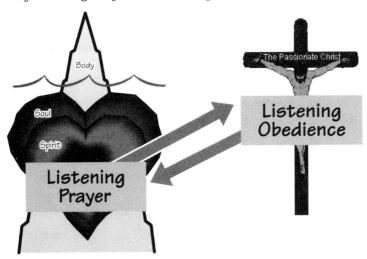

Five Steps of Listening Prayer
Step One: Seek
Open the sacred writings of the Holy Bible. Select a portion of Scripture to read. If you are not sure what to read, choose one of the first four books in the New Testament: Matthew, Mark, Luke, or John. Read a passage until a verse stands out to you, and then stop. Write out that verse or verses in your journal, and write down key words and phrases.

> *The word of God is living and active and sharper than any two-edged sword, and piercing as far as the*

division of soul and spirit, of both joints and marrow,
and able to judge the thoughts and intentions of the
heart. And there is no creature hidden from His sight,
but all things are open and laid bare to the eyes of Him
with whom we have to do.

(Hebrews 4:12-13, NASB)

Step Two: Reflect

Simply and very briefly write out your thoughts and meditations
to three questions:

- What are the key truths from the sacred Scriptures?
- Why do I need to know these truths?
- How do I apply these truths to my life?

Taking time to answer these three questions will bring simple and
profound depth to your meditation.

But his delight is in the law of the LORD, and in His
law he meditates day and night.

(Psalm 1:2, NASB)

Step Three: Respond

Talk to God about your meditations in the Scriptures and then
write out a prayer to Him from your time together.

Take words with you and return to the Lord.
Say to Him, "Take away all iniquity
And receive us graciously,
That we may present the fruit of our lips.

(Hosea 14:2, NASB)

Step Four: Listen

Having meditated on the Word of God, now sit back quietly to
listen. When you are quiet before the Lord, often He will lead
your heart and mind in ways that you cannot receive when you
are filled with the busyness and distractions of life. As you take
time to listen to God, write down what you are hearing.

This step will take time to develop. Most of us are not trained to listen in this busy culture. Our tendency is to talk to God more than listen to Him. Part of maturing is also learning how to weed out other thoughts:

- The fear, revenge, and lust of our humanness.
- The world's message of "Just do what feels good."
- The deceiver's confusion, "Did God really say you can't do _____ ?"

Many people confuse the voices of the flesh, the world, and Satan with the voice of God. God is always consistent with what He says in the Bible. If what you perceive does not line up with the principles of God's Word, you know it is not from God.

Listening prayer is the second way to experience the "Art of Receptivity." As you ask God to direct your heart, the core hunger in your spirit will start to be satisfied by the bread of life.

Pray, then, in this way:

> "Our Father who is in heaven, hallowed be Your name.
> Your kingdom come. Your will be done, on earth as it is
> in heaven. Give us this day our daily bread."
>
> (Matthew 6:9-11, NASB)

To daily eat of the bread of life will quicken and fill your spirit like no addiction or co-addiction ever can. The personal Word of God will continue to fill you all day long even after your daily reading of Scripture.

You may receive in listening prayer a peace that passes understanding in the midst of life's circumstances. It guards your heart and mind throughout the day. This step is the "receptivity" component of listening prayer.

> Therefore humble yourselves under the mighty hand of
> God, that He may exalt you at the proper time, casting
> all your anxiety on Him, because He cares for you.
>
> (1 Peter 5:6-7, NASB)

Step Five: Obey

Listening obedience is the "empowerment" component of listening prayer. When you choose to obey, the battle begins, and the Holy Spirit will empower you with the strength of God. At the moment you obey, you are choosing to radically defy the natural pull of the flesh, the world, and Satan. You are choosing to listen to and obey the Father.

> *He who has My commandments and keeps them is the one who loves Me; and he who loves Me will be loved by My Father, and I will love him and will disclose Myself to him.*
>
> —*Jesus (John 14:21, NASB)*

Write out your listening obedience—anything that you sense God wants you to do in response to your time with Him. He will provide you with the strength to obey if your heart is willing.

> *And He has said to me, "My grace is sufficient for you, for power is perfected in weakness." Most gladly, therefore, I will rather boast about my weaknesses, so that the power of Christ may dwell in me. Therefore I am well content with weaknesses, with insults, with distresses, with persecutions, with difficulties, for Christ's sake; for when I am weak, then I am strong.*
>
> *(2 Corinthians 12:9-10, NASB)*

As God gives you daily bread, your hunger will be fulfilled. As you daily draw a cup of cold water from His well, your thirsts will be quenched.

> *Jesus answered and said to her, "If you knew the gift of God, and who it is who says to you, 'Give Me a drink,' you would have asked Him, and He would have given you living water."*
>
> *She said to Him, "Sir, You have nothing to draw with and the well is deep; where then do You get that living*

water? You are not greater than our father Jacob, are You, who gave us the well, and drank of it himself and his sons and his cattle?"

Jesus answered and said to her, "Everyone who drinks of this water will thirst again; but whoever drinks of the water that I will give him shall never thirst; but the water that I will give him will become in him a well of water springing up to eternal life." The woman said to Him, "Sir, give me this water, so I will not be thirsty nor come all the way here to draw."

(*John 4:10-15, NASB*)

The Art of Receptivity and Empowerment

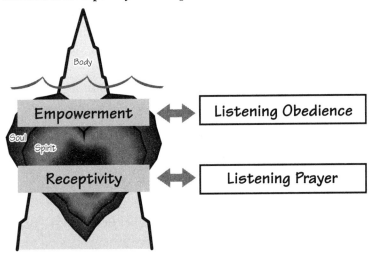

To go to God daily in listening prayer is to choose to feed your hunger with God's daily bread and quench your thirst with His living water. By doing this you kick out the twins of fear—emptiness and disempowerment—that have been cannibalizing you. This means war! The battle is the Lord's. His power can move the biggest boulders from the door of your spirit.

> *But you will receive power when the Holy Spirit has come upon you; and you shall be My witnesses both in Jerusalem, and in all Judea and Samaria, and even to the remotest part of the earth.*
>
> *(Acts 1:8, NASB)*

When the phenomenal power of God fills you, you will move mountains. The seeds of faith that have remained dormant in your head will now bloom in your heart. Drinking from the well of worship instead of the ditches of idolatry will unlock the warrior passion within that says, "I will now fight to represent the One who gave His life for me so that I could live!" Jesus came that you may have life and have it abundantly.

All my children do their listening prayer in less than half an hour each day with me. I started this spiritual discipline with them when the youngest was five and the oldest was thirteen. This process is building the biblical foundation for the houses of their spirits. The love and strength of the Lord are filling and empowering them at an early age.

I also teach participants at "Rekindling Your Spirit" conferences to take the time to daily fill and empower themselves with the love and strength of God. It is not surprising that adults struggle more with being quiet before the Lord and listening for His direction. We have dulled our hearing with the cacophonous voices of addictions and co-addictions so that we miss the quiet and yet powerful direction of the Spirit of God.

> *God whispers to us in our pleasures, speaks in our conscience, but shouts in our pains: it is His megaphone to rouse a deaf world.*
>
> *—C. S. Lewis*

If I had not listened to God and obeyed Him, I would not be alive today. Listening prayer was important in knowing what God was saying to me. However, it was equally critical for me to obey and go to see the urologist. Obeying the Lord has allowed me to live.

My son, do not forget my teaching,
But let your heart keep my commandments;
For length of days and years of life
And peace they will add to you.
Do not let kindness and truth leave you;
Bind them around your neck,
Write them on the tablet of your heart.
So you will find favor and good repute
In the sight of God and man.
Trust in the LORD with all your heart
And do not lean on your own understanding.
In all your ways acknowledge Him,
And He will make your paths straight.
Do not be wise in your own eyes;
Fear the LORD and turn away from evil.
It will be healing to your body
And refreshment to your bones.

(Proverbs 3:1-8, NASB)

May you experience God in a more intimate way through listening prayer and listening obedience. Like embracing God's presence, listening prayer is another way you can be daily refilled and daily reempowered.

The Art of Renewing Your Spiritual Vows

The art of renewing your vows is to daily go to the Cross and renew your spiritual commitment to Christ. As a marriage therapist, I wish all my couples would renew their wedding vows to each other every day. Can you imagine the impact that would have in the spirits of their marriages? The same principle applies to the holy wedding that occurred in your spirit the day you pledged your life to Christ. That day, you said in many ways, "For better or for worse, I do say now that You are my Lord and Savior until death do we meet."

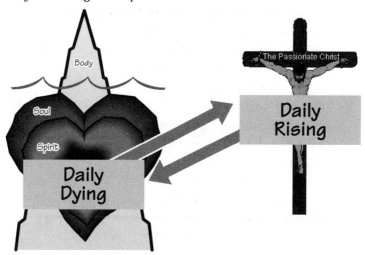

To daily renew your spiritual vows is really a way of daily renewing your baptism. If you have had a believer's baptism, you symbolically did two things that day in the witnesses of family and friends:

- You identified with the death and burial of Christ.
- You identified with the resurrected life of Christ.

The greatest picture of daily renewing your vows is found in the book of Romans. The two principles involved are daily dying with Christ and daily rising with Christ. Romans 6 describes this:

> *So what do we do? Keep on sinning so God can keep on forgiving? I should hope not! If we've left the country where sin is sovereign, how can we still live in our old house there? Or didn't you realize we packed up and left there for good? That is what happened in baptism. When we went **under the water**, we **left the old country of sin** behind; when we **came up out of the water**, we **entered into the new country of grace**— a new life in a new land!*

> *That's what baptism into the life of Jesus means. When we are **lowered into the water**, it is like the **burial***

119

*of Jesus; when we are **raised up out of the water,** it is like the **resurrection** of Jesus. Each of us is raised into a light-filled world by our Father so that we can see where we're going in our new grace-sovereign country.*

Could it be any clearer? Our old way of life was nailed to the Cross with Christ, a decisive end to that sin-miserable life—no longer at sin's every beck and call! What we believe is this:

__If we get included in Christ's sin-conquering death, we also get included in his life-saving resurrection.__ We know that when Jesus was raised from the dead it was a signal of the end of death-as-the-end. Never again will death have the last word. When Jesus died, he took sin down with him, but alive he brings God down to us. From now on, think of it this way: Sin speaks a dead language that means nothing to you; God speaks your mother tongue, and you hang on every word. You are dead to sin and alive to God. That's what Jesus did.

*But now that you've found you **don't have to listen to sin** tell you what to do, and have discovered the delight of **listening to God** telling you, what a surprise! A whole, healed, put-together life right now, with more and more of life on the way! Work hard for sin your whole life and your pension is death. But God's gift is real life, eternal life, **delivered by Jesus, our Master.***

(Romans 6:1-23, MSG, *emphasis added*)

Daily Dying with Christ

In order to daily die with Christ, you need to learn the art of daily releasing at the Cross. When you go to the Cross in prayer, picture the Cross of Christ, where He died for your sins. For many people, it is helpful to have a small wooden cross to hold in their hands as they release their sins and pain to the Lord Jesus.

Confess to the Lord Jesus at the Cross:
1. Your betrayal sin (how you have sinned against God or others).
2. Your betrayal pain (how you have been sinned against).

As you, in prayer, release your sin and pain to the Lord on the Cross, you will experience, through your spirit, your sin and pain going up, out, and onto the Cross.

Daily Rising with Christ
In order to daily rise with Christ, you need to learn the art of daily receiving at the Cross. After you have released your sins and pain to the Lord Jesus at the Cross, receive from Him:
- The gift of God's forgiveness and cleansing for your betrayal sin against God, yourself, and others.
- The gift of deliverance from the power of sin.
- The gift of God's healing for your betrayal pain.
- The gifts of the Holy Spirit for empowerment to live in obedience to God.

Walking Out Your Healing

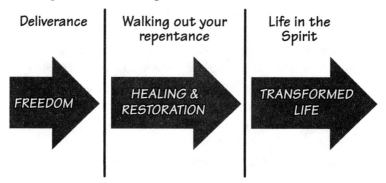

Deliverance | Walking out your repentance | Life in the Spirit

FREEDOM | HEALING & RESTORATION | TRANSFORMED LIFE

**"Blessed are those who mourn,
for they shall be comforted."**
(Matthew 5:4, NIV, emphasis added)

As you, in prayer, release your sin and pain and receive God's forgiveness, cleansing, deliverance, and empowerment at the Cross, you will start to experience freedom, healing, restoration, and transformation as you walk in the power of the Spirit.

Pray to receive God's forgiveness, cleansing, and the gifts of the Holy Spirit into the areas of your struggle. Also receive from Him the tenderness of His love and the strength of His love.

The people of God need the hand of God to free them from bondage to the flesh, the world, and Satan. Each day we need to be filled by the tenderness of God's love. Each day we receive a little more healing of our sense of belonging.

> *And you are also among those who are called to belong to Jesus Christ.*
>
> *(Romans 1:6, NIV)*

Each day we also need to receive the strength of God's love. Each day we receive a little more healing of our sense of being.

> *For in Him we live and move and have our being.*
>
> *(Acts 17:28, NIV)*

We also need to receive symbolically from God His fire to burn the bondage of Baal worship in our lives, His water of cleansing and forgiveness, and His oil of healing and anointing.

God has made clear that no altars to other gods are to remain among His people. We must daily destroy our altars of idolatry.

> *These are the decrees and laws you must be careful to follow in the land that the LORD, the God of your fathers, has given you to possess—as long as you live in the land. Destroy completely all the places on the high mountains and on the hills and under every spreading tree where the nations you are dispossessing worship their gods. Break down their altars, smash their sacred stones and **burn their Asherah poles in the fire;** cut down the idols of their gods and wipe out their names from those places. You must not worship the LORD your God in their way. But you are to seek the place the LORD your God will choose from among all your tribes to put*

his Name there for his dwelling. To that place you must go.

(Deuteronomy 12:1-5, NIV, emphasis added)

The people of the Lord needed to call on God to symbolically receive the water of forgiveness and cleansing as well.

*For I will take you from the nations, gather you from all the lands and bring you into your own land. Then I will **sprinkle clean water on you, and you will be clean;** I will cleanse you from all your filthiness and from all your idols. Moreover, **I will give you a new heart and put a new spirit within you;** and I will remove the heart of stone from your flesh and give you a heart of flesh. **I will put My Spirit within you** and **cause** you to walk in My statutes, and you will be careful to observe My ordinances. You will live in the land that I gave to your forefathers; so **you will be My people, and I will be your God.***

(Ezekiel 36:24-28, NASB, emphasis added)

Finally, God's people need to call on Him to symbolically receive the oil of healing and anointing.

*Is anyone among you sick? Then he must call for the elders of the church and they are to pray over him, **anointing him with oil** in the name of the Lord.*

(James 5:14, NASB, emphasis added)

To be empowered for the journey of recovery and healing, you need the hand of God with you.

Do not fear, for I am with you;
Do not anxiously look about you, for I am your God.
I will strengthen you, surely I will help you,
Surely I will uphold you with My righteous right hand.

(Isaiah 41:10, NASB)

To experience personal change from the inside out, you need the hand of God to uphold you as you:

- Look at your relational sin.
- Look at your relational pain.
- Look to the relational Cross.
- Take up the relational Cross.
- Follow Jesus all the days of your life.

Changing from the Inside Out

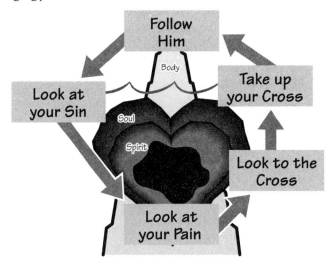

If you love Me, you will keep My commandments. *I will ask the Father, and He will give you another Helper, that He may be **with you forever;** that is **the Spirit of truth,** whom the world cannot receive, because it does not see Him or know Him, but you know Him because He abides with you and **will be in you.** I will not leave you as orphans; I will come to you. After a little while the world will no longer see Me, but you will see Me; because I live, you will live also. In that day you will know that I am in My Father, and you in Me, and I in you. He who has My commandments and keeps them is the one who loves Me; and he who loves Me will be loved by My Father,*

*and **I will love him and will disclose Myself to him.***

—Jesus (John 14:15-21, NASB, emphasis added)

To love Jesus is to daily take time to reflect on the spiritual reality that Jesus Christ lives in you. To love Jesus is to daily listen to and obey Him. To love Jesus is to daily die and rise with Him.

Three Daily Spiritual Disciplines

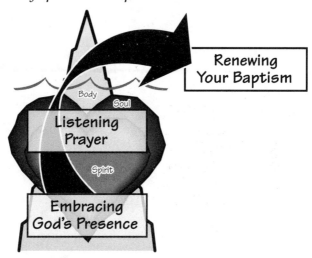

To experience Jesus is to release your guilt and shame onto the Cross. This is the whole, passionate reason He died for you! To experience Jesus is to be filled with His forgiveness and cleansing and be empowered with the gifts of the Holy Spirit. The overflowing love of God will cast out the twins of fear—emptiness and disempowerment—because God's perfect love does cast out all fear (1 John 4:18)!

The three tools of receptivity will restore your sense of belonging and being, will call forth your true self, and will define your life with a sense of purpose beyond all you could think or imagine! Are you ready to throw away your addictive and co-addictive lifestyle in exchange for a new life of godly worship?

As your addictive and co-addictive lifestyles die, you will be released to love God and your neighbor as yourself. In the process, your passion, giftedness, and purpose will be uncovered. This stage of your spiritual homecoming will keep you consistently filled and refreshed for the rest of the journey.

* * * * * * *

Personal Journaling and Small Group Questions
Spiritual Homecoming Assignment Six

Personal Journaling Questions

Follow the Five Steps to Listening Prayer found in this stage, abbreviated here:

1. Choose a passage of Scripture to use in your listening prayer. Read until a verse or verses jump out at you. Write them in your journal. Reflect on the verses, answering these questions:
   - What are the key truths in these verses?
   - Why do you need to know those truths in your life?
   - How can you apply them to your life?
2. Respond to God in prayer, talking about these verses. Write out a prayer to Him from your time together.
3. Sit back and wait quietly in the presence of God.
4. Write out your listening obedience—anything that you sense God wants you to do in response to your time with Him.
5. Share your experience with your small group or community. Ask a close friend or your group to keep you accountable to follow through and obey.

Small Group Questions

1. What... are the key truths that stood out to you in this stage?
2. Why... do you need to know these truths?
3. How... do you apply these truths to your life?
4. Your pain... What pain does this stage reveal in your life?
5. Your sin... What are you doing with your pain?
6. Repentance... What do you need to do differently?
7. Prayer... What do you need to ask God for help with?

127

STAGE SEVEN: Healing Your Story
The Art of Asking, Receiving, and Extending Forgiveness

Before moving through Stage Seven, experiencing the miracle of receptivity is crucial.

This is the miracle of being filled with the living love of God and being empowered by the living strength of God. God's incarnational love will empower you to do the work of this stage. Most people strive despite their emptiness, only to experience the exhaustion of performance and one-dimensional (external) behavioral management. However, as you make an intentional decision in your "being" to seek the only One who can fill you, you will be filled, and this will profoundly shape your "doing."

The Path to Deliverance, Healing, Restoration, and Transformed Living

This stage in your spiritual homecoming will be difficult but will bring you into profound freedom and healing as you do the difficult work of mourning—talk about what hurts and about your tendency to hurt others in passive or aggressive ways.

Blessed are those who mourn, for they shall be comforted.

(Matthew 5:4, NASB)

If you are willing to mourn, or talk to someone on the outside about what is hurting you on the inside, then you will be comforted. The Greek word for mourning is *penthountes*. It means to grieve or to sorrow. When you mourn, you are more than expressing sadness, you are revealing your internal state, letting it come into the open to be released.

Three Paths of Mourning
- The Path of Sadness—facing how you were betrayed.
- The Path of Grief—facing how you betray others and yourself.
- The Path of Sorrow—facing how you betray God. [12]

Many times, the grief of how you have violated your parents will point to how you violate God by projecting your painful parental images onto Him. This can bring you back to God so that He can help you with the sadness that may have brought you into therapy or counseling. Even though I am a Christian psychologist, I know it is far better to have God help you with your sadness than just a therapist! There are five aspects to this kind of mourning.

Facing How You Were Betrayed

You Must Face How You Were Betrayed by Others

The Path of Sadness: Mourning Betrayal

- Look at your relational sin. How do you betray God, yourself, and others?
- Look at your relational pain. How were you betrayed?
- Look to the Cross of Christ. Let your guilt and shame go up, out, and onto the Cross.
- Take up your own Cross daily. Die to your will and surrender to God's will. Be filled and empowered by the Holy Spirit who lives within you. Daily listen and daily obey God's voice.
- Follow Jesus. Daily die with Christ and daily rise with Christ.

To enter into your sadness and grief is painful. But remember that the way home is through the pain—through the hole in your spirit, not away from it.

First, seriously ponder that your mother and father are directly related to the receptivity in your human spirit. Through our mothers we receive the tender love of their spirits into ours. Even before birth, a baby receives a mother's love. Through our mothers we receive the capacity for receptivity. Through our mothers' tenderness of love we receive a sense of belonging and a sense of being. To have unresolved vows and judgments of unforgiveness toward your mother will block your capacity to receive and be filled by the tenderness of God's love within your own spirit.

Through our fathers we receive the capacity for empowerment. Through our fathers' strength of love we can walk out a sense of the true self and a sense of purpose. To have unresolved vows and judgments of unforgiveness against your father is to block your capacity to be empowered by the strength of God's love.

We need both parents to fill and empower our sense of being and sense of belonging. The good news is, if you are willing to deal with your vows and judgments with your mother and father, then God will also be able to deal with you! God describes Himself as a mother hen who gathers her chicks (Luke 13:34). That is a stunning picture of His tender, nurturing heart. However, your vows and judgments against your earthly mother can cut you off from being filled by the deep love of God.

In the New Testament, God is described as a father to the prodigal son. This is a picture of the strength of God's love. To have unresolved vows and judgments with your earthly father can cut you off from the power of the strength in God's love.

One Sunday evening I made my relational homecoming back to my own earthly father. That night I also made my spiritual homecoming back to my heavenly Father. I had no idea how directly linked the two were. In fact, that experience planted the seed for this book. My journey with my earthly father involved the dreaded forgiveness process. But the alternative to forgiveness is the prison of unforgiveness. Since that day I have been a free, healed and restored man, husband, father, and minister of the gospel.

It started when I was working with a client. As I counseled her, I sensed in my spirit that her father was dying and that she needed to fly home and be with him before he died. I did not say anything to her at the time, but the next week she confirmed the news. I was very sad for her because I knew she loved her father in spite of all the pain he had caused her.

My client flew home that week and had just enough time to give and receive forgiveness before saying goodbye to her father for the last time. They both had closure before he went on to the next world. It was a gift from her Abba Father to be able to make peace with her earthly father while he was still alive.

As I met with my client, I sensed that I needed to visit my own father as well. It was quite disruptive for me. I knew the Lord wanted me to ask my father for forgiveness. But I felt that my father was the one who had abandoned me—he should be the one asking for forgiveness. But God wanted me to humble myself and confess to my father how I had betrayed him. He did not want me to blame my father for how he had betrayed me by rarely being there for me. My father was a counselor as well. He was a very busy, professional man. Dad did love us as he could, but he wasn't there much, so it was a distant relationship. While growing up, I really longed for him to be involved with my life more than he was. Disappointment that he wasn't there when I had wanted him to be had built up and turned into anger. As a result of not experiencing some of the things that I wanted while growing up, my heart had been unloving toward my father.

I looked for every possible way to get out of it, but I knew that if I did not walk out the message I preached, God would not bless it.

A couple of days later, as I sat with my dad, I could not bring myself to tell him why I wanted to talk to him. Finally, he said, "Son, would you like to go to my office and talk there?"

I thought, *Great, I now have to tell my dad in his own office how I have abandoned him for all these years!*

So we went into his office, and I was frozen with the fear of doing what my Abba Father wanted me to do. I drew the blue iceberg with the big green heart and the smaller purple heart, and I launched into my confession of relational sin of betraying him for years with abandonment.

Finally, I said, "Dad, you know, for years I've really been angry at you for not being there for me the way I wanted you to be growing up. And many times when you have called and wanted to spend time with me, I haven't wanted to. I've just had a lot of anger toward you. It's frustrating because now that you're a grandpa, you want to spend time with me and the kids. Part of me is really frustrated with that, because when I needed you, you weren't there." My dad just listened.

I added, "Dad, to be really honest, I'm so angry at you that when you call, it's like I just want to say, 'Screw you, Dad!'"

As I shared with him the depths of my hurt, I entered into reality with my father, and he was finally solid and present with me. It was like a bubble that separated us had broken.

Then I said, "Dad, I do need to ask your forgiveness for how I've dishonored you with my anger, my unforgiveness."

My dad looked at me and responded, "Paul, I forgive you. I will always forgive you." And he went on to take responsibility for some of the issues in our relationship; he truly acknowledged the things that had caused me disappointment. Before we departed, my father gave me a hug. For the first time in my adult life, I could feel his strength and genuine love. He looked at me and thanked me for sharing my heart and asking for forgiveness.

That night, I spent time alone with God and played a song called "Forever My Friend," by Kelly Carpenter, over and over.

As I sang, the love of my Abba Father's Spirit filled me, and I realized that I had not only abandoned my earthly father, but I had also run away from my heavenly Father. I had unknowingly become the prodigal son.

Seven Steps to Facing Your Sadness:

Step One: Face how you were betrayed.

Step Two: Break your vows and judgments with yourself.

Step Three: Release your shame, and guilt if needed, at the Cross.

Step Four: Receive God's love, cleansing, deliverance, and healing at the Cross.

Step Five: Ask God to fill you and empower you.

Step Six: Repent from your unforgiveness.

Step Seven: Choose to shift from a life of unforgiveness to a life of forgiveness.

The dynamics of humbling myself and forgiving my earthly father opened my eyes to deeper truth. The heart of God thoroughly filled my heart in an intimate way. It's the first time in my life I felt so close to my "Abba Daddy"—the word Jesus used for His Father on the Cross was Abba, meaning "daddy." I didn't even want to move. I just sat there, and I sang. In my spirit, I could plainly feel my Abba Daddy in heaven holding me in a way, as a son, I'd never been held before.

After that conversation with my father, our relationship dramatically changed. The next day he invited my family to his home for a dinner, the kind that in my family is reserved for holidays and great celebrations. He really honored me and showed me a tangible offering of his love and regret for the mistakes of the past. Even though my father and I continue to have radically different views on life and religion, I have grown to love my daddy more than ever before.

I am convinced that if I had not listened and obeyed the Lord God's voice when He told me to ask my father for forgiveness, I would still be blocked in my relationship with God today. I am grateful to have had the Almighty rekindle my spirit. My heart awakened to the reality that God in heaven is our Father, His arms are open wide, and He's waiting.

The Path of Grieving: The Art of Asking for Forgiveness
The path of grieving is facing how you have betrayed others and yourself. It is a time to feel the impact of how you have used the knives of anger, contempt, and transference to wound the spirits of others and grieve the living God.

As you take an account of how you have betrayed others, you need to break any vows or judgments that you made in those betrayals. In the past, the vows protected you from facing your guilt and shame. When you break them, your shame and guilt will rise up. Let it do so. Release it to the Cross. God will extend His love, forgiveness, cleansing, deliverance, and healing. Receive it. Ask God to fill and empower you as you enter the path of relational repentance by choosing to love others rather than choosing self-protection. Relational repentance means that, from now on, you will act and respond differently to others.

*For all these things My hand has made, and so all these
things have come into being [by and for Me], says the
Lord. But **this is the man to whom I will look and
have regard:** he who is **humble** and of a **broken** or
wounded spirit, and who **trembles at My word** and
reveres My commands.*

(Isaiah 66:2, AMP, emphaisis added)

Facing How You Betray Others and Yourself

From whom do you need to ask forgiveness?

- Mother
- Father
- Spouse
- Children
- Friends
- Community members
- Spiritual Leaders

- Siblings
- Other Relatives
- Bosses
- Co-workers

Start by writing letters to those whom you have betrayed, asking
for forgiveness. You may not actually send the letters, but writing
them and going to the Cross with them will jump-start your
process of grieving. At the "Rekindling Your Spirit" conferences,
we provide a cross at the foot of the altar on which participants
nail their letters of grief.

I advise you to write initially one letter to your mother and one to your father. Honoring them with your relational repentance is central to rekindling your spirit. Let the Holy Spirit lead you concerning others to whom you should write and whether to mail the letters or simply nail them to a symbolic cross. However He guides you, allow your guilt and shame to come up, out, and onto the Cross. As you release at the Cross, receive His forgiveness, cleansing, and gifts of the Holy Spirit.

> *Therefore if you are presenting your offering at the altar, and there remember that your brother has something against you, leave your offering there before the altar and go; first be reconciled to your brother, and then come and present your offering.*
>
> *(Matthew 5:23-24, NASB)*

God asks us to make things right with others when we know we have sinned. When you seek forgiveness from those whom you have violated through betrayal, there are seven steps to follow:

Seven Steps to Asking Another's Forgiveness

Step One: Go symbolically to the Cross with the one whom you have betrayed and a few members of the body of Christ, as needed.

Step Two: Ask the person you have violated to tell you how your betrayals have affected his or her heart.

Step Three: Listen to his or her pain.

Step Four: Acknowledge that your betrayal was wrong.

Step Five: Share that you are sorry and ask forgiveness.

Step Six: Present a plan of repentance from your betrayal.

Step Seven: Offer restitution if necessary.

You also need to face how you have betrayed yourself with addictions and co-addictions. When you do, specifically break any vows or judgments that you have made about yourself, God, or others that have kept you from feeling your guilt and shame. As you grieve, release the guilt and the shame to the Cross. In return, once again, God will pour out His love, forgiveness, cleansing, deliverance, and healing. Take it all. Ask God to fill and empower you as you enter the path of repentance and shift from a life of idolatry to a life of worship. It is ideal to have an accountability partner who will pray for you and help you develop a specific plan of personal repentance from your addictions and co-addictions.

The Path of Sorrow: The Art of Receiving God's Forgiveness

The path of sorrow is facing how you have betrayed God. It is a time to feel the impact of how you have used the knives of substituting God (idolatry), ignoring God, and attacking God's name. As you do, break any vows and judgments that you have made. Until now, these have kept you from feeling your core guilt and shame. When those feelings swell, release them at the Cross. As you do, God will release His love, forgiveness, cleansing, deliverance, healing, and restoration. Receive it. Ask God to fill and empower you to love Him with all your heart as you enter the path of relational repentance with the Lover of your soul.

> *If we **confess** our sins, He is faithful and righteous to **forgive** us our sins and to **cleanse** us from all unrighteousness.*
>
> *(1 John 1:9, NASB, emphasis added)*

Facing How You Betray (Sin Against) God

Christ Restoring Your Relationship with Abba God

137

Seven Steps to Asking God's Forgiveness

Step One: Go symbolically to the Cross and kneel before the living God in Spirit.

Step Two: Name the betrayals you have committed against God and enter the path of sorrow.

Step Three: Break your vows and judgments against God.

Step Four: Renounce the betrayals you have committed against God.

Step Five: Have a plan of repentance with God.

Step Six: Let your guilt and shame go up, out, and onto Jesus.

Step Seven: Receive God's forgiveness, cleansing, deliverance, healing, restoration, and power for transformation.

Sorrowing at the symbolic foot of the Cross will bring you into greater intimacy with your Abba Daddy. Writing a letter to God and asking forgiveness is a good way to start. Tell God exactly how you have projected any distortions onto Him from your painful images of your mother and your father. Allow your guilt and shame to come up, out, and onto the Cross. As you release at the Cross, receive His forgiveness, cleansing, and gifts of the Holy Spirit. Nail this letter to a Cross or participate in some other symbolic action with it. Having a Christian spiritual leader or spiritual director pray for and encourage you as you continue to shift from a life of distortions to a life of seeing God accurately is invaluable.

Extending Forgiveness

The path of sadness is facing how you have been betrayed. It is a time to feel the impact of how you have been violated by the betrayal of others. The path of sorrowing and grieving involves releasing your guilt and shame up, out, and onto the Cross. However, the path of sadness involves inviting Christ to come into the areas where you have been hurt and shamed through the lives of others.

Let me start by telling the story of a woman who was stuck in unforgiveness with her mother. She was a sales manager in her late twenties and had been in therapy with various caregivers for three to five years. She was not personally changing and was discouraged. She had two young children who needed her to be there for them, but she was too checked out of life with depression and an overeating addiction.

One day in therapy, I saw how her mother had violated her trust. My client needed to forgive her, but she said she was not interested in addressing it. I told her my sense was that her unforgiveness of her mother was blocking her healing. That grabbed her attention because she wanted to be done with therapy!

In prayer, we asked the Lord to lead us through the house of her spirit. An unusual thing happened that day. We saw separately and together the same thing. We went down to the "basement" in the house of her spirit. It was pretty horrifying. She and I "sat" in a "large family room." However, on the other side of the family room there were three jail cells. In the middle cell sat her mother!

I said to her, "Sara [not her real name], would you like to let your mother out of the jail cell?"

She was not sure. She said, "Mom really hurt me. If I let her out, she will be off the hook! I am not ready to do that yet. She needs to pay for what she did to me. No, she can stay in there!"

I had to warn her that as long as Mom rotted in the basement, Sara would continue to rot with the bitterness of unforgiveness and that would block her receptivity to God's love and the empowerment of God's strength in her life as a woman, wife, mother, and entrepreneur.

She thought about it for half an hour. Finally, she said, "Okay, how do I let Mom out of the jail cell?"

I told her that she needed to talk to Jesus about it, and He would help her. We prayed and asked Jesus to come into the basement of the house of her spirit.

Jesus revealed Himself and brought the key to the jail cell. He said that she needed to make the choice to take the key and unlock the door of the cell. At the exact moment that she unlocked the door of her mother's jail cell, the structure of the living room came to light. Her living room was also a prison cell. As Sara unlocked the door of her mother's jail cell, the doors of the living room jail cell opened up as well, and both women became free at the same time.

Sarah was stunned. She saw it without telling me what she was seeing. I saw it without telling her what I was seeing. Then she wept considerably as something very deep was released in her. A flow of sadness came up, out, and went symbolically onto the Cross.

This woman experienced a sudden and profound freedom, healing, and restoration within months of this prayer session. The Lord showed me the following verse when that moment became reality for this young mother.

> *Is this not the fast which I choose,*
> *To **loosen the bonds of wickedness**,*
> *To undo the bands of the yoke,*
> *And to **let the oppressed go free***
> *And break every yoke?*
> *Is it not to divide your bread with the hungry*
> *And bring the homeless poor into the house;*
> *When you see the naked, to cover him;*
> *And not to hide yourself from your own flesh?*
> ***Then your light will break out like the dawn,***
> ***And your recovery will speedily spring forth;***
> *And your righteousness will go before you;*
> *The glory of the Lord will be your rear guard.*
> *Then you will call, and the Lord will answer;*
> *You will cry, and He will say, "Here I am."*
> *If you remove the yoke from your midst,*
> *The pointing of the finger and speaking wickedness,*
> *And if you give yourself to the hungry*

And satisfy the desire of the afflicted,
Then your light will rise in darkness
And your gloom will become like midday.
And the LORD** will continually guide you,**
And satisfy your desire *in scorched places,*
And give strength *to your bones;*
And you will be like a watered garden,
And like a spring of water whose waters do not fail.
(Isaiah 58:6-11, NASB, emphasis added)

This woman had a physical transformation that reflected the new life that reigned within her. She moved from a woman rotting with unforgiveness to a mother who could bond with her own little children because she was free from bondage with her own mother. When Sara shared her story with her mother at a later time, her mother was also set free from bondage with her mother. And it was not a therapist who prayed with her mother, it was her free and healed daughter.

I have heard it said that even if you do not feel like forgiving, choose this day to "will" to forgive, and your healing will come forth. This is profoundly true. "Will" to forgive and watch Jesus step in and bring forgiveness with deeper freedom, healing, restoration, and transformation to your spirit, soul, and body.

Extending forgiveness to those who have violated you through the sin of betrayal is a difficult challenge. It will swing open the prison doors of unforgiveness that have kept you locked up for years. But, it is time to come back into the light and experience the freedom, healing, restoration, and transformation that comes with forgiveness.

For My people have committed two evils:
They have forsaken Me,
The fountain of living waters,
To hew for themselves cisterns,

Broken cisterns
That can hold no water.

(Jeremiah 2:13, NASB)

It is time to seek God again. The cancer of unforgiveness kills our human spirit. His living waters bring life.

Pray, then, in this way:
"Our Father who is in heaven,
Hallowed be Your name.
Your kingdom come.
Your will be done,
On earth as it is in heaven.
Give us this day our daily bread.
And forgive us our debts, as we also have forgiven our debtors.
And do not lead us into temptation, but deliver us from evil. [For Yours is the kingdom and the power and the glory forever. Amen.]"

For if you forgive others for their transgressions, your heavenly Father will also forgive you. **But if you do not forgive others, then your Father will not forgive your transgressions.**

(Matthew 6:9-15, NASB, emphasis added)

Seven Steps to Extending Forgiveness

Step One: Go symbolically to the Cross and kneel before the living God in Spirit.

Step Two: Face how you were betrayed and enter the path of sadness.

Step Three: Release your pain and shame at the Cross.

Step Four: Ask Jesus to help you forgive.

Step Five: Ask God to fill you and empower you.

Step Six: Enter the process of repenting from unforgiveness.

Step Seven: Receive God's love, forgiveness, cleansing, deliverance, healing, restoration, and transforming power.

Then Peter came and said to Him, "Lord **how often shall my brother sin against me and I forgive him?** Up to seven times? Jesus said to him, "I do not say to you, up to seven times, but up to **seventy times seven.** For this reason the kingdom of heaven may be compared to a king who wished to settle accounts with his slaves. When he had begun to settle them, one who owed him ten thousand talents was brought to him. But since he did not have the means to repay, his lord commanded him to be sold, along with his wife and children and all that he had, and repayment to be made.

"So the slave fell to the ground and prostrated himself before him, saying, 'Have patience with me and I will repay you everything.'

"And the lord of that slave felt compassion and released him and forgave him the debt.

"But that slave went out and found one of his fellow slaves who owed him a hundred denarii; and he seized him and began to choke him, saying, 'Pay back what you owe.'

"So his fellow slave fell to the ground and began to plead with him, saying, 'Have patience with me and I will repay you.' But he was unwilling and went and threw him in prison until he should pay back what was owed.

"So when his fellow slaves saw what had happened, they were deeply grieved and came and reported to their lord all that had happened.

"Then summoning him, his lord said to him, 'You wicked slave, I forgave you all that debt because you pleaded with me. **Should you not also have had** *mercy* **on your fellow slave, in the same way that I had mercy on you?'** *And his lord, moved with anger, handed him over to the torturers until he should repay all that was owed him. My heavenly Father will also do the same to you, if each of you does not forgive his brother from your heart."*

(Matthew 18:21-35, NASB, *emphasis added*)

I would deeply encourage you to write a letter to your perpetrator(s) and extend to them forgiveness in the letter. Many people will say to me, "This is extremely difficult to do. I have tried it and it does not work!" I believe them because of my own journey of forgiveness. It is easy to forgive with your lips and not to forgive from your heart. However, be brutally honest with the picture of revenge that is going on in your soul. If you take a moment to close your eyes and look at the anger of revenge that has laced your soul with the spirit of murder, you will probably see a picture of you trying to strangle this person who dared to betray you and damage your life.

Then you want to release the person or persons in forgiveness to Jesus. It is very difficult to release your unforgiveness and anger. You are attached to that person both spiritually and emotionally by unforgiveness. In your anger, you want that person to pay for what they've done. If you let go, they'll be off the hook, so you keep hanging on with anger.

The paradox is that your healing comes at the point you release the person, let go of your anger, and forgive. As long as you hang on to him or her, you hang on to your anger and your bitterness.

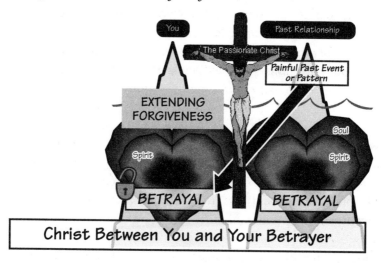

Christ Between You and Your Betrayer

In some cases, you might have experienced so much trauma with this person that you're paralyzed and can't let go. At that point, pray and ask Jesus to come right between you and that person. As Jesus stands between you, He releases them, and you are free. That's the point at which healing comes.

Don't hold on to unforgiveness; don't hold on to bitterness. Let God be the judge. He will hold people accountable. Forgiveness will release deliverance, healing, restoration, and transformation power into your spirit, your soul, and your body.

Men and women, it takes great courage to face how you were sinned against. Two of the most important people you may need to forgive are your mother and your father.

I had to forgive both my own mother and father for ways I felt hurt growing up. In the process, both of my parents also had the integrity to take responsibility for their issues and ask me for forgiveness as well. I believe that as I honored my mother and my father, God honored me by filling my emptiness and empowering me.

Regardless of how your mother or father respond, God will honor your forgiveness and bless you—filling your emptiness and empowering you, as he did me. That blessing outweighs any positive or negative response from a parent. Either way, ask the Holy Spirit to show you what it means to honor your mother and father.

I would also encourage you to have a Christian caregiver who will help you and strengthen you to continue to shift from a life of unforgiveness to a life of daily forgiveness. Have a specific plan in place for personal repentance from your anger of unforgiveness and the grace of extending mercy through a lifestyle of forgiveness.

Unforgiveness blocks your healing. The degree to which you withhold forgiveness is the degree to which you block your healing. On the other hand, forgiving others will profoundly impact your healing and your relationships. To forgive is to begin to heal!

Breaking Transference
Remember, transference is your response of anger toward a person in the present who triggers an unrelated experience in your past that caused you pain. If you are stuck in transference, you will need to make a choice with a neutral third party to address and release your pain and sadness symbolically at the foot of the Cross.

Have a counselor or pastor who understands transference help you identify your core longings that were betrayed and the resulting pain. Then, take some time to identify the painful vows and painful judgments that you made as a result of being betrayed.

All vows of self-protection need to be broken, or you will be choked by the strongholds of fear in your human spirit. I encourage you to:
- Confess your vows to your spiritual leader or community.

- Renounce your vows or take a stand against living in this type of self-protection that does not work.
- Repent of your vows by no longer living this way and start to find true spiritual protection in your spirit that will work.

Break your vows against your mother and father. This is central to breaking the pattern of transference. To successfully be released is to have your receptivity and empowerment restored so you have these two tools to help you get through the jungle of transference.

Many people at this moment can give up because of the pain that erupts with mother and father. However, it is so much better for the pain to come up and out of you than to let it rot inside of you long-term. At one level, transference now is a gift in setting you free to be healed and restored of unresolved past relational pain.

Just as self-protective vows must be broken, so all self-protective judgments of the soul need to be broken, or you will be choked by the strongholds of fear in your human spirit. I encourage you to do three critical actions to win the war on the strongholds of fear through your inner judgments in your human soul:
- Confess your judgments to your spiritual leader or community.
- Renounce your judgments or take a stand against living in this type of self-protection that does not work.
- Repent of your judgments by no longer living this way and start to find true spiritual protection in your spirit that will work.

Take the time to break your judgments with your mother and father, because this is so central to the disruption of transference. As hard as this is, the forgiveness process will help you to deeply heal from the inside out. This is also the time to invite Christ to start to heal you.

As you confess, renounce, and repent of your vows and judgments, your pain of betrayal and your anger of revenge will start to come up, out, and symbolically onto the Cross.

Jesus Coming Between You and Your Betrayer to Break Transference

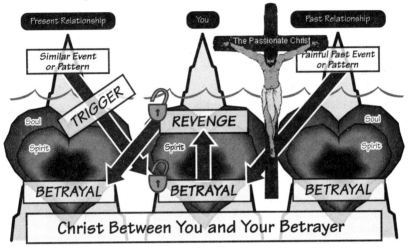

In prayer, you will probably see a picture of you and your betrayer. At that moment, invite Christ to come in between you and your betrayer. See what Christ does at that moment. As He helps you to become untangled from your betrayer, ask Him to help you start the process of forgiving your betrayer.

Experiencing Healing

I mentioned earlier, in Stage Five, that until I saw and experienced Jesus coming off the Cross for me, I knew what I believed but could not access the experience of my faith in my heart. Today, much healing has taken place in my head and heart coming together. I live very differently having deeply experienced in my heart what I know in my head.

One day I was in private practice with a male client who struggled with pornography and masturbation. On this particular day, Joe (not his real name) and I went symbolically into the elevator of his mind down into his heart. We went to the front door of his heart, and he left me there. Then he somehow went from the house of his heart to the house of his spirit. I just silently prayed for him as he started to profusely weep. This man had never cried in therapy before.

The counseling room began to be filled by the presence of God. It was so noticeable that I did not want to move. I did not want to disrupt at any level whatever was going on. After about half an hour of Joe weeping, I finally asked him what was going on. He said when he went into the living room of the house of his spirit, Jesus was standing there. He said he was so amazed that he bowed down to Jesus.

He said, "Master, I have been away from you for ten years. I have lived a life of pornography, masturbation, and sexual addiction. I am sorry for defiling you and leaving you. Today, I am coming back home to you. Will you forgive me and cleanse me?"

Jesus and he wept together. That day Joe experienced the grace of God in his spiritual homecoming. In his case, he was truly blind to his destructive behaviors, and from that day on, he could see.

I was astonished to see the living presence of Christ fill my client and the room in which we met. As a result of being filled by the love of God that day, Joe was finally empowered and within the year completed his therapy. His wife was so amazed by his personal change and the new clean intimacy they experienced that it made a believer out of her as well. Today, and three children later, they are doing well.

Later that same week, I had a female client who was stuck in her process of recovery from sexual abuse. I told her the experience of the man stuck in sexual addiction, and she asked if she could experience the same thing. I thought so, but this was new to me! She closed her eyes, and Christ met her in the house of her spirit as well. She also had a significant experience, and her recovery from sexual abuse progressed rapidly from that point.

Since I was the professional, I thought I should experience what my clients were also experiencing. So I asked the Lord if I could. This brings me back to the conference that I had attended, when I told God I would share my painful memory. You may recall that my stipulation to God was that no one laugh at my story.

I went to the workshop that afternoon, and no one volunteered to share. So I decided to be true to what I had told God. I publicly shared my painful memory. Someone laughed. It was a nervous laugh. Nevertheless, the laugh felt horribly shaming.

The workshop leader asked, "Would you like to have Jesus come into that memory?" I thought to myself, *I have already humbled myself and made myself vulnerable, and someone did laugh. What else do I have to lose?*

I closed my eyes, and within seconds the memory started to replay, and this time Jesus just stepped right into the memory. It was effortless and more amazing than when He met me at the Cross. Jesus took one hand and protected me from the impact of the pain, and with the other hand He comforted me. I was surprised and mesmerized at the same time. On one hand, I felt God's strength of love with His hand of protection. With the other hand, I felt His tenderness of love. I was filled with God's love and strength that day and for seasons to come.

1. GO to the Cross.

2. NAME the violations committed against you.

3. WILL to release the person(s) to Jesus.

4. ASK Jesus to come between you and your betrayer.

5. RELEASE your pain and anger... up, out, and onto the Cross.

6. In prayer, SEE what Jesus does.

7. RECEIVE His freedom, healing, restoration, and transformation power.

God wants to free you—untangle you—from the web of unforgiveness. As my clients and I experienced His freedom, healing, restoration, and transformation, I encourage you to ask for it as well. Ask Jesus to come in and heal the betrayal wound that is festering in you and fueling your unresolved anger. Let Him step between you and your betrayer and bring healing so that you can be unencumbered by any betrayals of the past. Unforgiveness will block your healing. The degree that you forgive is the degree to which you will be healed.

Personal Journaling and Small Group Questions
Spiritual Homecoming Assignment Seven

Personal Journaling Questions

1. List the top 24 people of whom you need to ask forgiveness.
2. List the top 24 issues for which you need to ask God's forgiveness.
3. List the top 24 people to whom you need to extend forgiveness.
4. Have you been in transference toward someone?
5. What memories do you want Jesus to heal? Ask Him to come right into those memories (Revelation 3:20).

Small Group Questions

1. What... are the key truths that stood out to you in this stage?
2. Why... do you need to know these truths?
3. How... do you apply these truths to your life?
4. Your pain... What pain does this stage reveal in your life?
5. Your sin... What are you doing with your pain?
6. Repentance... What do you need to do differently?
7. Prayer... What do you need to ask God for help with?

STAGE EIGHT: Turning from Idolatry
Recognizing the Mark of Baal in Your Life

Idolatry is worship of a false god. We all worship something. It is part of the human condition—we are hardwired for it. Worship is adoration and devotion for someone or something that you esteem. According to Dr. Edward Welch in Addictions: *A Banquet in the Grave,* idolatry is a worship disorder. What do you worship? Sometimes it is a conscious decision; other times we passively pay homage without even realizing it.

> *"Most of our culture ignores their pain*
> *And tries to go on with life,*
> *Letting their pain grow,*
> *Distancing their relationship with God*
> *Like a stray boat drifting out into the dangerous ocean of self*
> *And letting the currents of the world suck them in!"*[13]
> John-Paul Singh (My son at age 10)

Your idolatry is probably whatever you do when you're stressed out.[14] When life feels out of control, what habits crop up for you? Do you go online to a pornography site you weren't going to visit again? Do you lose yourself in the aisles of a store spending money you will regret spending? Do you block out your anxiety with fantasies and masturbation? Do you go on a drinking binge? Do you find relief in a dirty magazine or racy novel? Or, do you have no rest until you have fully and completely defamed to someone else the person who is causing you stress?

Idolatry is anything you use to try to fill the emptiness in your spirit that God is meant to fill. And frankly, it's an all-consuming quest because nothing else fills the emptiness that only God can fill.

> *My people have committed a compound sin: they've* **walked out on me,** *the fountain of fresh flowing waters, and then* **dug cisterns**—*cisterns that leak, cisterns that are no better than sieves.*
> (Jeremiah 2:13, MSG, emphasis added)

A LIFE OF IDOLATRY
* *Empty & Disempowered*
* *Taker*

Body

Soul

Spirit

LACK OF BELONGING

God's fresh flowing water is the only spiritual water that will satisfy the deep thirst of our human spirits. Jesus Christ called it "living water" (John 4:10). We turn from our fountain of water and hew cisterns instead; reservoirs that we think will hold everything that gives us life, but they don't hold anything at all. We are left thirsty and too weak to deal with the pain of life. False idols don't work, they are…false.

> Therefore **consider** the members of your earthly body as **dead to immorality,** impurity, passion, evil desire, and greed, which amounts to **idolatry.** For it is because of these things that the wrath of God will come upon the sons of disobedience, and in them you also once **walked,** when you were living in them.
> (Colossians 3:5-7, NASB, emphasis added)

Can you imagine what it means to be dead to immorality, impure passion, evil desire, and greed? Only your Abba Father, restoring your sense of being and belonging and filling you with His love, can give you the strength to be dead in your heart toward false pursuits. They are perversions of life. They are commitment to the

154

world rather than commitment to God. They are worship of the creature rather than the Creator. Our battle against sin includes battle against the world, our own flesh, and Satan (1 John 2). Being dead to these things means being able to really not go back to the website you weren't going to visit again. It means being able to hold back your tongue when a prime opportunity comes to slander the life out of someone who hurt you. To be able to walk past the aisle that is brimming with temptation. To be dead to sin and idolatry is to be alive to God. True worship of God brings transformation into your life.

> So, as those who have been chosen of God, holy and beloved, **put on** a heart of compassion, kindness, humility, gentleness and patience; bearing with one another, and forgiving each other, whoever has a complaint against anyone; just as the Lord forgave you, so also should you. Beyond all these things **put on love**, which is the perfect bond of unity. **Let the peace of Christ rule in your hearts,** to which indeed you were called in one body; and **be thankful.** Let the word of Christ richly dwell within you, with all wisdom teaching and admonishing one another with psalms and hymns and spiritual songs, singing with thankfulness in your hearts to God. **Whatever you do in word or deed, do all in the name of the Lord Jesus, giving thanks through Him to God the Father.**
>
> (Colossians 3:12-17, NASB, emphasis added)

The Idolatry of Baal Worship[15]

One of the false gods of the Canaanites and Phoenicians in ancient times was Baal, a fertility god. His female counterpart was Ashtoreth. In ancient Israel, when Elijah was God's prophet to the people, the whole land was infected with Baal worship, even those who believed in the living God. The drama unfolds in the book of 1 Kings, with the king and queen of Israel, Ahab and Jezebel, who made Baal worship the official practice of the nation. Jezebel was the daughter of the high priest of Baal worship.

155

When Ahab saw Elijah, Ahab said to him, "Is this you, you troubler of Israel?"

*He said, "I have not troubled Israel, but you and your father's house have, because **you have forsaken the commandments of the LORD and you have followed the Baals.** Now then send and gather to me all Israel at Mount Carmel, together with 450 prophets of Baal and 400 prophets of the Asherah, who eat at Jezebel's table."*

So Ahab sent a message among all the sons of Israel and brought the prophets together at Mount Carmel.

*Elijah came near to all the people and said, **"How long will you hesitate between two opinions? If the LORD is God, follow Him; but if Baal, follow him."** But the people did not answer him a word.*
                        (1 Kings 18:18–21, NASB, emphasis added)

Under the leadership of Ahab and Jezebel, Israel wandered from the pure worship of God to the addictive and co-addictive worship of Baal. The people were believers, just like us, who worshiped the living God but still did not know how to fill the holes in their spirits. The battle this passage depicts is not between Elijah and the prophets of Baal; it is the Lord making Himself known as Truth, and making Baal and all idolatry known as false.

Today, I use the term "Baal worship" to refer to idolatry, though all idolatry is not literally worship of the false god Baal. "Baal worship" is our effort to fill the core emptiness in our human spirits in our own ways and with our own means. Our ache for a love that is both tender and strong leads us to addictions and co-addictions that, metaphorically, are Baal worship. Idolatry drives the fear in your spirit that fuels the revenge in your soul and creates an addictive pull for relief in your body. The addictive dynamic of Baal worship is so diabolic that as soon as you possess what you think will fill you and give you life, it begins to possess you. (The word "Baal" literally means "lord possessor.")

Medicating Your Ache for Tenderness and Strength

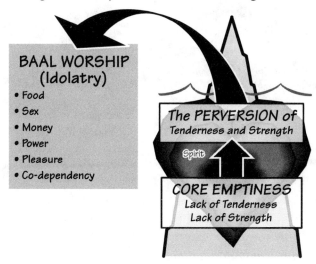

The influence of Baal is seen in many aspects of today's culture. Take, for example, television—which some call the "Baal Box." Every day, television pipes into the privacy of our homes images, erotic and non-erotic, that equate to Baal worship. We watch shows and commercials filled with every idolatry—from materialism, to abusive and using relationships, to immoral sexual activity. Most of us would never allow the behaviors that we see on TV to be witnessed by our children in real life. But somehow it's okay to see those types of behaviors—much of which amounts to pornography—in our homes through a plasma screen. As we see, think, and feel, so we become. Our children are being trained up as another generation of Baal worshipers by the constant media they consume.

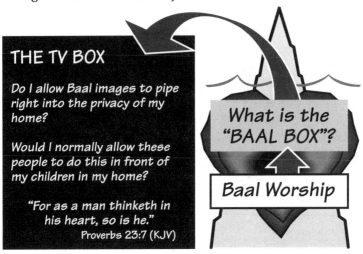

THE TV BOX

Do I allow Baal images to pipe right into the privacy of my home?

Would I normally allow these people to do this in front of my children in my home?

"For as a man thinketh in his heart, so is he."
Proverbs 23:7 (KJV)

What is the "BAAL BOX"?

Baal Worship

Leanne Payne was the first person to teach me about modern-day Baal worship. In her book *Healing Presence*, Leanne Payne says that "if we do not worhip our Creator, we will worship our procreative faculties in a fixation about men's & women's genitalia." Can you see how your Baal box pulls you into this? It is on your TV every day.

Sexuality in Baal Worship

As a fertility religion, ancient Baal worship had a strong, perverse, and addictive sexual component to it, a fixation upon female and male body parts. We can see the same preoccupation in today's obsession with external appearances rather than who or what someone is internally—in soul and, ultimately, in spirit.

Modern-day worship of genitals takes place in the forms of bikini contests, wet T-shirt contests, wet blue-jean contests, or rating men's or women's body parts. Modern-day "temples" of Baal worship include singles' bars, male and female strip clubs, adult bookstores, adult movie theaters, Internet pornography sites, phone sex lines, and even "mainstream" movies that include nudity and sexual activity.

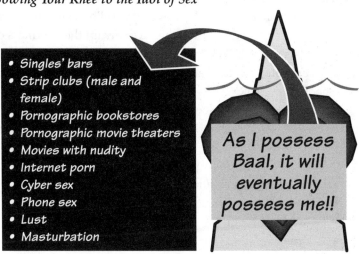

As a Christian church, we have become smug about what is acceptable idolatry and unacceptable idolatry. We condemn a man or woman who struggles with sexual immorality but look the other way for the man or woman struggling with food issues. For some, obsession with food is an addiction in the same way pornography is an addiction. For others, materialism is as besetting and destructive in their lives as sexual immorality in another's life.

Bowing Your Knee to the Idol of Food

Everyday Idolatry

All that God created is good. However, if we allow it to become as important to us as God Himself, then we corrupt the goodness of what God has made. This happens when we rely upon something to fill the emptiness in us that only God can fill. Then, that which God made good—like our sexuality or our appetite for food—becomes harmful to us. It doesn't fill us or meet our needs. It only makes the hole in our aching, longing, empty spirits even bigger.

What form does your idolatry take?
- Compulsive overeating
- Anorexia or Bulimia
- Other self-harm
- Pornography
- Cyber sex
- Masturbation
- Greed of money/Gambling
- Materialism
- Compulsive spending
- Perfectionism
- Control or power
- Putting work or ministry before family and relationships
- Gossip
- Escape

This is not a comprehensive list. Anything that seduces you away from honoring the true and living God to filling your emptiness in other ways is idolatry. That idolatry is just as detestable to God as the worship of Baal you read about above in 1 Kings.

What about co-addictions? What form do your co-addictions take in Baal worship?
- Inability to say NO to people
- Emotional dependence
- Enmeshed relationships
- Blurred boundaries
- Playing the role of the "martyr"
- Rescue of others from feeling their pain

160

The Idolatry Cycle in Your Spirit

Satan wages war on you and your loved ones on three levels: spirit, soul, and body. He promises relief, comfort, pleasure, and control. When you believe him, and obey him, you betray God.

- Guilt and shame deaden your receptivity to God's love.
- The twins of fear—emptiness and disempowerment—cut you off from God's strength.
- Empty and weak, you hide from God and will not let yourself be filled.
- Unable to be filled, you are unable to love God.
- You continue to take what the enemy offers you.
- Guilt and shame further deaden your receptivity to God's love, and the cycle repeats.

Spiritual Warfare in Your Spirit

To be free from Baal worship and idolatry and to be healed in your spirit, you will need to learn how to let the presence of the Trinity fill and empower your spirit with His love and strength. This is the first step to being able to listen and obey the voice of God. The tool of listening prayer is incredibly helpful here, disrupting the idolatry in our lives.

The Idolatry Cycle in Your Soul

The idolatry that takes root in your human spirit progresses to your soul.

- Unable to give or receive love, you look for relief, comfort, pleasure, and control.
- You believe, or choose to believe, whatever that promises for you—this is where addiction or co-addiction begins.
- You hide from others in your guilt and shame, yet you demand that the world and others meet needs that only God can meet.
- Dissatisfied, your soul responds with anger and the desire for revenge, which is the spirit of murder.
- The spirit of murder freezes your ability to feel.
- Unfeeling and angry, you are unable to give love to God and others, and the cycle repeats itself.

Spiritual Warfare in Your Soul

Part of the idolatry in the soul is in misogyny (the hatred of women) and misandry (the hatred of men). Misogyny is an attempt to kill the feminine spirit in women, to squelch tenderness of love. When women are dishonored, both women and men are blocked from receptivity—the feminine "art of being" and being filled in their relationships. To disregard the feminine is to close ourselves off from receptivity.

Examples of Misogyny:
- Lust for women or fantasies about women
- Jokes that degrade or dishonor women
- Pornography, masturbation
- Extramarital affairs
- Prostitution, rape, and other illicit sex
- Pin-up posters
- Cyber sex
- Adult bookstores, adult movies, strip clubs
- Mainstream movies, music videos, and websites that present women as sex objects
- Ridicule, disdain, or other disrespect toward women
- Disrespectful or contemptuous words to or about women
- Relating with your wife only through sexuality
- Disregarding the gifts of women in ministry

The reaction to misogyny is misandry, anger and hatred toward men and a desire to kill the masculine spirit. When men are dishonored, both men and women are blocked from empowerment in their spirits. To disregard the masculine is to disregard empowerment.

Examples of Misandry:
- Jokes that disrespect and dishonor men
- "Male-bashing," harsh criticism of masculinity, cutting down men in anger
- Belittling male character and performance
- Contempt for men
- Mainstream movies that emasculate men and father figures
- Lust for men or fantasizing about men; using them as sex objects
- Male pornography
- Male strip clubs

- Romance novels
- Extramarital affairs
- Male prostitution, rape, and other illicit sex
- The belief that you can get along just fine without them or their input

Feminism is a strong example of misandry as well. In the name of honoring women, it commonly disrespects and dishonors men rather than giving honor to either gender. The feminine and the masculine both need each other. One is not superior to the other; one cannot be complete without the other. They complement each other. Mutual respect and submission is necessary for the masculine and feminine to fully be as God designed them.

Souls that are wounded by a failure to receive what they demand from others often direct their anger toward whole groups of people instead of toward those who have disappointed them. This is why there is a great deal of misogyny and misandry where there has been worship of Baal.

The Idolatry Cycle in Your Body
The destruction caused by idolatry in your human spirit and your soul shows itself in your physical body—not only in destructive addictions, but even in sickness and medical maladies—as well as in your relationships.

- You act on the lies of misogyny, misandry, and worship of Baal.
- You try to numb your emptiness and pacify the spirit of murder with the spirit of lust.
- Your physical senses become numb to your pain, as well as to your passion, giftedness, and purpose.
- You keep acting out your addiction and co-addiction, even when you don't want to act it out.
- Your addictive and co-addictive worship begin to decay your soul and destroy your body's ability to respond to God and others, as well as respond to its own illness.
- Your relationships with God and others fail, and your health fails as well.

- In your weakness, you act on the lies of misogyny, misandry, and worship of Baal.

Spiritual Warfare in Your Body

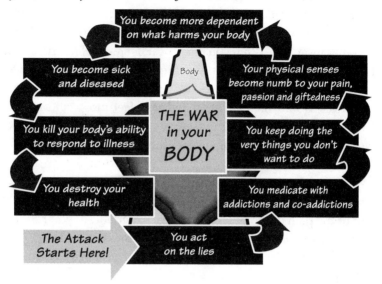

Food as an Idol

Compulsive overeating (or compulsive undereating) and food addictions start with disconnecting from your core spiritual pain (not experiencing the love and strength of God). Though you may know in your head that God loves you, that core spiritual pain comes when you are not able to feel it in your heart. That is worsened by the primary pain (not experiencing the love and strength of your mother or father)—even if you knew your parents loved you, but you felt disconnected from one or both of them. Any secondary pain (not experiencing the love and strength of others) you experienced on your journey from abusers exacerbates the core pain you feel. Secondary abusers can be anyone—classmates, teachers, boyfriends, girlfriends, or spouses.

The betrayal you felt from those experiences inhibits (or blocks entirely) the tenderness of love, strength of love and peace of love in your human spirit, and it creates an anger of revenge in your soul.

You overeat, wanting to soothe the emptiness in your spirit, feeding off the addictions in your body and co-addictions in your relationships, only to realize that the idolatry is feeding off you! Your core emptiness—spiritual starvation—increases as you are devoured by the very thing you thought would feed you. With greater emptiness, your drive to desperately eat more food becomes insatiable. What you really need is spiritual nourishment, but without identifying that, you are bound to physical comfort food and relational comfort food. This realization produces more helplessness and hopelessness, and you feel more cut off from God's love and strength. In essence, your food addiction is like worship of Baal—worshiping something that cannot fill you and cannot meet your need.

The Food Idolatry Cycle in Your Body

Out of the pain of the betrayals you've experienced, you listen to the lies of Baal that food can fill your emptiness.

- You try to fill your emptiness and assuage your anger with food.
- Your physical senses become numb to your pain, as well as to your passion, giftedness, and purpose.
- You keep acting out your addiction and co-addiction, even if you don't want to act it out.
- The addictive and co-addictive worship begin to decay your soul and destroy your body; your ability to respond to God and others is damaged, and your body is victim to many physical problems and illnesses as a result of your addiction.
- Your relationships with God and others fail, and your health fails as well.

We live in a culture of Baal worship that is destroying both the Church and the culture. In order to worship the true God, you must intentionally stand against idolatry in your life.

The Path Out of Idolatry

Even as Christians, without the tools of receptivity and empowerment, we daily run right into the arms of false gods. Our children and grandchildren will follow in that path as well if we do not change course—the sins of the fathers and mothers visiting generations to come. We must cleanse ourselves, our marriages, our homes, and our churches of being temples of Baal.

How did Elijah tackle this problem? He clearly knew he was called to do three things:

- To expose Baal worship
- To stand against Baal worship
- To call God's people away from Baal worship

Elijah knew that to go up against the King of the land would take the power of the Holy Living God. Elijah was filled by the presence of God; he listened and obeyed God and went forward in courageous faith, courageous hope, and courageous love.

Here is the story of what a simple man did to defend the name of the Living God, which was being defiled by both the pagans and the children of God. It is a story about how the passion of the Living God burns to rebuild the altars of holiness in all of His places of worship throughout the world.

> Then Elijah said to the people, "I alone am left a prophet of the LORD, but Baal's prophets are 450 men. Now let them give us two oxen; and let them choose one ox for themselves and cut it up, and place it on the wood, but put no fire under it; and I will prepare the other ox and lay it on the wood, and I will not put a fire under it. **Then you call on the name of your god, and I will call on the name of the LORD, and the God who answers by fire, He is God."**
>
> And all the people said, "That is a good idea."
>
> So Elijah said to the prophets of Baal, "Choose one ox for yourselves and prepare it first for you are many, and call on the name of your god, but put no fire under it."

Then they took the ox which was given them and they prepared it and called on the name of Baal from morning until noon saying, **"O Baal, answer us."** **But there was no voice and no one answered.** And they leaped about the altar which they made.

It came about at noon, that **Elijah mocked them and said, "Call out with a loud voice, for he is a god; either he is occupied or gone aside, or is on a journey, or perhaps he is asleep and needs to be awakened."**

So they cried with a loud voice and cut themselves according to their custom with swords and lances until the blood gushed out on them. When midday was past, they raved until the time of the offering of the evening sacrifice; but there was no voice, no one answered, and no one paid attention.

Then Elijah said to all the people, "Come near to me." So all the people came near to him. And he repaired the altar of the LORD which had been torn down. Elijah took twelve stones according to the number of the tribes of the sons of Jacob, to whom the word of the LORD had come, saying, "Israel shall be your name." So with the stones he built an altar in the name of the LORD, and he made a trench around the altar, large enough to hold two measures of seed. Then he arranged the wood and cut the ox in pieces and laid it on the wood. And he said, "Fill four pitchers with water and pour it on the burnt offering and on the wood." And he said, "Do it a second time," and they did it a second time. And he said, "Do it a third time," and they did it a third time. The water flowed around the altar and he also filled the trench with water.

At the time of the offering of the evening sacrifice, Elijah the prophet came near and said, "O LORD, *the God of Abraham, Isaac and Israel, today let it be known that You are God in Israel and that I am Your servant and I have done all these things at Your word. Answer me, O Lord, answer me, that this people may know that You, O Lord, are God, and that You have turned their heart back again."*

Then the fire of the Lord fell and consumed the burnt offering and the wood and the stones and the dust, and licked up the water that was in the trench. *When all the people saw it, they fell on their faces; and they said,* **"The Lord, He is God; the Lord, He is God."**

Then Elijah said to them, "Seize the prophets of Baal; do not let one of them escape." So they seized them; and Elijah brought them down to the brook Kishon, and slew them there.

Elijah said to Ahab, "Go up, eat and drink; for there is the sound of the roar of a heavy shower."
(1 Kings 18:22–41, NASB, emphasis added)

Elijah first exposed the idolatry in the land. He challenged the 450 prophets of Baal. Then he called their bluff. Their god could not answer the pleas of his followers. But when Elijah prayed, God answered swiftly and dramatically. The fire of God came down and burned the sacrifices in a supernatural display of His power! Then, the Lord God ordered justice: that all the prophets of Baal be executed. That is a picture of how the holy wrath of the living Holy God abhors the worship of Baal and its practices.

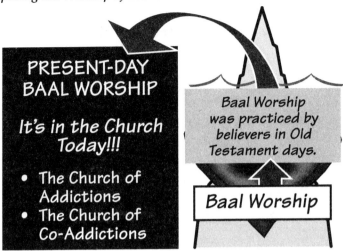

I pose the same question to you as Elijah posed: How long will you waver between two opinions? If the Lord is God, follow him; but if Baal—your addictions and co-addictions—is God, follow them.

The Call to This Generation

And I pray for you as Elijah prayed:

> *O Lord, God of Abraham, Isaac and Israel, let it be known today that you are God in Israel and that I am your servant and have done all these things at your command.* **Answer me, O LORD, answer me, so that these people will know that you, O LORD, are God, and that you are turning their hearts back again.**
>
> (1 Kings 18:36-37, NASB, emphasis added)

The stains of Baal worship, and its misogyny and misandry, are everywhere.

> **Or what agreement has the temple of God with idols?** *For we are the temple of the living God; just as God said, "I WILL DWELL IN THEM AND WALK AMONG THEM; AND I WILL BE THEIR GOD, AND THEY SHALL BE MY PEOPLE.*
>
> *Therefore, COME OUT FROM THEIR MIDST AND BE SEPARATE," says the Lord. "AND DO NOT TOUCH WHAT IS UNCLEAN; and* **I will welcome you. And I will be a father to you,** *and you shall be sons and daughters to Me," **Says the Lord Almighty.**
>
> (2 Corinthians 6:16–18, NASB, emphasis added)

The Lord Almighty invites you to leave your lifestyle of idolatry and make your spiritual journey back home to the living and compassionate heart of God.

"Have you given your children the gift of Baal?"

ADDICTIONS
• *Food, Alcohol, Smoking and Drugs*
• *Money, Power, Pleasure, Etc.*

CO-ADDICTIONS
• *Co-dependent Relationship*
• *Inability to Say "No" to People*

Baal Worship
Non-erotic Component

Ministry of Confession

In prayer, allow God's Spirit to show you the garden of your spirit as you take some time to pause and close your eyes in prayer. What are the weeds of unconfessed sin that have taken root in the garden of your spirit? Sit back and quietly let the living God show you what is choking out life in the garden of your spirit. Ask the Lord to show you what He wants you to do with the weeds of unconfessed sin that you see.

Clinically and spiritually, you are as sick as your secrets. The degree to which you keep a secret is the degree to which you will block intimacy with your loved ones. Unconfessed sin will block you from receiving God's tenderness of love and being empowered with God's strength of love.

> *Therefore **confess** your sins to each other and pray for each other so that you may be **healed**. The prayer of a righteous man [or woman] is powerful and effective.*
> (James 5:16, NIV, emphasis added)

The healing process in your spirit starts with confession. As you are known, you will be healed. To be known is to confess your sins of betrayal, disobedience, misogyny, misandry, and idolatry

172

to someone in the body of Christ who is worthy of your trust. When you name how you have been sinned against and how you sin against others, you disrupt the shame in your spirit in a life-giving way.

Three Steps of Confessing Sin:
1. Confidentially acknowledge and confess your sin and pain to someone you trust.
2. Take your sin and pain to the Cross, and release it to Jesus.
3. Receive at the Cross the forgiveness, cleansing, and healing of the Lord.

> *If we* **confess** *our sins, He is faithful and righteous to* **forgive** *us our sins and to* **cleanse** *us from all unrighteousness.*
>
> *(1 John 1:9, NASB, emphasis added)*

At "Rekindling Your Spirit" conferences, we set aside a time for the attendees to confidentially confess their sins to a prayer minister. This is the moment of breakthrough for many because the release of guilt and shame is so powerful when they hear another person declare that God has forgiven them, after they have confessed their sins to the Lord.

Three Steps of Turning from Idolatry and Baal Worship:
1. Confessing or acknowledging your addictions and co-addictions.
2. Renouncing your lifestyle of addictions and co-addictions; taking a stand against living the way you were.
3. Repenting of that addiction or co-addiction by choosing to have someone hold you accountable to turning from your addictive lifestyle as you choose to worship the Almighty God.

Perhaps you have not been involved in Baal or Ashtoreth worship, but your parents or grandparents or great-grandparents may have been. In that case, it is now infecting later generations. You must

173

tear down the altars to Baal that were erected by those who came before you. In Judges chapter 6, the Lord told Gideon to destroy his father's altar to Baal and Ashtoreth. Today, that is represented by the items, practices, and habits of idolatry in your family lines. Gideon was not personally guilty of Baal worship, but he had been stained by his father's Baal worship.

> *Tear down your father's altar to Baal and cut down the Asherah pole beside it. Then build a proper kind of altar to the LORD your God on the top of this height. Using the wood of the Asherah pole that you cut down, offer the second bull as a burnt offering.*
>
> *(Judges 6:25-26, NIV, emphasis added)*

The Scriptures say that the sins of the fathers and mothers will visit the generations of the children and their children's children (Exodus 20:5). Even though Gideon was not involved personally in Baal worship, the Lord wanted him and his household and future generations to be freed and healed from any Baal worship from prior generations. Gideon was filled with the presence of God. As Gideon listened and obeyed the voice of the Lord God, his masculinity was filled and empowered to stand against Baal and Ashtoreth worship and to actively call God's people from idolatry. He tore down his father's altar to Baal and the Asherah pole beside it. Many of our mothers and fathers have erected addictive and co-addictive Baal altars that we need to spiritually tear down through prayer. If we do not, the curses of the generations will be passed to us and our children.

We are called to do the spiritual equivalent of what Gideon did, spiritually tearing down, through prayer, the altars to Baal that those before us have erected. (If you are in spiritual and caregiving leadership, ask the Lord for humility in this area. Caregivers can be the most unwilling to acknowledge their own idolatry—you can help others with their Baal worship but be silent about your own.) Consider:

> *How can you say, "I am **not defiled,** I have **not gone**
> **after the Baals"?***
>
> (Jeremiah 2:23, NASB, emphasis added)

and

> *Not everyone who says to me, "Lord, Lord," will*
> *enter the kingdom of heaven,* but only he who does
> the will of my Father who is in heaven. Many will say
> to me on that day, "Lord, Lord, did we not prophesy
> in your name, and in your name drive out demons
> and perform many miracles? " **Then I will tell them**
> **plainly, "I never knew you. Away from me, you**
> **evildoers!"**
>
> (Matthew 7:21–23, NIV, emphasis added)

A person can stop certain behaviors but, like a dry drunk, continue the internal addictive thoughts, feelings, and choices by jumping to new, more culturally acceptable addictions like cigarettes, food, caffeine, TV, computer use or sports. The idolatry is deeper than physical, outward acts. For example, if you confess the use of pornographic material with your physical eyes, you also need to turn from entertaining pornographic thoughts in your imagination.

Modern-Day Misogyny and Misandry

MISOGYNY Anger toward the feminine by...	MISANDRY Anger toward the masculine by...
✔ The way you look at them?	✔ Engaging in "male-bashing"?
✔ The thoughts you fantasize about them?	✔ Cutting them down with your anger?
✔ The words you say to them or about them?	✔ Belittling their character and performance?
✔ The jokes you tell?	✔ The jokes you tell?
✔ Indulging in pornography?	✔ Using them as sex objects?
✔ Using them as sex objects?	✔ Overpowering them with words of contempt?
✔ Overpowering them with rape?	

When you confess, renounce, and repent of misogyny, misandry, and Baal worship or idolatry, the generational strongholds are severed and cut dramatically. This may be a quiet, reflective time for you, or it may be a time of weeping and lamentation. In either case, it is a time when many people experience a very deep release. The healing in their human spirits begins in earnest from that point forward.

Confession of Misogyny
- Confess the sin of misogyny in your own heart.
- Confess the misogyny of previous generations on your father's side and your mother's side.
- Confess the effect of misogyny on you and your household.
- Renounce misogyny, and announce your choice for you and your household to stand against it.
- Repent of misogyny with a specific plan of how to live differently from this point forward.
- Ask God daily to be filled by His tenderness of love, strength of love, and peace of love.

The Confession of Misandry
- Confess the sin of misandry in your own heart.
- Confess the misandry of previous generations on your father's side and your mother's side.
- Confess the effect of misandry on you and your household.
- Renounce misandry, and announce your choice for you and your household to stand against it.
- Repent of misandry with a specific plan of how to live differently from this point forward.
- Ask God daily to be filled by His tenderness of love, strength of love, and peace of love.

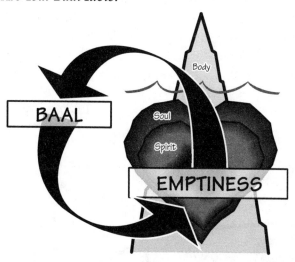

Confession of Baal and Ashtoreth Worship or Idolatry

- Confess the sin of Baal and Ashtoreth worship or idolatry in your own heart.
- Confess the Baal and Ashtoreth worship or idolatry of previous generations on your father's side and your mother's side.
- Confess the effect of Baal and Ashtoreth worship or idolatry on you and your household.
- Renounce Baal and Ashtoreth worship and idolatry, and announce your choice for you and your household to stand against it.
- Repent of Baal and Ashtoreth worship and idolatry with a specific plan of how to live differently from this point forward.
- Ask God daily to be filled by His tenderness of love, strength of love, and peace of love.

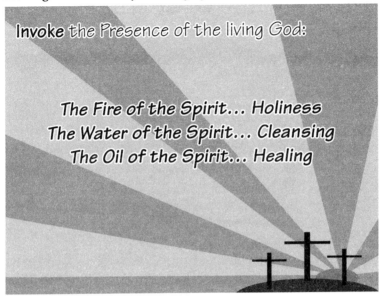

After you have confessed, renounced, and repented of the sins of misogyny, misandry, and Baal worship or idolatry, then, pray for God to destroy the strongholds of Baal in your life. Say with confidence, "The God who answers by fire—He is God" (1 Kings 18:24, 36-38). When the fire of God has destroyed the bondage of Baal in your life, holiness takes its place. This is the birthright of the children of God.

When people speak the words, "I renounce the god-idols of my father/mother, I renounce Baal," they often see the images of filthy, lustful, naked bodies. And the activities that have plagued their minds and spirits burn up and disintegrate before their eyes.[16]

Some men have reported that as the fire of God filled them, Jesus stood before them and pulled out reels of pornographic tapes that had been replaying in their minds for years. One woman who had been an object of Baal worship through sexual abuse saw the Holy Cross in the forefront of her mind burning with holy fire. She then saw the defiled images of herself and the Baal images and memories around the sexual abuse leave her and fly into the Cross and burn up.

Next, pray that the water of the Spirit would come and cleanse your spirit, soul, and body.

> *Then I will sprinkle clean water on you, and you will be clean;* I will cleanse you from all your filthiness and from all your idols. Moreover, *I will give you a new heart and put a new spirit within you;* and I will remove the heart of stone from your flesh and give you a heart of flesh. *I will put My Spirit within you and cause you to walk in My statutes, and you will be careful to observe My ordinances.*
> (Ezekiel 36:25-27, NASB, emphasis added)

In her book *Restoring the Christian Soul,* Leanne Payne teaches on how to make holy water and anointing oil. During "Rekindling Your Spirit" conferences, we use holy water and oil to anoint participants. Many people report that they knew they had been forgiven when they confessed their sins privately to God. However, through the ministry of the personal and corporate confessions of their sin, when they were sprinkled with the holy water, their hearts could then feel what their heads knew. Some did not think they could ever have the stains of Baal washed away from their lives and memories. Today these men and women testify to the power of the Cross in deliverance and healing.

> Are you sick? Call the church leaders together to **pray** and **anoint you with oil** in the name of the Master.
> (James 5:14, MSG, emphasis added)

The elements of the fire, water, and oil of the spirit are tools the Holy Spirit uses to minister to the whole person. They can help you feel in your heart what you know in your head. When your head and heart come together in freedom, healing, and restoration, life is good! As the hand of God brings modern-day deliverance, healing, and restoration to people who have been struggling with addictions and co-addictions, the filling and empowering by the Spirit of God becomes a new way to live.

This is not a one-time process, but one to repeat throughout your life as you continue to be affected by Baal and Ashtoreth worship in one form or another.

After this process, people often have amazing testimonies of how the Spirit of God brought new freedom and healing into their spirits, souls, and bodies. (Check our website blog for current testimonies: www.rekindlingyourspirit.com.)

Spiritual Warfare on Three Levels

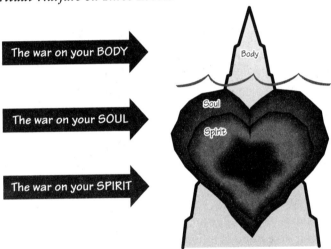

The Worship Cycle in Your Spirit

The key to experiencing worship in your human spirit is to daily embrace the presence of the Trinity who lives in your human spirit; you will be filled and empowered by the tenderness and strength of the presence of God—listening prayer. This fills your human spirit with the presence and voice of God. Each day, as you choose to listen to the voice of God, you will be filled and empowered by the voice of the real Father.

- By listening to and believing the truth from Father God, you reject and crowd out the voice of the father of lies.
- Father God restores your receptivity to His love.
- You seek to know Him and embrace His presence in your life.
- His strength empowers you to obey Him.

- Filled with love for God, you choose to obey Him and respond to Him with reverence and worship, longing to receive more of His love and truth.
- The love of God in your human spirit crowds out fear.
- Embracing the presence of God and listening to Him in prayer fills and empowers your human spirit with new faith and hope.
- You live with passion, giftedness, and purpose!

Filling and Empowering Your Spirit

Exchanging Idolatry for Worship
The Worship Cycle in Your Soul

The key to experiencing worship in your human soul is daily "Listening Obedience." As your human spirit is filled with the presence and voice of God, your soul will be empowered by the strength of God as you choose to listen and obey God.

- You listen to truth from God and fill your mind with it to displace and destroy the lies and doubts in your mind.
- Your heart is filled with new hope in "listening prayer."
- Through "listening obedience" you make wise choices.
- You lovingly engage others and rely on God to satisfy you rather than others.

- You are grateful and delight in God's law.
- You feel the full range of your emotions.
- You choose to love others instead of using them.
- You listen to truth from God and fill your mind with it, and the cycle repeats itself.

Filling and Empowering Your Soul

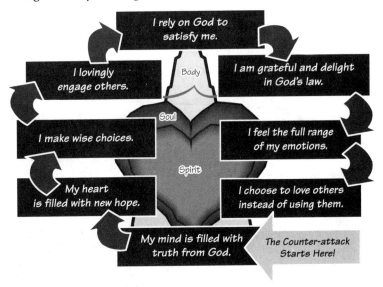

Listening obedience will empower you to live with a sense of purpose, to love God and love your neighbor as yourself.

The Worship Cycle in Your Body

Each day, as you choose to embrace the presence of the Trinity who lives in your human spirit and take the time to do your daily listening prayer and listening obedience, you will be equipped to counter the voices of addictions and co-addictions.

- By obeying God, acting on the truth, you reject and silence the voices of addictions and co-addictions.
- You stop medicating your pain and anger with addictions and co-addictions.
- You stop doing the addictive things that you don't want to do.
- Your physical senses come alive.

- You depend on God instead of on what harms your body and relationships.
- You choose what is good for the health of your body and relationships.
- You respond rightly to illness, addictions, and co-addictive relationships.
- You become healthier in spirit, soul, and body, and also in your relationships.
- You obey God, acting on the truth, and the cycle repeats itself.

Filling and Empowering Your Body

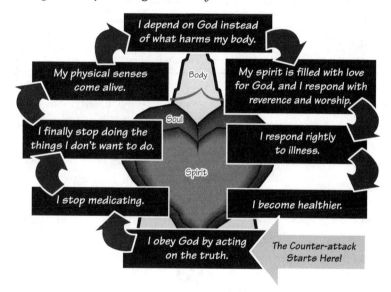

Three Tools for Spiritual Warfare

| Your FALSE SELF | SHIFTING → | Your TRUE SELF |

3
The Journey of Worship
Daily Loving Your Neighbor
Daily Loving God

2
Daily Dying and Daily Rising
Listening Prayer and Listening Obedience
Embracing the Presence of God

1
You Receive the Holy Spirit
Jesus Automatically Becomes Your Savior
Initially Make Jesus Your Lord

Each day as you choose to listen and obey the Voice of God, you will start to honor your body and your relationships. The choice to be filled and empowered in your spirit, soul, and body is yours. The choice to be filled and empowered in your relationship with God and others is yours! These are choices toward passion, giftedness, and purpose that expose, stand against, and call people away from the worship of Baal and Ashtoreth.

The Journey to Holiness

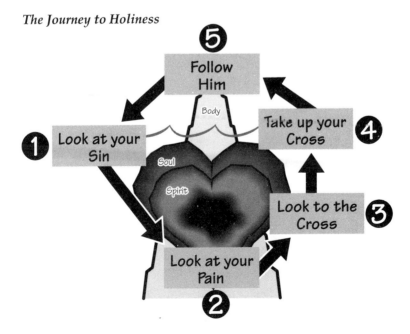

> *Don't let down your guard lest even now, today,*
> *someone—man or woman, clan or tribe—gets*
> ***sidetracked from GOD, our God, and gets***
> ***involved with the no-gods of the nations;*** *lest*
> *some poisonous weed sprout and spread among you.*
>
> (Deuteronomy 29:18, MSG, emphasis added)

As we turn from the worship of Baal and Ashtoreth and bend our knees to the Living God, we gain a vision for how the lost years can be restored to each and every one who no longer bows to Baal but to the living God Almighty.

> *Now that we know what we have—Jesus, this*
> *great High Priest with **ready access to God—let's***
> ***not let it slip through our fingers.*** *We don't have a*
> *priest who is out of touch with our reality. He's been*
> *through weakness and testing, experienced it all—all*
> *but the sin. **So let's walk right up to him and get***
> ***what he is so ready to give. Take the mercy, accept***
> ***the help.***
>
> (Hebrews 4:14–16, MSG, emphasis added)

Now is the time to turn from a life of idolatry and to return to the foot of the Cross! Now is the time to worship the great and almighty, true God.

* * * * * * *

Personal Journaling and Small Group Questions
Spiritual Homecoming Assignment Eight

Personal Journaling Questions

1. How do you engage in misogyny?
2. How do you engage in misandry?
3. List the ways in which you engage in Baal (idol) worship.
4. Go back in Stage Eight to the section on confession. Use it as a guide to confess, renounce, and repent from your misogyny, misandry, and Baal (idol) worship. When you repent, have a plan for how to live differently. Ask the friend praying with you to hold you accountable to it. Pray through generations back in your family as well. Do this with someone you trust. When you have confessed, that person can declare, "God has forgiven you!" Ask God daily to fill you with His tenderness of love, strength of love, and peace of love.

Small Group Questions

1. What... are the key truths that stood out to you in this stage?
2. Why... do you need to know these truths?
3. How... do you apply these truths to your life?
4. Your pain... What pain does this stage reveal in your life?
5. Your sin... What are you doing with your pain?
6. Repentance... What do you need to do differently?
7. Prayer... What do you need to ask God for help with?

186

STAGE NINE: Experiencing Holy Sexuality
Finding Ecstasy in Your Intimacy

When it comes to sex, men in general want to know how to get more sex! The chief complaint for men across the board is lack of it. A woman's radar, however, is on emotional intimacy. She wants to be cared for in a loyal, trusting friendship. She wants an engaging father for her children, a home in good repair, provision for the family's needs. She wants a lot of tender touch and kindness, and then some romance too!

Men tell me, "I send her roses. I give her chocolates. I rub her feet. I tell her she is beautiful. I tell her I love her. I have tried it all! I am the ultimate man. I clean the house and cook dinner. I have tried everything, and it still goes nowhere."

They are not sure what a wife really wants, but whatever it is, they are not doing it; and they are not getting the amount of sex they want. Men seem to constantly have sex on the brain. They compartmentalize life very easily—like a grid: Now it is time to work. Now it is time to eat. Now it is time to exercise. Now it is time for sex! It is very easy for the masculine soul to separate from all relationships, tasks, and emotions in life and say, "Honey, let's just have sex!" For women, however, relationships, tasks, and emotions are very intertwined. A woman needs to have peace or resolution in those areas in order to rest, relax, and enjoy herself sexually. This is difficult for men to comprehend:

"Sweetie, just forget about it all, and let's have a good time!" the husband says.

"That's the problem!" the wife responds. "You forget about it all, and I am the one who has to make sure everything gets done. Therefore I cannot rest. I cannot relax. Yes, I am uptight and not in the mood! Can't you get it?"

Men and women are fundamentally different in their sexual desires.

Four Desires in the Male Spirit

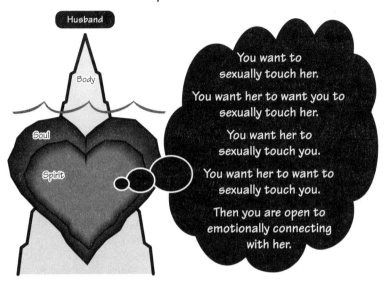

Four Desires in the Female Spirit

(If you are married, ask your spouse if the list is true of him or her. If you're courageous, ask where he or she thinks both of you are on the four "I wants." Then do something about it! Surprise your husband or wife...)

Sexual Desires of the Male Spirit
- I want to sexually touch her.
- I want her to want me to sexually touch her.
- I want her to sexually touch me.
- I want her to want to sexually touch me.
- Then I am open to emotionally connecting with her.

Sexual Desires of the Female Spirit
- I want to emotionally touch him.
- I want him to want me to emotionally touch him.
- I want him to emotionally touch me.
- I want him to want to emotionally touch me.
- Then I am open to sexually connecting with him!

As these lists describe, women want a more holistic approach to sexuality. Women tend to be interested in a great marriage relationship; men tend to be interested in a great marriage bed. Women are built to enjoy excellent sexual health if they are experiencing excellent spiritual health, relational health, and physical health. Men, if you are abandoning your wife to loneliness in any one of those three areas, you are in the doghouse!

On the other hand, men may just want great sex regardless of what is happening! Men, if you can come to understand the difference between sex and sexuality, you will be on the path to a much more frequent sexual relationship with your wife.

The Difference Between Sex and Sexuality
The body, the outer person, is only one-third of sexuality. Men tend to consider the erotic sexual component as the whole picture of sex. In actuality, the body-to-body bond is only a great, pleasurable one-third of sexuality! If you want the whole experience, you need to understand the other vital two-thirds of non-erotic sexuality.

189

Sex vs. Sexuality

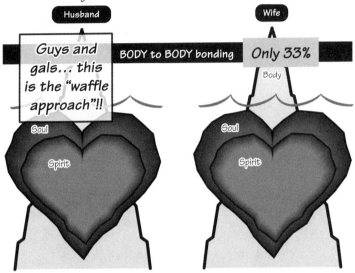

We know that men need to be sexually touched, but God created men with a need to be emotionally touched as well. Women want to be sexually responsive, but in order for that to happen, a woman must have an intermingled spirit-to-spirit and soul-to-soul connection with her spouse. She needs to be emotionally touched. When she experiences emotional touch, she can more naturally open to sexual touch.

The waffle approach is the man's ability to compartmentalize life.

Sex vs. Sexuality

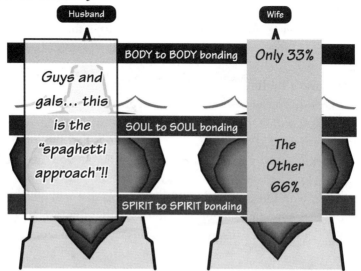

Contrary to the cultural messages that assault us daily, true and intimate sexuality requires bonding on all three levels of the spirit, soul, and body. Complete and fulfilling sexuality intertwines the desire phase of the spirit, the arousal phase of the soul, and the orgasm phase of the body. Each phase is one-third of the sexual experience.

The spaghetti approach is a picture of everything being intermingled for the woman's spirit, soul and body.

The Normal Sexual Phases

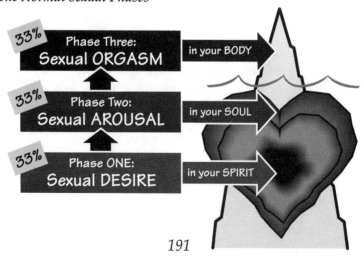

A normal sexual cycle is:

Phase One: Sexual Desire in your spirit (one-third)
Phase Two: Sexual Arousal in your soul (one-third)
Phase Three: Sexual Orgasm in your body (one-third)

A Husband's Toolbox

Men, how do you successfully engage in phase one and two when it is not as natural for you as phase three? If you have been empty and disempowered at your core, you have not had the internal resources to be truly relational with your wife. As you are filled by God's love and empowered by God's strength, He will enable you to grow in those areas. Here are five tools that will help you live out new strength of tenderness toward your wife, affecting all three phases of sexual desire, sexual arousal, and sexual orgasm.

1. Look at Her

When you look at her when she is talking, it tells her you are engaged with her and considering what she has to say. Men, when you and your wife are having a fight and you look into her eyes, it tells your wife that you value her in her pain and not just her body. When you look at your wife when she is crying, and she sees that her crying affects you, then she knows you really care about what is hurting her. It helps her to see your courage, that you are not afraid of her pain. When you see your wife and she sees you, you start to know her and you start to be known. Leaving your wife alone in her pain is relational abandonment, and it magnifies a woman's core emptiness and loneliness. This is one of the most cowardly acts we can do as men.

Wives, have patience with your husbands! A lot of men feel helpless about a woman's tears and do not know how to respond to pain. In moments of conflict, a man is searching to fix the problem at hand. Relational conflict tends to make a man feel very vulnerable and magnifies his core emptiness and inadequacy.

2. Talk to Her

Men, when you take the time to daily talk to your wife, this helps her know that you both are on the same page. She needs to know where your heart is and that your heart is exclusively hers. Let her inside by sharing the details of your day and listening to the details of hers, as well.

"Words are the tools that shape the heart."[17]

The fire of sexual desire can be birthed through sharing and listening to each other. Live with great loyalty to the woman of your heart, and the ecstasy of sexual orgasm will be privately and exclusively yours together as a couple.

Wives, sometimes when emotions are flying it is difficult for a man to collect his thoughts. And, it is difficult for the majority of men to put words to their emotions. Be patient with him.

3. Touch Her

Even though it is very challenging to give non-erotic touch to your wife when she is hurting, it can mean so much to her. A man's non-erotic touch speaks to a woman in a way that words cannot express. It lets her know that another human loves her and that she is valued and appreciated for her person and not what she can give or do for you, and that she is not alone in life. What you say from your heart verbally and non-verbally means a lot to a woman.

Wives, many husbands isolate themselves and like to be alone. They have to work hard at breaking through a high emotional barrier to reach out and touch you with non-erotic emotional touch. Encourage him with warm responsiveness to his tender touch for you.

4. Serve Her

Men, when you serve a woman with the hands of your heart, she feels valuable. When you help her with the kids and the home, you take a load off of her. When you turn from self-centered behavior

193

to other-centered behavior with your wife, she is freed to be "off task" and rest and enjoy "being."

Wives, let your husbands know in a gentle way where they can serve you. Husbands may not see the most obvious things—you may have to tenderly direct your husband to what you want done.

5. Pray with Her

When you pray with and for your wife, it speaks to the core of her being. Pray out loud with her; it's the deepest type of talking that you can do. Prayer can take on a new dimension as you feel the love of God in her tender spirit. It can rekindle the fires of unity, loyalty, and trust in each other.

Wives, it may take a while for a man to feel comfortable praying out loud. Pray for him that God would show him how to pray for you and your family.

A Wife's Toolbox

Women, men need to be respected. That says love to them. If you have been empty and disempowered at your core, you have not had what it takes to fully respect your husband. As you are filled by God's love and empowered by God's strength, He will enable you to love your husband with respect. Here are five tools that will help you live out new tenderness of strength toward your husband.

1. Honor His Reputation in Public

You are the one your man loves the most. You can be an excellent business partner for his inner world if you give him supportive feedback in private and honor his reputation in public. Show him respect in front of others; don't criticize him. When you address issues with him privately, if you approach him in a tenderness of love, he may be more able to listen to you. However, if you attack him, he will have trouble responding to your complaint positively.

"God also calls husbands and wives to use our words to push back the chaos and shape our lives into order and beauty."[18]

Men, when you feel verbally attacked, you may tend to either cower or explode in anger. Try instead to go to the core of the matter that is causing your wife to feel insecure or that a situation is out of control. Pray for the tenderness and strength you need to bring you both to a place of peace.

2. Support Him as a Father
Wives, if you want a strong and virile man in your relationship, enhance the strength of his masculinity. Show him respect in front of your children, and do not talk negatively about him to your children. Children can be easily poisoned by a critical spirit. Criticism of their father strips him of his authority and damages his relationship with them, as well as damaging their spirits and their concept of fatherhood.

Men, at the moment you feel your wife is undermining your respect with your children, graciously expose the situation and ask her to stop. If her concern is something that you can fix immediately or can come up with a solution to discuss for the future, you may diffuse her frustration as she realizes your strength even within your weaknesses or inadequacy.

3. Show Him Warmth and Affection
Wives, your husband is designed to receive the tenderness of strength from your feminine soul as you are designed to receive his strength of tenderness from his masculine soul. Show him your tenderness of strength in offering warmth and affection and trust, even if things are not perfect. To withhold sex from him because things are not perfect is controlling and self-protective.

Men, when a woman feels listened to, understood, supported and taken care of, the rewards can be great in the marriage bed. However, this path of sexual fulfillment takes patience. A wise man knows that the key to great sex is being a great husband to his wife when they're not in bed!

195

4. Serve Him

Women, be there for your man amidst the challenges of your day. Both you and your husband need to set aside time to talk and play together. After you have connected relationally, make it equally a priority to connect sexually. Many couples will take the early mornings during the week or on weekends before the kids get up. Whatever are your true priorities in serving each other, you will make the time for it. Be sure that in being a great mom and providing well for your children that you do not neglect your husband in the process.

Men, when women have children and a household to run, in addition to an outside job or other obligations, it can sap her energy. Make a point to take care of children and home matters from time to time so that she can unwind and transition to spend time with you. Also, take responsibility as the man to schedule—and keep to—time that you have set aside for each other, away from other responsibilities and away from the bedroom.

5. Pray with Him

Prayer is the most intimate talk you can have with your husband in the presence of the living God. Couples who pray together regularly are couples who have learned to fight for each other and not against each other. As you make it a priority to start your day together in prayer, or to end your day together in prayer, you will experience a spiritual glue that keeps you bonded throughout many storms.

Men, join a weekly men's group that will strengthen you and equip you to lead out spiritually with courage and integrity with your wife and your family. The Wild at Heart men's groups, based on the book by John Eldredge, are a great model for men to deepen spiritually within their masculinity.

Holy Sexuality: What We Want in Marriage

We have five fundamental and holy desires in marriage:

- We want to belong to God and each other—to experience the tenderness, strength, and peace of intimacy.

- We want to be with each other to experience our passion, our giftedness, and our purpose with each other.
- We want to offer each other our true selves.
- We want to live lives of purpose together.
- We want to experience God's love through each other.

Couples long to belong to God and to have the long-term security that they will belong to each other until death parts them. The marriage sense of belonging has the same elements of your personal sense of belonging: A healthy marriage flows out of a tenderness of intimacy through times of "being" together and sharing the vulnerable passions and pains of your hearts. A healthy marriage has the strength of intimacy in "doing" the kind acts of service for each other and the family that put the words "I love you" into action. Finally, a healthy marriage has the peace of intimacy that marks the couple with unity and a sense of rest in belonging to each other. This is the sense of belonging that we all want in marriage.

A sense of belonging in a marriage develops through the couple's sense of belonging with God. From that develops a sense of being. As a couple experiences the strands of tenderness, strength, and peace gracefully weaving together the sacred marriage cord, they start to share an intimate passion beyond the body. This is a spiritual passion that they offer to each other in an intimate giftedness that only the couple knows and shares. These elements of intimate passion and giftedness call forth a very intimate marriage purpose for the rest of their journey.

As this occurs for the couple, they will call forth the true self in each other by honoring the feminine spirit of the wife and honoring the masculine spirit of the husband. To honor the true feminine is the opposite of misogyny. To honor the true masculine is the opposite of misandry. Honoring each other brings unity in purpose. Filled by the tenderness, strength, and peace of God's love, the couple loves God and each other more completely and imparts sense of belonging and being to their children.

Baal Sexuality: What We Have in Marriage

When our marriage relationships pattern after Baal sexuality, we experience the opposite of what we really desire. Instead of the ecstasy God intended comes agony:

- We feel disconnected from God and each other, experiencing a lack of tenderness, strength, and peace of intimacy.
- Our marriage sense of belonging is ripped apart.
- We offer our false self to each other, unable to live in our true self.
- We live without real purpose together.
- We experience counterfeit love of the false self rather than God's love through each other.

As a marriage therapist, I generally have to help most couples with the intimate sexual issues in the marriage, and then the deepest issues of intimacy in their spirit, soul, and body immediately come to the surface. I believe that Christ-centered competent sex therapy takes a holistic approach to one's spirit, soul, and body.

Most couples who do not have a sense of belonging and being are starving for the tenderness, strength, and peace of God's love to fill up the cup of their human spirit. Sexuality generally reveals a lack of sense of belonging and being. This core emptiness drives each spouse to demand that they fill up each other. But we can only be filled with love and strength that God can offer. Your spouse can never love you as God can.

When you demand love, the first time your spouse disappoints you relationally or sexually by not giving the amount of tenderness or strength you expect, you become enraged—whether outwardly or inwardly. To demand that a human fill you, when that is something only God can do, is idolatry. It is also an abuse of your spouse and a display of your self-centeredness. If you do not look to God to fill you, you will end up going to other forms of idolatry when your spouse disappoints you—whether pornography, co-dependent relationships, or other dysfunctions.

Six Sexual Styles in the Marriage Bed

Agony in the marriage infiltrates our marriage beds. When a husband and wife's relationship is tied to Baal and they are operating out of their false selves, their marriage bed is riddled with the false relational styles we discussed in Stage One. After years of providing marriage therapy, I have noticed how those styles operate in the context of sexuality. As you read these styles, you may find that parts of all six sexual styles apply to you, but most people have a primary style of relating sexually and a secondary style. No one fits a particular sexual style exactly; these are just generic categories that help identify sexual dysfunction and help you shift into sexual health and passion. (Healthy sexual relational styles are discussed later in this chapter.)

False Sexual Styles in the Marriage Bed

Adapted from the work of Dr. Dan Allender- Graduate School 1989

Dysfunctional sexuality is rooted in male avoidance and female control, which is a result of the fall of humankind recorded in Genesis 3.[19] Passive avoidance or passive control refuses strength and perverts tenderness. Aggressive avoidance or aggressive control refuses tenderness and perverts strength. Most couples need Christ-centered, competent help in dealing with their false relational styles.

Little-Boy or Little-Girl

The "little boy" adult sexual relational style or "little girl" adult sexual relational style refers to those over eighteen who have not found the strength to grow up and take on the tasks and responsibilities of life. They are adult men and women who are constantly in some type of crisis and constantly pull on others to rescue them. They have not grown up emotionally and relationally. They will pull on others for illegitimate tenderness and touch through covert emotional manipulation. They can sexually manipulate their spouses by sexually stealing—taking from them under the guise of sexually giving—to receive illegitimate sexual tenderness and touch. When confronted, people with this relational style generally deny it or move into a depressive, pouting funk of helplessness and hopelessness.

Good Boy or Girl

The good boy or good girl is sexually nice and extremely compliant with his or her spouse. They rarely offer any sexually honest feedback about what they want or what they are experiencing in bed. Sex is very stable, but bland and boring. He or she will do whatever it takes to keep a spouse sexually happy, even if disgusted by it. Good boys or girls can let themselves be used to avoid relational conflict. The good boy or girl experiences a lot of co-dependent sex—meeting the sexual needs of the spouse to avoid facing the relational and sexual emptiness of the marriage.

Religious Boy or Girl

Religious boys or girls want clean desire, clean excitement, and clean orgasm, but do not feel that the words pleasure and holiness can coexist. Pleasure is often associated with dirtiness and guilt, so the religious boy or girl can actually be scared of pleasure. They often have "sweet saccharin" sex, making sure they never become too sexually passionate. Prim and proper sexual etiquette is the routine for this couple, even though they long for much more. It is more vulnerable to be emotionally naked than physically naked. Sometimes they will hide in spiritual chatter to avoid real honest sharing of themselves to each other.

Though religious boys and girls may be followers of Christ, they may still be empty and disempowered at the core. As discussed in Stage One, there is a difference between being sealed with God's Spirit at conversion and being filled and empowered by God's Spirit on a daily basis. God longs for each of us to know His love for us; He wants to lavishly pour His love over us daily! However, for many religious boys and girls, this is not a reality. For many of them, "faith" means trying to obey the rules. Doing this without being filled with God's love, they have to resort to what they think they "should" do instead of what they desire.

Party Boy or Girl

Party boys or party girls engage in seductive and addictive entertainment. This keeps the painful reality of lack of belonging and being in his or her spirit at a distance. While emotionally and relationally checked out, the party boy or girl can avoid the spiritual and emotional pain of life through the momentary relief of sexual and addictive pleasure in the body. These never bring the deep authentic tenderness and strength for which they hunger. And, until that core hunger is met, party boys or girls will stay sexually disconnected from a spouse through empty, addictive sex. Both can struggle with pornography, masturbation, and affairs.

Party boys generally have a very charming relational style with women. They can flirt at the drop of a dime. The party boy is interested in sex and would not mind having sex twice a day and seven days a week. The party boy's main goal is to have a good time regardless of the cost or the painful outcome. Party boys are fun in the beginning but are a walking disaster when it comes to faithfulness and relational responsibility.

The party girl is very seductive in what she wears and how she talks and moves. As she is in emotional starvation of tenderness and strength, her spiritual deprivation drives her into one-night stands, prostitution, and situations where she is vulnerable to rape. Her spirit has lost the hope of life and clean sexuality. She feels like damaged goods and that she will never be desired by the man of her dreams. In a hopeless, helpless funk, she has sold out to being the object of sexual pleasure. This woman is secretly dying within the daily violations of misogyny she experiences.

Driven Boy or Girl

Driven boys and girls are extremely task oriented, competent, and

201

very successful. They are driven by their desire to avoid feeling and facing their core sense of belonging and being pain. They are often surrounded by friends and awards and are not aware of their pain. However, deep inside they are empty, and tired, and they long to taste relational tenderness and passion.

For many driven boys or girls, activity in the marriage bed can be just another task. Neither know how to rest and relax in desire and intimacy. The driven boy loves sex without intimacy—it is more efficient that way! But often the driven boy is so tired at the core that he turns to pornography because it is less relational work. Often the driven girl avoids sex because she is so tired and has so much to do. When she does have some down time, she may turn to reading romance novels and masturbation as a substitute for the lack of intimacy in her marriage. The result is a distant and cold marriage bed.

Tough Boy or Girl

The tough boy or tough girl relational style is the opposite of the little-boy or little-girl sexual relational style. Tough boys or tough girls infect the marriage bed with their refusal to be relationally and sexually tender, using power plays to receive what they want or avoid what they do not want. They may demand to have their needs met through overt emotional, physical, and sometimes sexual manipulation of their spouses. Ultimately, they will meet their sexual needs by themselves if their spouses do not bend to their aggressive narcissism (self-centeredness).

If you are courageous, talk to your spouse about your sexual relational style. Ask your spouse to tell you how he or she experiences your relational style. Then, do something about it! Make the changes needed to surprise him or her beyond words. As you discuss your sexual relational styles with your spouse, note that this private information should never be shared with others outside of a marriage therapist or spiritual counselor. To share this information with another mutual couple, first ask your spouse if he or she is comfortable with that. If not, wait until you both can agree about how and whom to bring into your private world of sexuality. "Rekindling Your Marriage and Sexuality" conferences are also a resource to help you through these issues.

The Baal Sexual Cycle
- Phase One: Baal Sexual Fantasy (one-third)
- Phase Two: Baal Sexual Lust (one-third)
- Phase Three: Baal Sexual Indulgence (one-third)

When two people are empty and disempowered at the core, they will start to fantasize and desire the illegitimate issues of the flesh, the world, and Satan. A good passion starts to shift to bad passion, and they start to feed off erotic and non-erotic idolatry. They begin to try to fill their core emptiness with sexual addictions, food addictions, materialism, power, or co-dependent relationships. Those Baal desires in the spirit turn into sexual lust in the soul—longing for the forbidden, whether erotic or non-erotic.

The Baal Sexual Phases

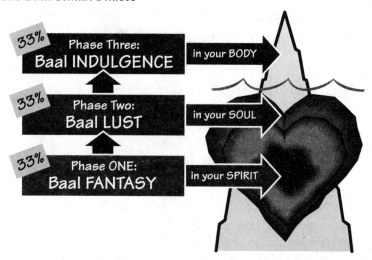

Baal sexual desires, Baal sexual fantasies, and Baal sexual indulgences are perverted forms of tenderness and strength. These perversions squelch your passion, giftedness, and purpose. They keep husbands and wives stuck in their false selves with only numbness to offer each other. At that point, they may try to use sexuality like a narcotic to try to come alive with some sense of feeling, but it only ends up increasing the numbness.

Misogyny and misandry are two powerful, pervasive tools characteristic of Baal sexuality. As we have discussed, misogyny is the hatred of women or what is feminine, and specifically men degrading women, using them as objects to satisfy their erotic and non-erotic passions of the flesh. Misandry is the hatred of men or what is masculine. Often this shows itself by women degrading men verbally or seeking vengeance against them.

Baal Blockades to Great Sex

As Baal sexuality works to destroy the human spirit, it works to destroy the spirit of a marriage as well. These are some of the blockades that smear good, passionate desire with shame and guilt.

The In-Law Blockade

Pain in your marriage due to your in-laws can be one of the biggest blockades to sexual frequency and satisfaction. Many times one spouse does not follow the biblical admonition to leave his or her mother or father and cleave (join or connect) to a spouse. This issue is central to most conflict in marriage.

> For this reason a man will **leave** his father and mother and be **united** to his wife, and they will become one flesh. The man and his wife were **both naked,** and they felt **no shame.**
>   (Genesis 2:24-25, NIV, emphasis added)

You need to leave your parents to cleave and weave to your spouse! Loyalty to your new spouse honors and blesses the marriage bed. Continued loyalty to a mother or father betrays the marriage bed, and you will lose out!

Is your parent in your marriage bed? When a husband needs to protect his family's time commitments during the holidays, but cannot say no to his mother, his wife may say no to him in the marriage bed. The wife says in no uncertain terms, "It is your mother or me. If you cannot say 'no' to her, then I will say 'no' to you. Got it? Who is your queen, Baby? It better not be your mama!"

The Sexual Abuse Blockade

Past unresolved sexual abuse pain can keep violating the present marriage relationship through the dynamics of frozen shame in the spirit, frozen revenge in the soul, and sexual dysfunction in the body, as discussed in Stage Two. One of the most devastating arrows of betrayal that one can experience growing up is the arrow of sexual abuse.

Sexual abuse is when someone looks at or touches you in a way that should not be done by anyone but your spouse. If sexual abuse is not addressed, normal sex within marriage leaves a woman or man feeling betrayed and degraded. Those who have been sexually abused may feel guilty or unclean; they may long for a place to get rid of the stain of shame, filth, and damage that has marred their sexuality.

The Wounded Heart by Dr. Dan Allender is an excellent resource on sexual abuse. Dr. Allender says that the closer in relationship the perpetrator is to a victim, the more severe the damage is. Someone who has been sexually abused has been an object and a victim of Baal worship; they were used to fill someone else's core emptiness.

Shame and hopelessness are the greatest hurdles a sexual abuse victim must overcome. He or she might use depression to suppress his or her anger toward the perpetrator, or might medicate the pain with multiple addictions. An abuse victim will sexually disconnect or dissociate from his or her spouse while making love. He or she will also distance him or herself out of anger and disrupt the sexual relationship. A spouse who has been sexually abused will experience significant sexual dysfunction until the couple can pursue freedom and healing together. When these wounds are left unattended, the God-given sense of pleasure dies.

If a spouse continues to make love as the other dissociates, the one who has been abused will feel violated and used all over again, every time.

The Sexual Addiction Blockade

Sexual addiction is doing something sexually that no longer feels like a choice. Expressions of sexual addiction include:

- Viewing pornography via the Internet, TV, magazines, or other media
- Masturbating
- Visiting adult bookstores
- Viewing adult movies
- Frequenting strip clubs
- Having an affair
- Sharing spouses
- Committing incest
- Engaging in prostitution

Pornography is a rampant problem. When someone looks at pornography, he or she is lusting after another person—violating that person and sinning against his or her own spouse.

> You have heard that it was said, "YOU SHALL NOT COMMIT ADULTERY"; but I say to you that everyone who **looks** at a woman with lust for her **has already committed adultery** with her **in his heart.**
> (Matthew 5:27-28, NASB, emphasis added)

Oftentimes pornography is followed by masturbation. Masturbation is self-sex that takes away your desire for your spouse or even the desire to be married someday. When you falsely meet your sexual needs by yourself, you reject the "spirit-to-spirit" and "soul-to-soul" bonding that is the essence of a holy sexual relationship. You settle for the lonely orgasm and deny your spouse (and yourself) the oneness of sexual desire in the spirit, sexual excitement in the soul, and sexual orgasm in the body.

The Sexual Transference Blockade

Sexual transference is the most common struggle I see in couples in private practice. You will want to read Stage Three and the section on transference, if you have not already, to understand this section of this stage. It starts with a sexual betrayal—a painful sexual event or pattern of the past produces a sense of sexual betrayal in the spirit. As a result, the person self-protects by numbing the pain with addictions in the body and/or co-addictions in relationships. When a spouse acts in a similar manner or pattern to the other's previous abuse experience, the frozen sexual betrayal is triggered. The present thaws the frozen sexual revenge of the past, and all of the unresolved rage and unforgiveness toward past betrayers is transferred onto the spouse. The sexually betrayed becomes the sexual betrayer. Unless the Cross intersects your sexual betrayal and sexual revenge, sexual transference will raise its ugly head every time something similar to your past triggers this festering relational pain and relational sin. The cycle is self-perpetuating, and the spouse may engage in counter-transference sparked from his or her own betrayal experiences that the spouse in transference is now triggering.

To unravel this transference and find a door to new freedom and healing, a husband and wife need a trained, Bible-based, third party and, ideally, a small group community. A couple cannot accomplish this process alone—a person cannot do anything about someone else who is in transference with him or her. They both need a third party to give objective help. The best book I have read on transference is by Valerie McIntyre called *Wolves in Sheep's Clothing*.

The Affair Blockade

> *Adultery is not merely sex with the wrong person; it is union with someone who will never require us to face our sinfulness or draw forth our glory so that we are more and more in awe of God.*[20]

In a marriage betrayed by an affair, there is a sense of helplessness and hopelessness that a sense of belonging and being will ever be restored to the marriage. It seems like the marriage passion, giftedness, and purpose will be shut down forever. How can you trust again when such sexual betrayal has taken place?

First, the spouse who had the affair must confess it, renounce it, and repent of it. Then a prayer minister calls on the sword of the Holy Spirit to sever all ties (spirit-to-spirit, soul-to-soul, and body-to-body) that were formed during the affair. Miraculously, God uses the sword of the Spirit to bring about deliverance and healing to couples and restores even years of betrayal. As the marriage sense of belonging is healed, so is the marriage sense of being.

Throughout seventeen years of being a marriage therapist, my clients have experienced their sexual passion, sexual giftedness, and sexual purpose being redeemed, re-symbolized, and restored! Only the tender and strong hand of the living God can do this level of resurrection work in marriage.

> Marriages are the crucible not only for sin to be exposed but also for forgiveness to restore relationship and intensify our hope of heaven.[21]

When you have had an affair, the degree to which you keep a secret is the degree to which you block intimacy in your marriage relationship. Secrecy is not allowing your spouse to see into you. The degree to which you are known is also the degree to which you will be healed.

Sexual confession may drop a boulder on an already shaky foundation. In fact, your marriage may quickly end, especially if your spouse falls into transference. As a marriage therapist and pastor, I recommend that you pray about first confessing your sexual sin to a trained biblical third party and then to confess it to your spouse. Have a third party on hand to help with this very explosive process.

It is critical that you and your spouse be involved in a Christ-centered, biblical community with a leader you trust. He or she must be a trained leader who will extend grace and have a goal of restoration in your counseling. Such a person can give support to help you work through sexual confessions and sexual transference. See the appendix for the process of working through sexual addiction or a sexual affair.

* * *

The following portion of this stage is primarily written for those who are married or who are contemplating marriage. Some unmarried people may wish to read it as well to understand the battles of those who are married. Others will want or need to wisely avoid it rather than contemplating the concerns of erotic sexual relationships.

The Sexual Desire of the Spirit

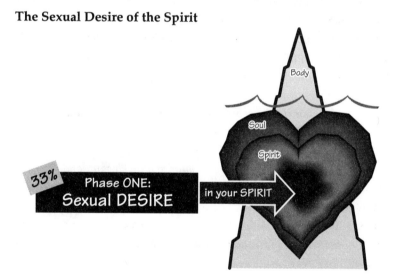

The normal sexual cycle flows from the desires within the human spirit. Contrary to the cultural messages that assault us daily, true and intimate sexuality requires bonding on all three levels of the spirit, soul, and body. Complete and fulfilling sexuality intertwines the desire phase of the spirit, the arousal phase of the soul, and the orgasm phase of the body. Each phase is one-third of the sexual experience.

A normal sexual cycle is:
> Phase One: Sexual Desire in your spirit
> Phase Two: Sexual Arousal in your soul
> Phase Three: Sexual Orgasm in your body

The sexual desire in the human spirit is another word for sexual anticipation. When your desire is consistent with how God made you, your sexual anticipation can be built on a clean foundation of legitimate, intimate, erotic pleasure. The clearest picture of this is in the book of the Song of Solomon.

> *You're so beautiful, my darling, so beautiful, and your dove eyes are veiled.*

> *By your hair as it flows and shimmers, like a flock of goats in the distance streaming down a hillside in the sunshine.*

> *Your smile is generous and full—expressive and strong and clean.*

> *Your lips are jewel red, your mouth elegant and inviting, your veiled cheeks soft and radiant.*

> *The smooth, lithe lines of your neck command notice—all heads turn in awe and admiration!*

> *Your breasts are like fawns, twins of a gazelle, grazing among the first spring flowers.*

> *The sweet, fragrant curves of your body, the soft, spiced contours of your flesh*

> *Invite me, and I come. I stay until dawn breathes its light and night slips away.*

You're beautiful from head to toe, my dear love, beautiful beyond compare, absolutely flawless.

Come with me from Lebanon, **my bride. Leave** Lebanon behind, **and come.** Leave your high mountain hideaway.

Abandon your wilderness seclusion, where you keep company with lions and panthers guard your safety.

You've captured my heart, dear friend. You looked at me, and I fell in love.

One look my way and *I was hopelessly in love!*

How beautiful your love, dear, dear friend—far more pleasing than a fine, rare wine, your fragrance more exotic than select spices.

The kisses of your lips are honey, my love, every syllable you speak a delicacy to savor.

Your clothes smell like the wild outdoors, the ozone scent of high mountains.

Dear lover and friend, you're a secret garden, a private and pure fountain.

*Body and soul, **you are paradise,** a whole orchard of* **succulent fruits** —

Ripe apricots and peaches, oranges and pears;

*Nut trees and cinnamon, and all **scented** woods;*

*Mint and lavender, and all herbs **aromatic;***

A garden fountain, sparkling and splashing, fed
by spring waters from the Lebanon mountains.

Wake up, *North Wind,* **get moving,** *South Wind!*

Breathe on my garden, *fill the air with spice*
fragrance.

Oh, let my lover enter his garden!

Yes, let him eat the fine, ripe fruits.

I **went** *to my garden,* *dear friend,* **best lover!**
breathed the sweet fragrance.

I **ate** *the fruit and honey, I* **drank** *the nectar and*
wine.

Celebrate with me, friends! Raise your glasses—
"To life! To love!"

(Song of Solomon 4:1–5:1, MSG, emphasis added)

This is a picture of clean, sexual foreplay. Unfortunately, sexual imagery has been so corrupted by the Baal culture that only the Holy Spirit can purify and renew our symbolism. As you see in Song of Solomon, sexual imagery does not have to be ungodly. In this picture of holy, sensual, sexuality, the imagery is described as captivating, inviting, exotic, succulent, and fragrant. This is good and enjoyable! Notice that it is built through conversation between the spouses. Conversation has always been the way to woo your lover's heart and stimulate arousal.

To desire each other is to start to anticipate what it is that you want and what it is that your spouse wants. The sexual dance of tenderness and strength plays itself out when you want to love each other well because your spirit is filled with God's love. The spirit is where the desire to please your spouse is birthed. From

212

there, God's strength of love can empower you to please your spouse in a holy, sensual way.

Sexual Arousal of the Soul

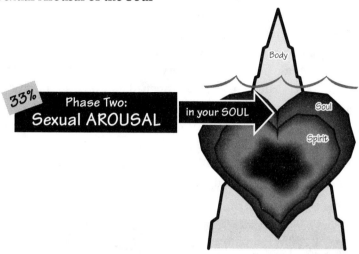

As your human spirit fills with sexual desires (sexual hungers and sexual thirsts), your human soul will be empowered with sexual arousal. Whereas men can be easily aroused visually, women are greatly affected by words of loyalty, adoration, and powerful commitment to an exclusive relationship. Foreplay for a woman is based on how she is treated relationally every day. Her capacity for arousal is like a pool or underground stream that wells up and remains over time, reflecting the health of the relationship. A consistent, intentional, intimate spirit-and-soul bonding greatly affects body-to-body bonding!

Most people do not realize that while masculine arousal is quick and to the point, feminine arousal can be steady and long lasting. (That is good news, men!) However, an argument can drain a woman's well of desire in seconds. As soon as the fight ensues, sex will be on hold until a man can bring strength of love into the resolution.

I have seen husbands in my practice who decided to intentionally connect spirit-to-spirit and soul-to-soul with their wives each day and, predictably, unless their marriage was experiencing one of the blockades to great sex mentioned earlier, most of these men were not complaining about a lack of sexual frequency in their marriages. These husbands learned how to be consistently filled with God's love and empowered by God's strength to relationally pursue their wives, even in conflict. When the wife tasted her husband's humility, courage, and strength of love in the heat of the moment, it was natural for her to respond in kind. The man's new strength called forth and reopened his wife's tenderness. Men, if you can learn how to be other-centered with great strength of love in serving your wife within the heat of the battle, your reward will be great!

Sexual Orgasm of the Body

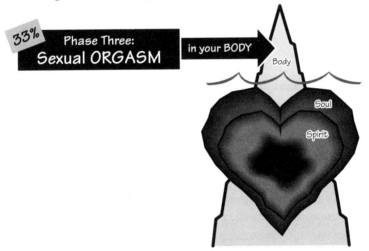

As desire continues to build in the spirit and the fires of arousal start to flame in the masculine and feminine souls, the man and woman will experience something called vascocongestion. For most men, desire in the spirit and excitement in the masculine soul causes an engorgement of blood in the penis and therefore an erection. Desire in the spirit and arousal in the feminine soul causes an engorgement of blood in the vaginal passage and therefore enlargement of the vaginal tissue. When a woman has soundly experienced the desire phase of the spirit, and the excitement phase in the soul, so that she can rest and trust, orgasm in the body naturally follows. When a man waits on his wife and honors her with a holistic approach to sexuality, she will also honor him beyond his wildest dreams!

To experience great sexuality, both husband and wife need to connect with each other on all three levels of sexuality in the spirit, soul, and body. Complete and fulfilling sexuality intertwines the desire phase of the spirit, the arousal phase of the soul, and the orgasm phase of the body. As a marriage therapist, when I saw couples pursuing complete sexuality, they naturally became more sexually active with each other.

- The spirit of the marriage…births sexual desire
- The soul of the marriage…deepens sexual arousal
- The body of the marriage…enjoys sexual orgasm

The husband and wife toolbox section gives you an initial picture of spirit-to-spirit and soul-to-soul bonding. As a couple seeks to have the spirit and soul of their marriage rooted and established in love, the body of their marriage will be empowered and revitalized with new potency and ecstasy. As this occurs, the couples' libido (sexual drive) starts to increase, and new sexual health occurs right into the golden years!

Note: It is important to realize that some issues in the outer body have nothing to do with the inner body. Physical problems can also affect your sex life and should be addressed by a physician.

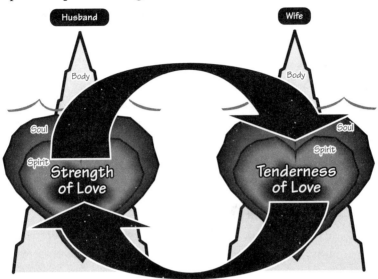

Your sexual relationship is really a mirror of your relationship or lack of relationship with God. If your spirit-to-spirit bond is lacking, you and your spouse will use and abuse each other, demanding that the other fill his or her own core emptiness with empty sex with your bodies. But if your spirit-to-spirit bond is being filled by God's love and strength, you will know it, feel it, and experience it far beyond the bedroom. You will just look at each other and know that tenderness and strength of love is being released into you, and you are both glad to receive it.

In spirit-to-spirit bonding, your spouse needs to know that you are filled with God's love, empowered by His strength, and can forgive him or her.

Forgiveness
Are you willing to forgive your spouse when he or she disappoints you or betrays you on the marriage journey? Your marriage will reveal the relationship you have with God. Forgiveness is an issue of the human spirit. If you have never experienced God's forgiveness, it will be very difficult for you to forgive your spouse's betrayal of you. Couples betray, or sin against, each other daily.

Unforgiveness in the spirit of the marriage blocks couples from recovery and healing. And, unforgiveness kills sexual desire in the marriage bed.

Acceptance

Are you willing to embrace your spouse when he or she feels defective, undesirable, and inadequate as a man or woman? Rather than fixing him or her, can you trust God with your spouse? Acceptance is an issue of the human soul. When any of us are accepted for who we are, regardless of how we look or perform, we can relax and be more honest and intimate with each other. A lack of acceptance in the soul of the marriage kills sexual excitement. But the couple that truly forgives, truly trusts, truly loves, and truly accepts each other will have the greatest sexual experience in the body.

> *The goal of marriage is twofold: to reveal the glory of God and to enhance the glory of one's spouse.*[22]

A Desire for Tenderness

A mature husband really wants to release the strength of tenderness into his wife's spirit, soul, and body. The man's passionate strength of tenderness will naturally call forth the tenderness of strength found in the passion of the woman. That is how the Potter made the human clay.

The man's emotional desire is that the woman would want his strength of tenderness and would receive his strength of tenderness. Why? If the woman receives his strength of love, she will naturally respond with a tenderness of love that wants him. This is how God built holy, sensual sexuality for the man and the woman.

As both spouses are filled and empowered by God's love and strength, the couple can bond on a rare spirit-to-spirit level that few experience. Being cherished and honored results in a holy sexuality that is very sensual, intertwining spirit, soul, and body! That is the way we are meant to be.

Releasing Sexual Guilt and Shame

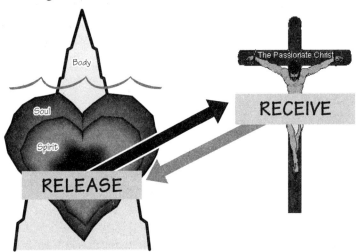

The man who has struggled with the guilt of sexual addiction (pornography, cybersex, masturbation, or other addiction) can release that guilt and shame at the Cross. He can have a clean spirit with his wife when they make love. The Cross is where he releases his sexual guilt and sexual shame to receive God's forgiveness, cleansing, and healing. When a man continually bows before the Cross in his daily spirit-to-spirit relationship with God, he will be filled with the love of God for his tender bride. The man who is clean, filled, and empowered in spirit is going to take his wife to new heights!

The woman who has experienced sexual abuse or struggled with body shame can release that shame at the Cross so that she too can have a clean spirit with her husband when they make love. The Cross is where she can release her pain and sin and be filled with forgiveness, cleansing, and healing. When a woman faces the Cross each day in her spirit-to-spirit relationship with God, she can sensually embrace her groom with a phenomenal passion. The woman who is clean, filled, and empowered in spirit is going to respond to her husband with a sensuality that is passionate and exclusive to their relationship.

When husband and wife stand at the foot of the Cross in prayer as relational sin and relational pain occur throughout the years of marriage, they will receive forgiveness, cleansing, and healing. However, as their sin and pain go onto the Cross, their deep sexual passion will also be released to each other. As a couple receives this private sexual gift from each other, the weaving of spirit, soul, and body brings them both into a new taste of glory.

Soul-to-Soul Bonding

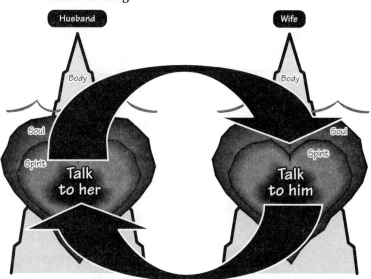

Soul-to-soul bonding is an overflow of spirit-to-spirit bonding. In soul-to-soul bonding, your spouse needs to know that you can shift from a self-centered relational style to an other-centered relational style and that you intimately embrace him or her.

Rest in the Feminine Soul
Husbands, for your wife to experience tender, intimate, holy sensuality, she needs to be at rest so she can relax, let go, and have a good time! By enabling her to rest, you build a strong relational foundation for your marriage that will benefit you both!

These are the elements that she needs in order to rest:

- To have a holy (non-Baal), cherishing love in which she can trust
- To feel secure and taken care of
- To feel a togetherness and partnership with you
- To have a nest that is fixed and beautiful to her
- To be romanced with intimate and tender embrace; kind and caring words

Honor in the Masculine Soul

Wives, for a man to experience intimate, holy sensuality, he needs to feel strong and respected so he can be potent in spirit, soul, and body. These are the elements he needs to feel respected:

- To have a holy, cherishing love in which he can trust
- To be able to feel strong in his masculinity
- To be able to feel respected by you and in his life work
- To be affirmed by the softness of his wife's support toward him
- To enjoy sexual, erotic touch

As a husband holds the key to a wife's tenderness, she holds the key to his strength. However, contempt of his masculinity or the criticism of how he operates differently from you chops away at his soul. As you are tender and yet honest with your husband, your feminine tenderness will call out his masculine strength to change and "to be" with you. As your husband honors you spiritually, emotionally, and physically, honor him back spiritually, emotionally, and physically.

Body-to-Body Bonding

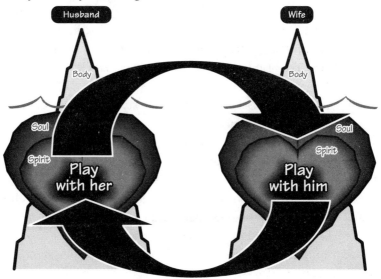

The body-to-body bond flows out of the spirit-to-spirit and soul-to-soul bonds. All are interrelated. The body-to-body bond is an expression of the inner health of each couple.

> *And the man and his wife were **both naked** and **were not embarrassed or ashamed in each other's presence.***
>
> *(Genesis 2:25, AMP, emphasis added)*

At one time, the first married couple looked at their own nakedness and each other's nakedness and felt no shame. When a man and woman feel the security of knowing that they will be forgiven and accepted for who they are, the marriage bed starts to rock! Wanting to offer each other the gift of pleasure is not just for the honeymoon. It really can—and should—become better and better as the marriage grows older!

> *A successful marriage is one in which two broken and forgiving people stay committed to one another in a sacrificial relationship in the face of life's chaos.*[23]

What happens to these false relational styles when a man or woman begins to experience restored sense of being and belonging and is filled with God's tenderness of love and strength of love? A man begins to give strength appropriately. Passivity begins to yield to initiative; insecurity begins to yield to confidence; control begins to yield to release. The godly strength in a man naturally draws out his wife's sexual desire and calls out her tenderness. Control begins to yield to mutual submission, fear begins to yield to security and confidence, manipulation gives way to genuine satisfaction.

As God fills both husband and wife with His tenderness and strength of love, they give to each other relationally and sexually in the ecstasy of a clean, erotic, holy, passionate, sexual relationship. They are freed to experience the joy of each other in ways they have not previously experienced.

True Sexual Styles in the Marriage Bed

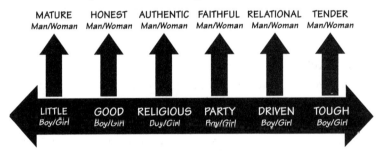

| MATURE Man/Woman | HONEST Man/Woman | AUTHENTIC Man/Woman | FAITHFUL Man/Woman | RELATIONAL Man/Woman | TENDER Man/Woman |

| LITTLE Boy/Girl | GOOD Boy/Girl | RELIGIOUS Boy/Girl | PARTY Boy/Girl | DRIVEN Boy/Girl | TOUGH Boy/Girl |

Embodies True Strength   **Values True Strength**
Values True Tenderness   **Embodies True Tenderness**

Little Boys Shift to Sexually Mature Men
When a little boy who formerly needed to be rescued experiences healing in sense of belonging and sense of being, he will start to

move like a masculine man as he engages boldly with his wife relationally and sexually. He will develop a new capacity to lead out with a tenderness and strength in his spirit, soul, and body. When a feminine soul does not have her husband's masculine strength filling her, her soul may become the strong one who is engaging relationally and sexually. When she is in this state, she cannot sexually rest or relax. But when a little boy becomes a mature man, his wife will begin to rest, relax, and experience authentic climax within his sexual strength. His new sexual strength can become a new way to sexual pleasure for both of them. He will probably be bolder in a tender way of bringing her into more intense sexual desire, deeper sexual arousal, and erotic orgasm with his new intensity of strength. As she responds to him with more sexual tenderness, he will respond with more sexual virility, and their sexual experience can skyrocket!

Little Girls Shift to Sexually Mature Women

The little girl who is shifting to become a mature woman is starting to find authentic tenderness and new strength in her spirit. While her core is being filled with God's love and empowered by God's strength, she can start to spiritually rest and relax. This foundational rest in her feminine spirit prepares her to relax with her husband regardless of how imperfect he is. Her climax is intermingled with three layers of rest within her femininity. In her spirit, she is built to have spiritual rest with God. In her soul, she is designed to have relational rest with her husband. In her body, she is built to have physical rest. This former little girl used to refuse strength and, therefore, could not rest. Now, as she is filled with strength in her spirit, soul, and body, her sexual desires are called forth in rest and she can be aroused. Her new tenderness of strength starts to compel her husband's strength of tenderness in a clean, erotic weaving that brings them into sexual maturity in their marriage. As this woman experiences rest and relaxation in her spirit, soul, and body, she is able to let go and have a great time with her husband. As she trusts in God's strength and in her husband's new strength coming around her, she will relax with a new security that enables her to take time to play, be enjoyed, and delight in giving erotic, sensual pleasure!

Good Boys Shift to Sexually Honest Men

When the good boy who formerly needed to draw strength from others' affirmation starts to shift into honest relational and sexual engagement with his wife, the rewards can be stunning. She has likely been living without masculine strength for years and, in her contempt, has raised the drawbridge of the castle to keep him out on all counts! However, his courage to take her on with disruptive nobility and strength of tenderness is very sensual to her feminine soul. When a woman feels strength of tenderness from the masculine soul of her husband—her modern-day knight fighting on her behalf—she can abandon herself to him sexually as a way to enjoy his newfound strength. As this man conquers his fears of conflict and rejection, he is more willing to try new, tender sexual play with her without the fear of rejection. His new strength may allow him to be more creative in different sexual positions and creative tender embraces. This couple can shift from boring sex to the creative fine art of sexual arousal and erotic orgasm. As they both explore new sensual moves, they will delight in erotic vitality for years, "'til death do us part!"

Good Girls Shift to Sexually Honest Women

When the good girl shifts into being a sexually honest woman, a lot of disruption initially happens in her marriage bed. Since this former good girl could never say no to her husband, one mark of her growth is to now be able to say no periodically. As she grows in the sense of belonging and being to walk in who God created her to be, her no will be no, but her yes will become a passionate, fully responsive, YES! Her husband will initially experience sexual rejection from her "no"s. However, as she begins to bring pleasure, not out of compliance but out of passion, his natural response will be in strength of tenderness. Since the former good girl wants to naturally please, when her husband allows her the dignity of sexual choice, she is empowered. Then, when she chooses to respond to his strength, her responses will tantalize him and bring new desire and excitement to the bed. When this newly honest woman wants to sexually touch her husband, her desire for him will emotionally and sexually charge him. She has great power to call forth his sexual strength, which is reserved for

224

her alone. Together they can celebrate the erotic dance of weaving and cleaving.

Religious Boys Shift to Sexually Authentic Men

Religious boys who have been bound up in guilt and shame have to grow to embrace the concept of clean, holy, erotic sexuality. They know God is the author of sexuality and that holy sexuality is the opposite of Baal sexuality. However, to be fully honest with his wife about his clean sexual desires may still seem risky. To no longer be afraid of passionate sexuality and to start to desire clean, sensual lovemaking with his bride brings this man back to the dreams of his honeymoon. And, in many ways, his real authentic honeymoon is about to start!

As the religious boy becomes the authentic man relationally and sexually, his wife will notice! It is evident to her that a miracle has occurred for her husband and herself. The previously legalistic marriage bed just became real, alive, and unpredictable. His new openness to sexual desire brings their sexual arousal to new heights, making them both feel young and frisky again. It is evident to both that God is at work when tenderness and strength redeem legalistic sexuality, restoring it to healthy, happy, erotic joy.

Religious Girls Shift to Sexually Authentic Women

As the religious girl shifts into becoming an authentic woman, her character is marked by an authentic tender love that allows her to walk in the strength of dignity and grace. This shift of being filled at her core with the love and strength of God that will unlock new, authentic passion in her initially feels a little wild. As she realizes that sensuality can be holy and clean, she will have a new vision for holy pleasure with her husband. This woman wants to feel fully alive in passionate sexuality as long as it is God's design for her.

As this authentic woman responds to the love and strength of her God and her husband, she will start to rest within the chaos of this world. The nature of godly strength is to pierce through

225

disorder and bring order. This wife will have a tender strength to embrace her man with pleasure and delight that reflect her inner glory and her commitment to his inner glory as well. Glorious, holy sexuality climaxes with a great sensual celebration of God's love within each other!

Party Boys Shift to Sexually Faithful Men

The party boy will be blown away with holy sexuality. If he thought he had intense libido and sexual desires before the healing of his sense of belonging and being, he is in for a big awakening. His former Baal sexual obsession actually buried his God-given passion. The tender and strong love of God awakens the deepest passions that were buried below all of the addictive medications in which the party boy indulged.

The tenderness and strength of God will unlock the holy libido of the former party boy. This new, faithful man has the real thing and he will share with his wife a passion that is so other-centered that she may wonder who he is. The faithful man will offer her relational tenderness and strength. He will sexually give to her and no longer sexually prostitute her. As his wife starts to experience his new loyalty and faithfulness, she will be drawn more to this God of tenderness and strength as well. This couple is on the road to experiencing great sexuality!

Party Girls Shift to Sexually Faithful Women

The party girl will transform into a faithful woman as she tastes the faithful, tender care of a loving, powerful God in her life. As she realizes His loyalty to her well-being, a new vision in her heart arises about how to passionately come alive. She no longer needs to engage in sexual seduction to get what she wants. She wants to be offered loyal strength so she can rest in her husband's love and willingness to take care of her. As she finds her core needs for spiritual rest in her new relationship with God, her core passion starts to come alive. This woman can now offer pure, tender passion to her man. Her new tenderness naturally calls forth his virile strength, and she becomes beautiful and desirable to him.

This couple can have great sex if there is an exclusive relational and sexual commitment to each other. For this woman to have the greatest ecstasy within an orgasmic climax, she needs to know and feel that her husband is committed to her above all women for the entire journey. To this woman, trust is seeing and believing, and ecstasy is letting go and inviting him to have a great time with her! Faithful women can throw great private parties in the exclusivity of the marriage bed!

Driven Boys Shift to Sexually Relational Men

When the driven boy experiences the healing of his sense of belonging and being, his emotions are restored with a depth of richness that makes his transformation very noticeable. His relational and sexual skills become a new, vivid delight to his formerly lonely wife. This relational man can now offer new rest to his wife. The climax for his wife can be ecstatic because she can finally let go and have a great time in his new strength. The rest in her feminine spirit paradoxically charges her sexual desires with intense erotic passion. This woman is ready to share in the sexual delights that tender and strong love embody. The party is just beginning for this couple!

Driven Girls Shift to Sexually Relational Women

When the driven girl shifts into the relational woman, her husband is in for a great marriage bed surprise. However, it is a fight to convince the driven girl that she will not be lazy and nonproductive if she takes the time to slow down and play in bed. The driven girl is sexually available if her world is ordered and sexually turned off if her world is disordered. However, when she is filled and empowered by God, she realizes that her security in having order is really no security at all. The love and strength of God empowers her more effectively in ordering her world than trying to do it herself. The wonder of the gospel is that as she chooses to slow down and receive God's love and be empowered by God's strength, she will also start to enter into rest. The driven girl, deep down, wants to rest and play, but she is built in a way that says responsibility comes before pleasure. The pull to put tasks before her relationship is a lifelong struggle.

As she matures in her relationship with God, His relational tenderness and strength will transform her into a relational woman. However, she needs to choose to take daily time to be filled and empowered by God. Then this woman will have a greater capacity to order her relationship over tasks. When this woman rests, she is able to respond to her husband with a powerful sexual drive and enjoy an incredible time of arousal with her man.

Tough Boys Shift to Sexually Tender Men

As the tough boy heals from his sense of belonging-and-being wounds, he starts to taste the tender and yet strong love of his Abba Daddy. This new tenderness in the former tough boy awakens him to something he has been searching for his whole life. This man of tenderness also starts to discover that he has more real strength in his spirit, soul, and body than he ever had as a tough boy. Virility is definitely holistic for this man and his now lucky wife.

His new strength of tenderness will start to bring healing and rest to his wife who was formerly beaten down by his violent attitudes or actions. His new tenderness is a spiritual rebirth — a stunning testimony of the transforming power of the living God. This man's new tenderness will also bring his wife into deep rest and secure relaxation. It will only take a look in her eyes for him to know that his tenderness is unlocking the sexual desires she thought she had permanently put away. As her sexual arousal starts to peak in her soul, she will take the first steps again in trusting him—sharing the intimate and vulnerable climax experience with him. If the first climax is safe, embraced and desired, she will be on the road to new, tender climaxes. Her husband will also enjoy the strength of tenderness in the responsive gifts of trust and pleasure. This couple will influence their world for Christ as they live out His tenderness and strength in their marriage and sexuality.

Tough Girls Shift to Sexually Tender Women

The tough girl's transformation into becoming the tender woman is an incredible picture of the power of the living God. The tough girl thinks that her perverted power and refusal to be tender is the safest way to live life. However, her hardness of control blocks the love and strength of God from filling her and empowering her. Once she realizes that her emasculating control keeps her separated from God's empowering, she is angry because she knows the only way to be safe is to be with God. Interestingly, when she lets go of her control and becomes vulnerable to God's love, God's strength will empower her to live with more protection than when she tried independently to protect herself. The miraculous dynamic of receiving God's love is that it tenderizes hard hearts and empowers with loving strength.

As the tough girl starts to become a tender woman, her sexuality is invigorated with a soft passion that no longer competes with her husband's strength. This, in turn, will call forth his strength. When he starts to fight on her behalf, she will have moments of authentic rest in her life. To no longer be alone in this journey and to finally be supported by a man who is strong enough to care for her will birth a new tenderness within her spirit.

This woman will be open to sexual play because she no longer has to live in the strength of the masculine. A new world of tender responsiveness is open to her. If she can count on her husband to be strong on day-to-day tasks and relationships, she can then afford to discover all the intimate and vulnerable passions and desires that she was running from. As this tender woman now has the space to look into her heart, she will discover that she wants an emotional connection with her husband. She wants to be known, and she wants to know him. She wants to be listened to, and she wants to listen to him. She wants to be enjoyed, and she wants to enjoy him. She wants to have sexual touch, and she wants to touch him. The relational woman can embrace her sensuality and passion; she is released in her spirit to be aroused and to play. However, this time she is happy to have him lead sexually and be the recipient of uninhibited, erotic pleasure that brings them back into the wedding dance again!

Talking about Passionate, Hot, Erotic, Holy Sexuality
If you and your spouse have taken the time to bond spirit-to-

spirit and soul-to-soul, then you are probably enjoying the gift of giving clean, tender, orgasmic, passionate pleasure to each other. However, most married spouses do not talk about their sexual relationship—with each other, anyway! To have holy sensual sexuality, you need to honestly share your sexual desires with your spouse. You need to tell him or her what you do and do not want sexually. Begin with these questions:

- What is pleasurable?
- What isn't pleasurable?
- What do you want me to do more?
- What do you want me to do less?
- What do you want me to change?
- Are you comfortable with…?
- What will honor and delight you the most?

Can you see how these questions can only be discussed when spirit-to-spirit and soul-to-soul bonding is taking place?

The Beginning of the Climax

Many married women have never experienced a sexual climax. About one-third of women report not ever experiencing a sexual climax.[24] Most women also report feeling like they have to manage the responsibilities of marriage and family life. They fear that if they do not, it will not get done. It is not coincidence that women burdened by responsibility cannot rest and relax in order to climax sexually.

Husbands, if you are honoring and serving your wife, give her body time to catch up with your spirit-to-spirit and soul-to-soul bonding. Her feminine body will naturally respond to the spiritual security and relational embrace. A woman's sexual response is gradual. Remember, your wife's sexuality is determined by how you treat her every day. If you have taken the time to rap on the door of her spirit and soul, it is only your privilege to rap on the door of her body. If she lets you in, Glory! However, it is her choice. If you have done your part of building sexual desire in her spirit and sexual excitement in her soul, then allow her slower arousal to bring her into the sacred trust of letting go and enjoying an orgasm in her body.

However, gentlemen, to be quite honest and straight forward, when the time comes, you have to find your wife's clitoris to be able to bring her into an orgasm. Why? Clinically, all orgasms are clitoral. The best way to discover your wife's clitoris is not by reading a book, which will probably be pornographic in nature. If your wife trusts you and wants you, she will show you the one part of her body that demands extreme tenderness and craves the strength of pleasure. That is a private party just for the two of you. Exploring together and having fun together is part of healthy, redeemed sexuality!

The Strength of Potency

Women, men are built with sexual speed that only you can tame. The lion within your husband can be a great ride, but you have to help him out. Even though a man is turned on by sight and your tender sexual touch on his entire body, he is more deeply empowered by your words of trust and respect. Tell him what works for you and what does not work for you. However, after telling your man what you sexually desire and what will bring sexual excitement to you, let him then lead sexually. For the woman to lead the man sexually is like pouring cold water on his sexual fires. However, if the man understands how to lead with humility, holiness, and passion, he will consider other-centered steps in the sexual weaving. Your tenderness of strength will invite your man to be himself with you and only you.

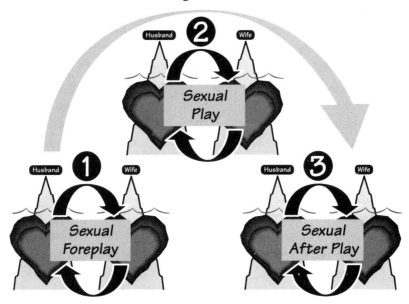

Phase 1: Erotic Sexual Foreplay

Foreplay for both men and women will determine the quality of sexual play for each couple. Husbands, think through what creative tenderness looks like for your wife, and you will relationally live out "sexually being" all week. Allow her to feel the strength of your physical embrace for non-sexual reasons. Wives, your husband needs to hear privately and publicly that he is your man above all men, and that you want him! He needs the same creative romance that you do.

Phase 2: Erotic Sexual Play

In the sexual play, whatever you both mutually agree upon is fine in the marriage bed. However, the key is that you both feel it is right, pleasurable, and mutual. God created sexuality, and God is the one who gives you the capacity to release and receive clean, holy pleasure. Have fun!

Phase 3: Non-Erotic Sexual Afterplay

Sexual afterplay is the slow descent from a memorable ride together. As you both are sexually satisfied, holding each other in

232

gratitude expresses the awe of the sexual dance of tenderness and strength of love. The afterplay moments validate the authenticity of the foreplay and the sexual play. Some of the most profound moments of bonding in spirit, soul, and body occur in times of rest and thankfulness after experiencing the holy, sensual, excellent mystery of sexuality with the one made especially for you and you alone.

"A strong husband will draw forth the strong tenderness of his wife, and a tender wife will birth the tender strength of her husband."[25]

The mystery of holy, sensual sexuality is that the husband's strength of love draws out the tenderness of love of his wife. Strength calls forth rest and relaxation in the feminine spirit. The wife's tenderness of love calls forth strength and potency in the masculine spirit. Tenderness brings the mystery of awe into the spirit. Strength brings the mystery of gratitude into the spirit.

In your relationship with God, tenderness, awe, strength, and gratitude are the core of intimate worship. In your relationship with your spouse, tenderness, awe, strength and gratitude are the core of holy, sensual sexuality! When a husband and wife touch each other authentically in spirit and soul, the mystery of their tender weaving becomes a physical expression of God's love and strength.

Personal Journaling and Small Group Questions
Spiritual Homecoming Assignment Nine

Personal Journaling Questions

1. How does your false self reveal itself in the marriage bed? What is your relational style?
2. Do you have betrayals from the past that are affecting your marriage relationship? Spend time releasing them at the Cross.
3. Reread the section on Rest for the Feminine Soul or Respect for the Masculine Soul. Write down three ways you can meet the needs of your spouse that you have not been meeting.

Small Group Questions

1. What... are the key truths that stood out to you in this stage?
2. Why... do you need to know these truths?
3. How... do you apply these truths to your life?
4. Your pain... What pain does this stage reveal in your life?
5. Your sin... What are you doing with your pain?
6. Repentance... What do you need to do differently?
7. Prayer... What do you need to ask God for help with?

Private Husband and Wife Questions

Husband, ask your wife: Are the four "emotional wants" true for you?

Sexual Desires of the Female Spirit:

- I want to emotionally touch him.
- I want him to want me to emotionally touch him.
- I want him to emotionally touch me.
- I want him to want to emotionally touch me.
- Then I am open to sexually connecting with him!

Wife, ask your husband: Are the four "sexual wants" true for you?

Sexual Desires of the Male Spirit:

- I want to sexually touch her.
- I want her to want me to sexually touch her.
- I want her to sexually touch me.
- I want her to want to sexually touch me.
- Then I am open to emotionally connecting with her.

Husband, ask your wife: Give me some feedback on how I am doing in all three phases of "complete sexuality."

Marriage sexuality cycle:

- Phase One: Sexual Desire in your spirit (one-third)
- Phase Two: Sexual Arousal in your soul (one-third)
- Phase Three: Sexual Orgasm in your body (one-third)

Wife, ask your husband: Give me some feedback on how I am doing in all three phases of "complete sexuality."

Marriage sexuality cycle:

- Phase One: Sexual Desire in your spirit (one-third)
- Phase Two: Sexual Arousal in your soul (one-third)
- Phase Three: Sexual Orgasm in your body (one-third)

Husband, ask your wife: With which tool do I need to honor you the most?

- Look at her
- Talk to her
- Touch her
- Serve her
- Pray with her

Wife, ask your husband: With which tool do I need to honor you the most?

- Honor His Reputation in Public
- Support Him as a Father
- Show Him Warmth and Affection
- Serve him
- Pray with him

Couple, ask each other: On which of the five fundamentals do we need to work?

- We want to belong to God and each other—to experience the tenderness, strength, and peace of intimacy.
- We want to be with each other to experience our passion, our giftedness, and our purpose with each other.
- We want to offer each other our true selves.
- We want to live lives of purpose together.
- We want to experience God's love through each other.

Husband, ask your wife: In which area do I need to bring you rest?

- To have a holy (non-Baal), cherishing love in which you can trust
- To feel secure and taken care of by you
- To feel a togetherness and partnership with you
- To have a nest that is fixed and beautiful for you
- To be romanced with intimate and tender embrace

Wife, ask your husband: In which area do I need to bring you respect?

- To have a holy, cherishing love in which you can trust
- To enable you to feel strong in your masculinity
- To be able to feel respected by me and in your life work
- To be affirmed by the softness of my support toward you
- To enjoy sexual, erotic touch

Couple, take turns asking each other the following questions:

- What is my sexual relational style?
- How do you experience my sexual relational style?
- What do you want my sexual relational style to be?
- What do you want more of and less of in sexual foreplay?
- What do you want more of and less of in sexual play?
- What is pleasurable and not pleasurable to you?
- What do you want more of and less of in sexual afterplay?

STAGE TEN: The Art of Intimate Worship
Living in Awe and Gratitude

The art of intimate worship is the most restful stage of the spiritual homecoming. This is a stage of experiencing great wonder and reverence for who God is despite the chaos of our world. In this stage, receptivity and empowerment infuse your spirit, moving you into a passionate dance of celebration! This is a stage of deep gratitude for what God has done for you. In *Desiring God,* John Piper states that we were designed to glorify God by enjoying Him forever.

Living in Awe and Gratitude

Resting in God
Rather than "being" the Church, the people of God just "do" church. We do not spend time in awe of God. Without awe, we lack gratitude, and this fuels our frenetic pace of "doing" in our own strength. Instead, we should be resting in Him, who He is, and who we really are.

To "be" the Church, we need to submit to a position of receiving. Rest does not come from our core pain being healed, but from repenting of our core rebellion. When we spend time in awe and gratitude of His grace and mercy, we rest and come alive in celebration of worship.

Intimate relationship with God brings a follower of Christ into the Sabbath each day of his or her life. To "Sabbath in the Spirit" is to rest in your spirit as your soul and body are empowered to go forth and "do" in love only and exactly as you are called to do.

Many leaders in the Church do not feel the freedom to rest. "Rest is not the cessation of passion nor activity, but it is the freedom to not act."[26] Out of intimate rest, you will have great passion to boldly live out the gospel as the Lord God leads you.

When you are at rest, you will experience the intimate heart of God pouring His Spirit into you. When you are at rest, your spirit will be washed by God's merciful rains. You will passionately dance for joy like King David because you are forgiven! A dance of passion and empowerment will overflow from a heart of rest and receptivity.

As you rest in God, you will begin to see the greatness of God, and you will see the smallness of humanity. The greatness of God is reflected in the wonders of His beauty and strength. This is a God of great mercy toward the sons and daughters who once rebelled against Him and left Him to pursue empty lives of addictions and co-addictions. This is the God of compassion who runs to us when we turn back toward home. He has a tender embrace for us and says, "Welcome home My sons and daughters. I love you. I have patiently been waiting for your return. Welcome back home to My heart!"

Worshiping in Spirit
Worshiping the False Gods
To understand a life of intimate worship, you will need to think more deeply through the world of addictions and co-addictions. In the first half of this book, we defined addiction and co-addiction as behavior that no longer feels like a choice. At the deepest level, addictions and co-addictions are not just born out of human need—our meager attempts to fill our emptiness—but their foundation is really in human refusal to show gratitude to God.[27]

For the wrath of God is revealed from heaven against all ungodliness and unrighteousness of **men who suppress the truth in unrighteousness,** because that which is known about God is evident within them; for God made it evident to them. For since the creation of the world His invisible attributes, His eternal power and divine nature, have been clearly seen, being understood through what has been made, so that they are without excuse. **For even though they knew God, they did not honor Him as God or give thanks,** but they became futile in their speculations, and their foolish heart was darkened. Professing to be wise, they became fools, and exchanged the glory of the incorruptible God for an image in the form of corruptible man and of birds and four-footed animals and crawling creatures. **Therefore God gave them over** in the lusts of their hearts to impurity, so that their bodies would be dishonored among them. **For they exchanged the truth of God for a lie, and worshiped and served the creature rather than**

239

the Creator, who is blessed forever. Amen.
(Romans 1:18-25, NASB, emphasis added)

When you refuse to honor God and thank Him, you block all healing of sense of belonging and sense of being. Our deepest betrayal of God is a life that does not acknowledge Him, honor Him, and give thanks to Him.

The word "suppress" in this verse means to hold down. It is a picture of forcing something down that wants to be released. Truth wants to be released in your spirit, soul, and body. However, we suppress truth with the wickedness of addictions and co-addictions. A life of bondage is the opposite of a life of honoring and thanking God.

We were built for worship. To bend our knee to Baal in addictions and co-addictions is to worship false gods. With all addictions, we are looking to the creature and not the Creator to feel passion, giftedness, and purpose. The evidence of idolatry in your life is bondage, being stuck in addiction or co-addiction. When you bow your knee to the true living God, you will experience deep freedom to live out your passion, giftedness, and purpose.

Rebellion in Your Soul

240

*So I tell you this, and insist on it in the Lord, that you must no longer live as the Gentiles do, in the futility of their thinking. They are **darkened** in their **understanding** and **separated from the life of God** because of the ignorance that is in them **due to the hardening of their hearts.** Having lost all sensitivity, they have given themselves over to sensuality so as to **indulge in every kind of impurity, with a continual lust for more.***

(Ephesians 4:17-19, NIV, emphasis added)

In this passage, the phrase "with a continual lust for more" expresses the empty nature of the false worship of addictions and co-addictions. You have a compulsive urge to indulge in something or someone that will not satisfy you at the core. This is rebellion against God because He wants to fill you; you were created for His filling. Rebellion to seek your satisfaction elsewhere only results in pain because others' attempts and other sources cannot fill you. Only God can fill you.

Living a Life of Idolatry

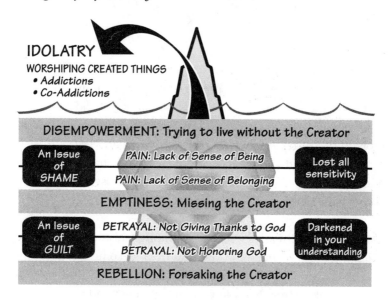

Addictions and co-addictions begin with the darkening of the heart (spirit and soul). As you harden your heart with Baal worship, you start to lose your sensitivity to life. You no longer feel alive. You feel nothing or numb in the core of your being; you have no sense of belonging or being. Hardness of heart produces deadness of spirit, soul and, eventually, body.

Rebellion in Your Body

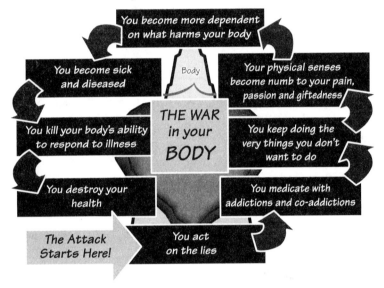

You become more dependent on what harms your body

You become sick and diseased

Body

Your physical senses become numb to your pain, passion and giftedness

THE WAR in your BODY

You kill your body's ability to respond to illness

You keep doing the very things you don't want to do

You destroy your health

You medicate with addictions and co-addictions

The Attack Starts Here!

You act on the lies

Addiction and co-addiction try to produce feeling and passion within the emptiness and numbness of life. The addiction or co-addiction tries to conjure up life. The more you bend your knee to false gods, the darker your heart (spirit and soul) will be. With more darkness comes more hardness of heart and greater loss of sensitivity—deadness. This cycle entices you further into sensual addictions and co-addictions because they falsely promise to revive your senses.

The man who struggles with pornography feels dead at his core. When he starts to look at pornography, he becomes aroused and the inner deadness seems to go away. The intensity of the sexual arousal imitates real life. No relational conflict and no relational pain mar this momentary illusion of the dark world of Baal worship. However, more and more pornography is required to keep up the illusion. The more a man possesses Baal, the more Baal will possess him.

Baal worship blocks the spirit and soul from receiving love and strength. Baal worship further blocks the spirit and soul from receiving light. The heart only hardens as the spirit and soul darkens with Baal passion and Baal images.

As a man continues, entrenched in Baal worship, he loses sensitivity to the Holy Spirit of God. As deadness of his senses and deadness to the Holy Spirit sets in, he is driven even further into a life of worship to Baal in sexual addiction.

The same principle applies to a food addiction of overeating. The overeater feels dead and empty in his or her inner person. To try to come alive inside, he or she is aroused by sight, smell, and cravings, and chooses to eat. To choose to come alive apart from God is arrogant and never works. The overeater rebels against God by idolizing food. As with all idolatry, food addictions leave you feeling deader inside, and more food is required to bring the illusion of life into your deeper sense of deadness.

Romans chapter one exposes addictions and co-addictions as a perversion of worship—a shift from worshiping the Creator to worshiping the creature. Ephesians chapter four connects the hardening of the heart (spirit and soul) to insensitivity to the Holy Spirit, which drives addictive and co-addictive worship.

Worshiping the True God

To worship God is to express authentic awe and gratitude.[28] Over the years, I have discovered the fundamental truth and mystery in those words. Awe is a sense of being overwhelmed by the greatness of the Creator, to see the vast beauty and strength of the One who created you and the universe in which you live. The sunset, the stars on a clear night—the King's universe reflects His royalty each evening! His majesty is shown every day through magnificent vistas, rainbows, and every living creature. All of creation displays awe and reverence for the living God.

Each of us knows deep down that we are responsible for our choices that betray God and others. The sin of betrayal is death, eternal death. We all have an internal sense of justice that intuitively knows that we deserve judgment for our sins of betrayal—not loving God and not loving our neighbors as ourselves.

To have a holy wonder is to be receptive to the Son of God in your spirit, to revere the Gift Giver by receiving the gift! There is a feminine quality to receiving the tender love of God. To take time daily to be in awe of God is to daily honor God.

Gratitude is recognizing God's mercy to forgive you of your sins of betrayal. When you receive Jesus as your Lord and Savior, you know that you are forgiven forever! However, gratitude also knows the delight of God. The Creator of the universe so loves His creatures; He delights when you receive His tenderness and strength within the intimacy of a relationship with Him. Gratitude is loving God and others in return for the love He has given you. First John 4:19 says that we love because He first loved us!

Gratitude also brings empowerment to your spirit. There is a strong masculine quality in releasing love to God and others. However, you cannot have such gratefulness without first having awe. The dance of awe and gratitude is the expression of worship on the journey of a lifetime. It leads you straight into the celebration of the Son—the Lamb of God who takes away the sin of the world!

The Mystery of Awe
To develop a life of awe toward God, you must address the core issue of your rebellion toward God and embrace the presence of God by receiving His Son into your human spirit As you realize the living presence of the Son, the Father, and the Holy Spirit, you will experience the tenderness, strength, and peace of God.

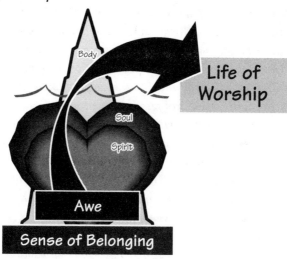

Before you can address the core issue of rebelling against God, God must first embrace you with His mercy and grace. He did this by sending His Son to earth as a man to reconcile humanity through His death. God has always had the compassion and mercy—the tenderness of love and strength of love—to make the first move in our human lives.

The story of the prodigal son applies to any prodigal child—both sons and daughters. The father in this story had the tenderness of love to receive his returning child with a compassionate embrace. However, the father also had the strength of love to run toward his child in holy passion and delight! The prodigal child needed both the tenderness and strength of the parent to feel the peace and security of being welcomed home after his foolish choice to rebel against the great love of his parents.

The Embrace of the Prodigal
We all have lived lives of idolatry this side of heaven. Like the prodigal son or daughter, we all have left Father God to live in the pigpen of addictions and co-addictions. We all have bent our knee to the worship of false gods.

245

*A man had two sons. The younger of them said to his father, "Father, give me the share of the estate that falls to me." So he divided his wealth between them. And not many days later, the younger son gathered everything together and **went on a journey into a distant country, and there he squandered his estate with loose living.** Now when he had spent everything, a severe famine occurred in that country, and he began to be impoverished. So he went and hired himself out to one of the citizens of that country, and he sent him into his fields to feed swine. And he would have gladly filled his stomach with the pods that the swine were eating, and no one was giving anything to him.*

(Luke 15:11-16, NASB, emphasis added)

In the story, the son finally hits bottom in his life and comes to his senses. Most of us are too arrogant to come to the Cross without experiencing some level of pain in life. For many of us, we have to have a crisis before we will truly turn from our rebellion and emptiness of Baal worship.

But when he came to his senses, *he said, "How many of my father's hired men have more than enough bread, but I am dying here with hunger! 'I **will get up** and **go to my father,** and **will say to him,** "Father, I have sinned against heaven, and in your sight; I am no longer worthy to be called your son; make me as one of your hired men."'"*

(Luke 15:17-19, NASB, emphasis added)

The prodigal son is an authentic story of spirit-to-spirit embrace with God. The child says that he will get up and go to his father. This is a picture of repentance and not rebellion. The child has decided to stop running and is going back to his father. And the prodigal is honest about it. Unlike our spiritual forefather, Adam, who tried to hide from God and blame God, the prodigal chose to enter into relationship with his father by confessing how he had sinned against him.

For us to embrace God's presence is to go to the Cross and confess our sins of betrayal to our Father God. The prodigal was not all talk—he did what he said he would. However, watch what happens before he arrives home. The mystery of the gracious and merciful embrace of the living God occurs.

> *So he got up and came to his father. But while he was still a long way off, **his father saw him and felt compassion for him, and ran and embraced him and kissed him.***
>
> (Luke 15:20, NASB, emphasis added)

The father sees his son from a distance; he does not passively wait for his return, but he runs with passion to his son. He welcomes his son home with a tender embrace of love. This is a picture of the tenderness and strength of a good parent.

The Father God of the universe also sees you right now. The God of the universe has relentlessly pursued His prodigal sons and daughters by the tender sacrificial death of His only beloved Son so that we may live now and forever with Him. The death of the innocent Son is the epitome of holy tenderness and holy strength.

> *And the son said to him, "**Father, I have sinned** against heaven and in your sight; I am no longer worthy to be called your son." But the father said to his slaves, "**Quickly** bring out the **best robe** and put it on him, and put a **ring** on his hand and **sandals** on his feet; and bring the **fattened calf,** kill it, and let us **eat** and **celebrate;** for this son of mine was **dead** and has come to **life** again; he was **lost** and has been **found."** And they began to **celebrate.***
>
> (Luke 15:21-24, NASB, emphasis added)

The choice to daily honor God by returning to Him means allowing God's presence to saturate your spirit, soul, and body. The mystery of receptivity enables you to experience three things: Jesus takes you to the Father, the Father fills you with the Holy Spirit, and the Holy Spirit releases His gifts within your spirit. The prodigal is filled with awe and gratitude.

The Mystery of Gratitude
Gratefulness is the only proper response to awe. Gratitude comes from fully acknowledging how you've betrayed others and fully receiving the truth that you are forgiven and cleansed. When a man or woman has received the mercy of forgiveness, an extravagant delight wells up in them to say, "God, thank You!"

Life of Worship

Gratefulness overflows in a stream of clean, authentic, intimate love. Tasting the love of God will profoundly fill you in a way that will affect your entire being. As you eat the bread and drink the living waters of His love, you will start to love God in the greatest way possible. You will start to love God with all of your heart, with all of your mind, with all of your soul, and with all of your strength. To have gratitude in your spirit is to release the gift of love back to God and to love your neighbor as yourself.

Worship in Spirit
The Cycle of Receptivity and Empowerment in the Human Spirit
The choice to love God and to not rebel starts here:
- You listen to God and believe His truth.
- God restores your receptivity to His love.
- Receiving God's strength empowers you to obey Him.
- You seek to know God and embrace His presence.
- Full and strong, you choose to obey God.
- Your spirit is filled with love for God, and you respond with reverence and worship.
- You long to receive more of God's love and truth.
- You love God deeply and responsively.
- You live with passion, giftedness, and purpose!

Worship in Your Spirit

When you choose to take the daily time to listen to God, you will hear His voice in spirit and in truth. When you are listening to the voice of God, you will be filled with desire to be loved and enjoyed by the Almighty! God's love powerfully restores your sense of belonging and your sense of being. Within that restoration, a tender awe will fill you with the strength of gratitude. As you experience listening prayer with the Lord God Almighty, your spirit will be washed with fresh, daily mercy, which will also bring you great delight.

To come alive at your core unlocks great passion and spiritual desire. As passion and giftedness are released, your spiritual purpose will unfold as you boldly live out the gospel with tenderness, strength, and peace.

A daily life of embracing God's presence, listening prayer, and listening obedience is the path to standing against your own rebellion and idolatry. When you continue to bend your knee to false gods, your betrayal is like spitting in the face of the true God. But when you come back home to God in spirit and truth, you receive the everlasting love and kindness God has for you.

Worship in Soul
To worship in your soul is to allow your new sense of belonging and sense of being to transform your false self into your true self. This is the result of being spiritually reborn: you become filled with love for your Creator and empowered to love your Creator.

In Stage Six, you read about daily renewing your spiritual vows to the Lord Jesus Christ. To daily die with Christ is to daily release at the Cross of Christ. As the Holy Spirit embraces you each day, and as you think about who it is that lives within you, the Trinity living within your spirit will give you the strength to release at the Cross. As you release your flesh, the impact of the world, and the impact of Satan at the Cross, you will be daily delivered with new freedom in the spirit.

The Cycle of Receptivity and Empowerment in Your Soul
The choice to stop rebelling and love others starts here:
- Your mind is filled with truth from God.
- Your heart is filled with new hope.
- You make wise choices.
- You lovingly engage others.
- You rely on God to satisfy you.
- You are grateful and delight in God's truth and grace.

- You feel the full range of emotions.
- You choose to love others instead of using them.

Worship in Your Soul

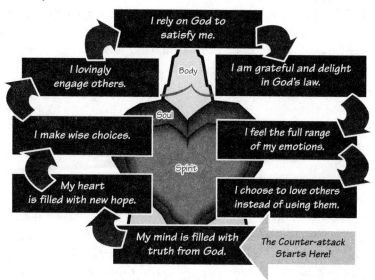

As you choose to live out your journey through listening obedience, you will be filled with the power of the Holy Spirit. It is a mystery to spend time in listening prayer and then to be blessed with strength from the Holy Spirit. As you listen and obey the Lord God, your emptiness will be filled with belonging and being in Christ. As you become reborn in the spirit, you live and move and have a vibrant sense of being.

How does the false self shift to the true self? When you receive strength as the Holy Spirit fills and empowers you each day, the symbolic confusion in your mind is cleared by the holy light of Christ. As the light of Christ comes into your soul, the truth of God transforms the images and beliefs in your mind. As your mind is filled and empowered by symbolic truth, it changes how you feel about yourself. The lack of well-being that can produce anxiety, depression, restlessness, and dissatisfaction starts to shift to a sense of well-being. To feel good from the inside out, without the use of addictions and co-addictions, is to know and experience the love, strength, and peace of the living God.

As your capacity to think and feel is daily empowered by the Holy Spirit, your disempowered will shifts to an empowered will. Instead of legalistically performing, you choose to act out of passion, giftedness, and purpose. You choose to repent from rebelling toward the living God by responding to Him out of love. To love God is to listen and obey God because your heart has been drawn into holy intimacy with Him. God has always seen you; however, you now see God. And you run home to embrace Him in wonder and gratitude!

As you return to the living God, your relational style will shift from self-protection to loving. The tough boys and girls become tender men and women as they experience the tender awe of God. The little boys and girls become mature men and women as they grow up in the strength of gratitude toward God. The good boys and girls become honest men and women as they proclaim the truth that the culture is trying to suppress. The religious boys and girls become authentic men and women of faith as they are genuinely filled and empowered by the Holy Spirit. The party boys and girls become faithful men and women because the power of the Holy Spirit will awaken them to their passion, giftedness, and purpose. The driven boys and girls become relational men and women who take the time to rest and experience the mystery of receptivity.

These become the new parents of homes of tenderness, strength, and peace. These are the parents who will live naturally out of the filling and empowerment of the Holy Spirit. This is the path to true relational health in the futures of their children.

This is also the path to disrupting the ugly hate of racial transference. To love God is to love your neighbor as yourself. That means all of your neighbors. People of all races think that if they act appropriately in public and in passing, that is enough. We don't fool each other! We can detect whether love is genuine or superficial, whether the bias of hatred is still buried in one's spirit and played out in one's thinking.

To repent of the rebellion of racism, you will need to go to the roots of the racism in your human spirit. When your spirit is filled and empowered by the love and strength of God, you can start to break the vows and judgments you made when you first learned such prejudices.

Think of the vows and judgments that you've made. Perhaps you judged that all people of another race are bad. Or perhaps you vowed never to trust someone of a certain race. Perhaps you separate yourself from certain races when it comes to issues of intimacy and commitment.

To shift from hatred to love is to bring Jesus into your betrayal memories. To do this, confess your vows and judgments with another person at the foot of the Cross. Then close your eyes and invite the Jesus of Revelation 3:20 into that memory, and see what Jesus does.

Worship in Body
To worship God in your body may be as disruptive physically as turning from issues like racism in your soul. However, freedom from addictions and co-addictions will bring you into new health in every arena—including physical health.

The Cycle of Receptivity and Empowerment in Your Body
The choice to stop rebelling against God and to honor your body and relationships starts here:
- You obey God by acting on the truth.
- You choose to stop medicating.
- You finally stop doing the things you don't want to do.
- Your physical senses come alive.
- You depend on God instead of on the object of your addiction.
- You choose what is good for the health of your body.
- Your body is able to respond rightly to illness.
- You become healthier.

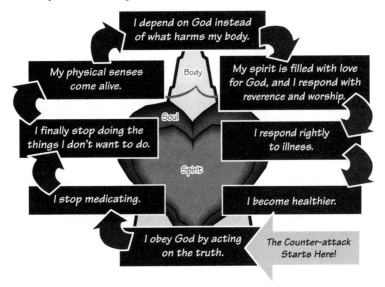

The reason you could not stop your addictive or co-addictive behavior before is that you were in rebellion against God. Rebellion leaves you empty and disempowered, unable to stand against your own compulsive behavior. Trying harder is not effective!

To take responsibility for your sin is to own your rebellion.

- The father of lies continually causes you to doubt the truth that God wants to fill and empower you.
- Doubt triggers vulnerability to your abandonment pain, which comes from a lack of belonging and lack of being.
- You start to listen to the lies of the flesh, the world, and Satan.
- You eventually obey the lies of the flesh, the world, and Satan.
- You ultimately betray others, yourself, or God.

When you are rebelling, you are cut off from receiving God's love, and you are cut off from being filled by God's strength. That leaves you empty and disempowered, stuck in your sinful, false self of betraying God and others.

When your inner person is empty and disempowered, your outer person will be in bondage to addictions and co-addictions. Inversely, when your outer body is in bondage to addictions and co-addictions, your inner person will be empty and disempowered. This is the spiritual war we are in.

The opposite of rebellion is surrender. As you listen and obey the voice of the Holy Spirit, you will go from being empty to being filled, from being disempowered to being empowered, to having what you need to deal with addiction and co-addiction, shifting from rebellion to surrender.

One of the tools that enables you to repent of your rebellion and take responsibility for your sin is listening prayer and listening obedience. Through listening prayer, you can hear the voice of God and become filled with the tender love of God. Through listening obedience, you can be filled with strength and empowered to finally work through sexual immorality, food addiction, co-dependence, or whatever your struggle is.

When you recognize your rebellion against God, life may get worse before it gets better. To turn from your rebellion and to stop medicating your pain with addictions and co-addictions will thaw your frozen pain. I live in the tundra of Minnesota. When you have been out in the bitter cold and come inside, your body has to warm up again to stay alive. The thawing process hurts like the blazes! However, the only way to function properly is to thaw; to remain in the cold too long leads to frostbite, gangrene and, ultimately, death.

As you choose to stop numbing your pain and sin with addictions and co-addictions, the guilt and shame of your rebellion against God can be released at the Cross. When the guilt and shame in your spirit are released, even your physical body is affected. The strength of your immune system will increase as you progress through the deliverance and healing process in your spirit, soul, and body.

Your life of surrender and obedience to God will enable you to receive God's tenderness and strength of love and empowerment to stand against addiction.

After battling cancer, I finally had to learn how to take care of my body. Our bodies are the temple of the Holy Spirit. Previously, my diet consisted primarily of meat, dairy, refined carbohydrates, and caffeine. I may have taken a vitamin once in a while, and occasionally I'd have a glass of water. I was too busy to do any regular exercise, and between a busy private practice and a large, busy family, I did not allow time to rest and relax. I was not honoring God with the choices I made. Cancer was a wake-up call for me—one I hope you do not have to experience before you decide to take care of your temple.

The reality is that our culture is brimming with junk food; filled with conveniences that limit the need to move our bodies; riddled with toxins; and loaded with activities that keep us too busy to rest and pray. All of this entices us to lead a lifestyle of haste and convenience without the necessities of nutrition, exercise, rest, and prayer. To live this way is like going into a battle without any weapons. Take an honest look at your own life. When it comes to taking care of your body, does your lifestyle reflect the bondage of idolatry or the freedom of a life of worship? Are you honoring God in the choices you make regarding your physical body?

Here is a thought for you: If you do not provide what your body needs, it will not function the way it was designed. It will not be equipped to fight the battle. It's similar to taking care of a car. If you don't add the right fuel and provide appropriate maintenance, then it will not perform at its full potential. It will probably be in and out of the repair shop and end up in the graveyard prematurely. The problems may not surface right away, but day by day, neglect will cause damage. The same is true for our bodies! If we put in the right fuel and do the preventative maintenance, we have a much better probability of avoiding health problems. Being sick, tired, or dying prematurely is not God's plan. He designed our bodies to work. It's up to us to steward them properly so they will.

What if the car you are driving was borrowed from a friend? Would that affect how you drive and care for it? Knowing it wasn't your car, would you be even more careful about fueling it, cleaning it, making sure you didn't put unnecessary miles on it? Your body is not your own; God bought and paid for you—all of you, including your body! Our bodies are vehicles to be used in service to God. We have the privilege and the responsibility to use and care for them while we are here on this earth.

As you confess, renounce, repent, and begin to listen and obey, God will forgive you, fill you, and empower you to make choices for your body that will honor Him.

What does the stewardship of our bodies look like? As you are empowered to move from a life of idolatry to a life of worship, it is essential to know how to make good choices. Through my experience I've learned that there are at least five keys to good health.

Five Keys to Good Health

(Note: I am a licensed psychologist, not a nutritionist, so please consult a qualified health professional regarding the treatment of your medical problems. This information is not intended to provide medical advice or take the place of medical advice and treatment from your personal physician. Neither the publisher nor the author takes any responsibility for any possible consequences from any treatment, action, or application of medicine, supplement, herb, or preparation to any person regarding or following the information contained in this section.)

1. Nutrition

We cannot eat junk and expect to be healthy! The apostle Paul tells us God's will in 1 Corinthians 6:20: Honor God with your body. That means putting the right things into your body. Pastor Bill Hybels of Willow Creek Church says, "Don't ask God to bless junk food and miraculously transform it so that it has nutritional value. Doing that is acting like the fifth-grader who, after taking the geography test, prayed, 'Dear God, please make Detroit the capital of Michigan.' That's not how God works."[29] Our bodies have nutritional needs that are only found in the foods God designed for us.

*Then God said, "I give you every seed-bearing **plant**
on the face of the whole earth and every tree that has
fruit with seed in it. **They will be yours for food.***
(Genesis 1:29, NIV, emphasis added)

Most of us breeze through the produce section thinking of fruits and vegetables as an optional side dish. In reality, they should be our main fare. Fresh fruits and vegetables, along with whole grains, legumes, nuts, and seeds provide the nutrients our bodies need. Most of a typical grocery store is nothing more than a graveyard for processed foods void of nutrition and loaded with additives, preservatives, and other toxic ingredients that no one can pronounce. When our bodies don't get what they need, we end up with disease and illness.

Nutrition is clearly a key ingredient for a healthy body. I encourage you to pay close attention to what you are eating. Since battling cancer, I have a new desire to eat well and take care of my body. I've started reading food labels to really know what I'm getting, and I try new recipes every week of dishes that are heavy on vegetables, whole grains, and legumes, and light on meat and cheese. I feel like this diet has really improved my physical, mental, and spiritual health.

2. Exercise
Physical exercise is also a key for good health. Many of us drive to work, take an elevator to our offices, sit at desks, order takeout for dinner, use machines to accomplish our chores, and watch TV in our leisure time. But our bodies need to move! Our muscles— including our heart—need to be challenged in order to be healthy and strong. Our bones need weight bearing exercises; our muscles need to be stretched to remain flexible.

We benefit in spirit, soul, and body from regular exercise. Being overweight increases the risk for almost every disease plaguing Americans today. It is good stewardship to invest the time and energy it takes to get your body in good physical shape. It is not a luxury to be in good shape—it's a necessity. God needs your vehicle in good working order. He has work for you to do. Is your body fit enough to do it? You can either choose to make time to prevent problems today, or you will be forced to make time for the inevitable breakdowns later.

I try to walk every day, and I have realized that I do not need a lot of equipment to do strength-training exercises—just an exercise band or a few dumbbells. I stretch for flexibility and to prevent back pain, and our family makes exercise a family affair. We've found it doesn't really matter what we do; the key is to do it often and consistently.

3. Cleansing (Detoxification)

Beyond taking a shower, cleansing or detoxifying my body was a new concept to me. To cleanse is to render clean; to free from filth, pollution, infection, guilt, etc.; to clean.[30] Living in a fallen world, there are plenty of ways our bodies get contaminated. We ingest toxins in the water we drink, and we pollute our bodies with the air we breathe and the food we eat. Food today is sprayed with chemicals, preserved with chemicals, decorated with chemicals, and flavored with chemicals. Food manufacturers use all kinds of chemicals to make their products look good, taste good, and last a long time sitting on a shelf. Many of these chemicals are toxic to your body. I believe that the best foods for your body are those with only one ingredient and grown organically, without the use of chemicals.

4. Rest

God rested and He gave us the gift of rest, too.

> *"Remember the Sabbath day by keeping it holy."*
> *(Exodus 20:8, NIV, emphasis added)*

Rest is simply essential for good health. We need eight to ten hours of sleep each night. Have you ever stayed up all night? How did you feel the next day? Fired up and ready to tackle the world? Or were you slogging through the day just trying to survive? Daily rest is essential and God wired us to need sleep every day. We also benefit from resting from our work once a week. Think about Jesus – He took time to get away from it all once in a while. We also need vacations periodically. We Americans are working ourselves into an early grave. Look how far we lag behind comparable countries when it comes to average annual vacation time.

Italy	42 days
France	37 days
Germany	35 days
Brazil	34 days
United Kingdom	28 days
Canada	26 days
Korea	25 days
Japan	25 days
U.S.	13 days

[31]

What are the results? A nation of people who are stressed, tired, and heading toward burnout. Over time, a lifestyle without rest will lead to health problems. God gives us rest because we need it. Let's accept this gracious gift and make time for the rest we so desperately need.

> It's **useless to rise early** and **go to bed late,** and work your worried fingers to the bone. Don't you know **he enjoys giving rest to those he loves?**
> (Psalm 127:2, MSG, emphasis added)

I make sleep a priority now; I try to go to bed on time to make sure I get enough rest. I rest daily with the Lord by spending some quiet time alone with Him. I take a day off every week—the Sabbath is a gift from God. Sunday is now our family re-group day to rest, relax, and have fun together just as a family! This is the one day of the week to celebrate life and make fun lasting memories. We also try to take a relaxing vacation every year. (A fast-paced trip that leaves me more exhausted than when I left may be fun, but does nothing for my need for rest!) I seek to spend time every day just hanging out with my kids, and I spend time with Beth every day, as well. This is not only restful, but it is essential to keep my marriage healthy and growing within the storms of life.

5. Prayer

Do you remember back in Stage Six when I told you how God saved my life through listening prayer? If I had only listened to my doctor, I would probably not be here today. I would be like King Asa:

> *In the thirty-ninth year of his reign Asa was **afflicted** with **a disease** in his feet. Though his disease was severe, even in his illness **he did not seek help from the** LORD, **but only from the physicians.** Then in the forty-first year of his reign Asa died and rested with his fathers.*
>
> *(2 Chronicles 16:12-13,* NIV, *emphasis added)*

The medical industry is even starting to see the correlation between prayer and physical healing of patients. The power of prayer simply cannot be overestimated. We need to have two-way conversation with the Lord each day. It is through time spent with Him that we get to know Him and His ways. As you know, willpower is simply not powerful enough to change your health habits for very long. Real and lasting change is only possible through the supernatural power of the Holy Spirit. Only God can break the spiritual strongholds that keep us from being good stewards of our bodies. It is God who is able to heal us. Sometimes God heals us instantly, but often He chooses to partner with us to bring healing. Consider the story of Naaman, who had leprosy. He sought the Lord through the prophet Elisha, and here is what he told him:

> *"**Go to the River Jordan and immerse yourself** seven times. **Your skin will be healed** and you'll be as good as new."*
>
> *Naaman lost his temper. He turned on his heel saying, "I thought he'd personally come out and meet me, call*

on the name of GOD, wave his hand over the diseased
spot, and get rid of the disease. The Damascus rivers,
Abana and Pharpar, are cleaner by far than any of the
rivers in Israel. Why not bathe in them? I'd at least
get clean." He stomped off, mad as a hornet.

But his servants caught up with him and said, "Father,
if the prophet had asked you to do something
hard and heroic, wouldn't you have done it? So
why not this simple 'wash and be clean'?"

So he did it. *He went down and immersed himself in*
the Jordan seven times, **following the orders of the**
Holy Man. His skin was healed; *it was like the skin*
of a little baby. He was as good as new.
(2 Kings 5:10b-14, MSG, emphasis added)

Naaman sought God's advice, he listened, he obeyed, and then he was healed. God may ask you to do something you don't want to do or something you may not understand in order to be healed. I am evidence that it pays to listen and obey!

My son, **pay attention** *to what I* **say; listen** *closely*
to **my words.** *Do not let them out of your sight, keep*
them within your heart; for **they are life to those**
who find them and health to a man's whole
body.
(Proverbs 4:20-23, NIV, emphasis added)

Now, more than ever, I make listening prayer a daily priority. I seek the Lord, listen to Him, and obey. I pray for God to heal me when I'm sick, and I confess, renounce, repent, and ask forgiveness and cleansing for the ways I may have neglected to properly steward my temple. I ask the Lord to show me specifically what I need to work on with regard to my physical body. I believe He will empower me to do what I need to do to maintain and restore my temple.

It has taken me three years post-cancer to start to implement these changes in caring for my physical body. They have been coming slowly, but they are becoming a new way of living for me. When I lapse, I think about how my selfish decisions could impact my wife and children's lives if I were to die. That usually helps me to cry out to God for His help. When I ask Him to fill me and empower me, I can make decisions that flow out of a life of worship in loving God and loving my wife and children in spirit, soul, and body.

I pray that I will live a long and healthy life. I pray for God to fill me and empower me each day to make choices in my physical body that honor God and do not rebel against how He wants me to steward my body. As someone once said, "I work like it is all up to me. I pray like it is all up to God."

And I pray the same for you:

> *Beloved, I pray that in all respects you **may prosper** and be in **good health,** just as your soul prospers.*
> *(3 John 1:2 NASB, emphasis added)*

Through our receptivity and empowerment, God brings deliverance, healing, and restoration to our spirits, souls, and bodies so that we can worship Him in spirit, soul, and body.

The Hand of Blessing
The first verse that helped me to see God's strong heart to bless a life of worship unto Him was Isaiah 1:19 (NIV, *emphasis added*).

> *If you are **willing** and **obedient, you will eat the best from the land.***

We can only be willing and obedient as the Almighty embraces us with His grace and mercy. The book of Deuteronomy shows that God's hand of blessing upon you, your family, and your generations to come is directly related to your obedience:

263

Now it shall be, if you diligently obey the LORD your God, being careful to do all His commandments which I command you today, the LORD your God will set you high above all the nations of the earth. All these blessings will come upon you and overtake you if you obey the LORD your God: Blessed shall you be in the city, and blessed shall you be in the country. Blessed shall be the offspring of your body and the produce of your ground and the offspring of your beasts, the increase of your herd and the young of your flock. Blessed shall be your basket and your kneading bowl. Blessed shall you be when you come in, and blessed shall you be when you go out.

The LORD shall cause your enemies who rise up against you to be defeated before you; they will come out against you one way and will flee before you seven ways. The LORD will command the blessing upon you in your barns and in all that you put your hand to, and He will bless you in the land which the LORD your God gives you. The LORD will establish you as a holy people to Himself, as He swore to you, if you keep the commandments of the LORD your God and walk in His ways. So all the peoples of the earth will see that you are called by the name of the LORD, and they will be afraid of you. The LORD will make you abound in prosperity, in the offspring of your body and in the offspring of your beast and in the produce of your ground, in the land which the LORD swore to your fathers to give you. The LORD will open for you His good storehouse, the heavens, to give rain to your land in its season and to bless all the work of your hand; and you shall lend to many nations, but you shall not borrow. The LORD will make you the head and not the tail, and you only will be above, and you will not be underneath, if you listen to the commandments of the LORD your God, which I charge you today, to observe them carefully, and **do**

not turn aside from any of the words which I
command you today, to the right or to the left, to
go after other gods to serve them.

(*Deuteronomy 28:1-14, NASB, emphasis added*)

The Hand of Cursing

However, Isaiah 1:20 (NIV, *emphasis added*) is a sobering verse of how God will curse a life of idolatry:

"But if you resist and rebel, you will be devoured by the sword." For the mouth of the LORD has spoken.

God curses those who bend their knee to false gods. Three types of disasters occur from such idolatry, shaking our fists of rebellion toward God—personal disasters, man-made disasters, and natural disasters.

This passage in Deuteronomy further shows how God's curse on you, your family, and your generations to come is directly related to your rebellion.

But it shall come about, if you do not obey the LORD your God, to observe to do all His commandments and His statutes with which I charge you today, that all these curses will come upon you and overtake you: Cursed shall you be in the city, and cursed shall you be in the country. Cursed shall be your basket and your kneading bowl. Cursed shall be the offspring of your body and the produce of your ground, the increase of your herd and the young of your flock. Cursed shall you be when you come in, and cursed shall you be when you go out.

The LORD will send upon you curses, confusion, and rebuke, in all you undertake to do, until you are destroyed and until you perish quickly, on account of the evil of your deeds, because you have forsaken Me. The LORD will make the pestilence cling to you until

He has consumed you from the land where you are entering to possess it. The LORD *will smite you with consumption and with fever and with inflammation and with fiery heat and with the sword and with blight and with mildew, and they will pursue you until you perish. The heaven which is over your head shall be bronze, and the earth which is under you, iron. The* LORD *will make the rain of your land powder and dust; from heaven it shall come down on you until you are destroyed.*

The LORD *shall cause you to be defeated before your enemies; you will go out one way against them, but you will flee seven ways before them, and you will be an example of terror to all the kingdoms of the earth. Your carcasses will be food to all birds of the sky and to the beasts of the earth, and there will be no one to frighten them away. The* LORD *will smite you with the boils of Egypt and with tumors and with the scab and with the itch, from which you cannot be healed. The* LORD *will smite you with madness and with blindness and with bewilderment of heart; and you will grope at noon, as the blind man gropes in darkness, and you will not prosper in your ways; but you shall only be oppressed and robbed continually, with none to save you. You shall betroth a wife, but another man will violate her; you shall build a house, but you will not live in it; you shall plant a vineyard, but you will not use its fruit. Your ox shall be slaughtered before your eyes, but you will not eat of it; your donkey shall be torn away from you, and will not be restored to you; your sheep shall be given to your enemies, and you will have none to save you. Your sons and your daughters shall be given to another people, while your eyes look on and yearn for them continually; but there will be nothing you can do. A people whom you do not know shall eat up the produce of your ground and all your labors, and you will never be anything but oppressed* and crushed continually. You shall be driven mad by the sight of what you see. The LORD will strike you on the knees and legs with sore boils, from which you cannot be healed, from the sole of your foot to the crown of your head.

The LORD will bring you and your king, whom you set over you, to a nation which neither you nor your fathers have known, and there you shall serve other gods, wood and stone. You shall become a horror, a proverb, and a taunt among all the people where the LORD drives you. You shall bring out much seed to the field but you will gather in little, for the locust will consume it. You shall plant and cultivate vineyards, but you will neither drink of the wine nor gather the grapes, for the worm will devour them. You shall have olive trees throughout your territory but you will not anoint yourself with the oil, for your olives will drop off. You shall have sons and daughters but they will not be yours, for they will go into captivity. The cricket shall possess all your trees and the produce of your ground. The alien who is among you shall rise above you higher and higher, but you will go down lower and lower. He shall lend to you, but you will not lend to him; he shall be the head, and you will be the tail. **So all these curses shall come on you and pursue you and overtake you until you are destroyed, because you would not obey the LORD your God by keeping His commandments and His statutes which He commanded you.** They shall become a sign and a wonder on you and your descendants forever. **Because you did not serve the LORD your God with joy and a glad heart,** for the abundance of all things; therefore you shall serve your enemies whom the LORD will send against you, in hunger, in thirst, in nakedness, and in the lack of all things; and He will put an iron yoke on your neck until He has destroyed you. The LORD will bring a nation against you from afar, from the end of *the earth, as the eagle swoops down, a nation whose language you shall not understand, a nation of fierce countenance who will have no respect for the old, nor show favor to the young....*

(Deuteronomy 28:15-50, NASB, emphasis added)

The horrific curse continues on through verse 68, including the utter demise of those who have gone against God—to the point of cannibalizing their children. A gruesome picture indeed.

As we live in this culture of Baal worship and its addictions and co-addictions, I see the good heart of God wanting to bring His Holy fire to burn up all of our bondage to false gods. The fire of God is bringing His holy light into the hearts of men and women who are seeking Him with all of their hearts.

Hard and callous hearts of all peoples of the earth are being mercifully shattered by the fresh forgiveness of God. All tribes and nations are being beckoned to the foot of the Cross to receive the miracle of awe and to release the miracle of gratitude.

A new sensitivity of our spirits to the Holy Spirit is causing the people of this earth to come alive after living for years in deadness and addiction. The holy fire of God is bringing back reverence for His holiness and the wonders of His character. The psalms in the Old Testament are alive with the sound of worship.

The celebratory worship dance of awe and gratitude is filling houses of prayer again. The humility of being in a position of receptivity is filling the culture with the tenderness of God's love. The result of receptivity to the Spirit is the empowerment of the human spirit that is filling the culture with the strength of God.

*And the four living creatures, individually having six wings, were full of eyes all over and within [underneath their wings]; **and day and night they never stop saying, Holy, holy, holy is the Lord God Almighty (Omnipotent), Who was and Who is and Who is***

*to come. And whenever the living creatures **offer*
***glory and honor and thanksgiving to Him** Who*
sits on the throne, Who lives forever and ever (through
the eternities of the eternities), the twenty-four elders
(the members of the heavenly Sanhedrin) fall prostrate
*before Him Who is sitting on the throne, **and they*
***worship Him Who lives forever and ever; and*
***they throw down their crowns before the throne,*
***crying out, Worthy are You, our Lord and God,*
***to receive the glory and the honor and dominion,*
***for You created all things; by Your will they were*
[brought into being] and were created.

(*Revelation 4:8-11,* AMP, *emphasis added*)

Then I looked, and I heard the voices of many angels
on every side of the throne and of the living creatures
and the elders [of the heavenly Sanhedrin], and
they numbered ten thousand times ten thousand
and thousands of thousands, saying in a loud voice,
***Deserving is the Lamb, Who was sacrificed, to*
***receive all the power and riches and wisdom and*
***might and honor and majesty (glory, splendor)*
***and blessing!** And I heard every created thing in*
heaven and on earth and under the earth [in Hades,
the place of departed spirits] and on the sea and all
that is in it, crying out together, To Him Who is
seated on the throne and to the Lamb be ascribed
the blessing and the honor and the majesty (glory,
splendor) and the power (might and dominion)
forever and ever (through the eternities of the
eternities)! Then the four living creatures (beings)
said, Amen (so be it)! And the elders [of the heavenly
Sanhedrin] prostrated themselves and worshiped Him
Who lives forever and ever.

(*Revelation 5:11-14,* AMP, *emphasis added*)

The delight of God in your spiritual homecoming, and the spiritual homecoming of many, is bringing a new spiritual feast into this century. Spiritual homecoming is being celebrated by the kiss of embrace, royal robes, international sandals and great food, drink and music for all the tribes and nations to enjoy together.

The time has come to sound the trumpet! The beginning of life is about to arrive in glory and splendor.

But there is far more to life for us. We are citizens of high Heaven! We are awaiting the arrival of the Savior, the Master, Jesus Christ, who will transform our earthly bodies into glorious bodies like His own. He'll make us beautiful and whole with the same powerful skill by which He is putting everything as it should be, under and around Him.

The host of this party is about to return for His guests; the invitations to this wedding party of the times have been issued.

*The Angel said to me, "Write this: **'Blessed are those invited to the Wedding Supper of the Lamb.'"** He added, "These are the true words of God!"*

I fell at his feet to worship him, but he wouldn't let me. "Don't do that," he said. "I'm a servant just like you, and like your brothers and sisters who hold to the witness of Jesus. The witness of Jesus is the spirit of prophecy."

*Then I saw Heaven open wide—and oh! a white horse and its Rider. The Rider, named **Faithful and True**, judges and makes war in pure righteousness. His eyes are a blaze of fire, on his head many crowns. He has a Name inscribed that's known only to himself. He is **dressed in a robe soaked with blood,** and he is addressed as **"Word of God."** The armies of Heaven, mounted on white horses and dressed in dazzling white linen, follow him. **A sharp sword comes out of his mouth** so he can subdue the nations, then rule them with a rod of iron. He treads the winepress of the*

*raging wrath of God, the Sovereign-Strong. On his
robe and thigh is written, KING OF KINGS, LORD
OF LORDS.*

*I saw an Angel standing in the sun, shouting to all
flying birds in Middle-Heaven, "**Come to the Great
Supper of God!** Feast on the flesh of kings and captains
and champions, horses and their riders. Eat your fill of
them all—free and slave, small and great!"*

*I saw the Beast and, assembled with him, earth's kings
and their armies, ready to make war against the One
on the horse and his army. The Beast was taken, and
with him, his puppet, the False Prophet, who used
signs to dazzle and deceive those who had taken the
mark of the Beast and worshiped his image. They were
thrown alive, those two, into Lake Fire and Brimstone.
The rest were killed by the sword of the One on the
horse, the sword that comes from his mouth. All the
birds held a feast on their flesh.*

(Revelation 19:9-21, MSG, emphasis added)

A day will come when all of the enemies of God will be vanquished
and utterly destroyed. That is the day the Son of God takes His
bride, and there will be a wedding feast like no other. The bride
is His Church—you and me. We will rejoice forever with Him in
Heaven for His victory over our addictions, our co-addictions,
over Baal and every other false God—over Satan, the father of
lies.

IDOLATRY
WORSHIPING CREATED THINGS
• Addictions
• Co-Addictions

WORSHIP
WORSHIPING THE CREATOR
• Loving God
• Loving Others

EMPOWERMENT: Living in the Strength of Love of the Creator

HEALING: Sense of Being

HEALING: Sense of Belonging to God

BECOMING FILLED: Receiving the Creator's Tenderness of Love

GRATITUDE: Thanking God for His Mercy & Love

AWE: Approaching God in Wonder & Reverance

REPENTANCE: Returning to the Creator

We wait in a life of worship before the sounds of waves and thunder bring us into the roaring glory of the Lion and the Lamb! The final celebration of awe and gratitude is about to begin!

Personal Journaling and Small Group Questions
Spiritual Homecoming Assignment Ten

Personal Journaling Questions

1. Describe how you can shift from "doing" to "being" and allow yourself to rest in a new life of worship unto God.
2. Consider your addictions and co-addictions and describe why they are idolatry and rebellion against God.
3. How do you rebel against God by listening to the voice of Satan?
4. How do you rebel against God by obeying the voice of the enemy?
5. List three instances of awe of God that you experienced recently. (Note: consider small things and great things, anything that moved you to awareness of the greatness of God.)
6. Did you experience gratitude in your experiences of awe? Spend time in prayer now in gratefulness to God. Revisit your experiences of awe and thank Him. Then spend ten minutes with God listing each thing that comes to mind for which you are grateful.

Small Group Questions

1. What... are the key truths that stood out to you in this stage?
2. Why... do you need to know these truths?
3. How... do you apply these truths to your life?
4. Your pain... What pain does this stage reveal in your life?
5. Your sin... What are you doing with your pain?
6. Repentance... What do you need to do differently?
7. Prayer... What do you need to ask God for help with?

STAGE ELEVEN: Releasing Passion, Giftedness, and Purpose
Living in Sacred Intimacy with God

As the worship dance of awe and gratitude fills your spirit, soul, and body, your spiritual homecoming will take on a deep intimacy with God and have a significant effect on your world. The awe in your relationship with God will bring you into deep rest. Rest will disrupt your frenetic "doing," and instead your actions will flow from gratefulness to God and rest in God. You will be able to love God and love your neighbor with passion, giftedness, and purpose!

Your Passion, Giftedness, and Worship

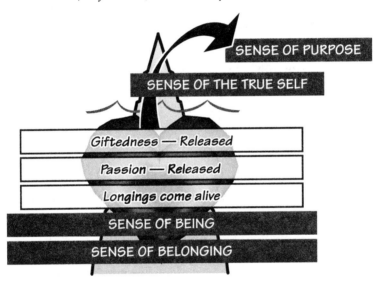

Releasing Your Passion

> *Now there was a man of the Pharisees, named Nicodemus, a ruler of the Jews; this man came to Jesus by night and said to Him, "Rabbi, we know that You have come from God as a teacher; for no one can do these signs that You do unless God is with him." Jesus answered and said to him, "Truly, truly, I say to you, unless one is born again he cannot see the kingdom of*

*God." Nicodemus said to Him, "How can a man be born when he is old? He cannot enter a second time into his mother's womb and be born, can he?" Jesus answered, "Truly, truly, I say to you, **unless one is born of water and the Spirit he cannot enter into the kingdom of God.** "That which is born of the flesh is flesh, and that which is born of the Spirit is spirit. "Do not be amazed that I said to you, 'You must be born again.' "The wind blows where it wishes and you hear the sound of it, but do not know where it comes from and where it is going; so is everyone who is born of the Spirit."*

(John 3:1-8, NASB, emphasis added)

Passion

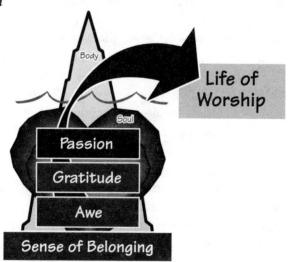

When you are spiritually born again, your human spirit is filled with deep passion and empowered by enormous strength through the Holy Spirit. Your core guilt and core shame are automatically released to the Cross. Your passion, which guilt and shame had tried to bury, is then called forth in you by the power of Jesus Christ.

You may know a lot of people who profess to be reborn and yet their lives seem no different. I do too. When you are reborn in the spirit, that is not the end of the story, but the beginning. A reborn life is where the personal battle and spiritual warfare play themselves out.

When you say yes to Jesus Christ, making Him Lord of your life, you are turning from a life of rebellion toward a life of obedience to God. You are saying no to the Baal worship of addictions and co-addictions. You are releasing your relational sin and relational pain to the Cross.

Unfortunately, the enemy attacks you through the seduction of artificial passions. A life of idolatry promises to be better than the real thing. This is the point at which you struggle with the forces of good and evil. When you betray God through idolatry, new guilt and shame begin to bury your passion again.

If you are not daily thinking about the reality that Jesus Christ lives in you, you will start to think more about self and will go back down the road to self-centeredness—narcissism. If you are not daily listening and obeying God, you will live out further rebellion, which results in deeper emptiness, more addictive idolatry, and another layer of deadness will be on the pile!

If you are not daily releasing at the Cross (daily dying) and daily receiving at the Cross (daily rising), the strongholds of addictive and co-addictive bondage will continue to strangle the life out of your spirit, further burying passion, giftedness, and purpose. However, the miracle of awe and gratitude can fill you with the power of the Holy Spirit to change from the inside out.

> *Do not get drunk on wine, which leads to debauchery. Instead, be filled with the Spirit. Speak to one another with psalms, hymns and spiritual songs. Sing and make music in your heart to the Lord, always giving thanks to God the Father for everything, in the name of our Lord Jesus Christ.*
>
> (Ephesians 5:18-20, NIV)

This verse references getting drunk on wine, but apply it to your own struggle. Do not take comfort in reckless spending, which leads to relational strife and financial problems. Instead, be filled with the Spirit…. Do not fill your mind with pornographic images, which dishonor your sexuality. But be filled with the Spirit…. Do not gorge on junk food, which leads to obesity and health problems. But be filled with the Spirit…

As you already know, Jesus takes you to the Father, and the Father releases the gifts of the Holy Spirit within your human spirit. The Holy Spirit within you offers extraordinary power. Only when you are empowered by the Holy Spirit can you make a lifestyle decision not to rebel against God. The unmatchable strength of God is what you need to fight the personal battles of your human nature, the world around you, and Satan. The power of the Holy Spirit is your supernatural artillery for the frontlines of your spiritual warfare.

> *Finally, **be strong in the Lord and in his mighty power.** Put on the full armor of God so that you can take your stand against the devil's schemes. For our struggle is not against flesh and blood, but against the rulers, against the authorities, against the powers of this dark world and against the spiritual forces of evil in the heavenly realms. Therefore **put on the full armor of God,** so that when the day of evil comes, you may be able to stand your ground, and after you have done everything, to stand. **Stand firm** then, with the **belt of truth** buckled around your waist, with the **breastplate of righteousness** in place, and with your feet fitted with the readiness that comes from the **gospel of peace.** In addition to all this, take up the **shield of faith,** with which you can extinguish all the flaming arrows of the evil one. Take the **helmet of salvation** and the **sword of the Spirit,** which is the **word of God.** And **pray in the Spirit on all occasions** with all kinds of prayers and requests. With this in mind, **be alert** and always keep on praying for all the saints.*
>
> *(Ephesians 6:10-18, NIV, emphasis added)*

Five Critical Spiritual Homecoming Questions

Ask yourself the following questions each day of this spiritual battle.

1. What is my relational sin—the daily choices I make to rebel against God?
2. What is my relational pain—the emptiness I feel of not being loved and not loving others well?
3. What is the relational Cross—my daily releasing and receiving at the Cross?
4. How do I take up my Cross daily? How do I listen to God and obey Him daily?
5. How do I follow Christ, daily dying and daily rising with Him?

The Spiritual Homecoming Process

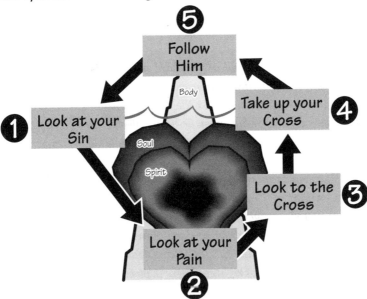

As you choose to daily repent of your rebellion against God, you will be empowered by the Holy Spirit. This process will unlock something very deep and passionately alive within the core of your being, as though the Creator has just breathed new life into you. In fact, you will experience daily healing in your sense of belonging and sense of being as the Holy Spirit daily empowers you. The love of God will continue to unlock your deep passion. You will journey with new giftedness and new purpose!

Releasing Your Giftedness

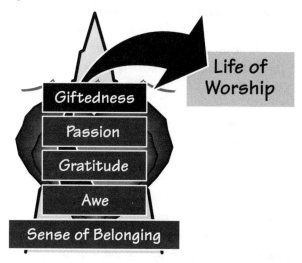

As the love and strength of God releases your passion through a new level of intimacy with Him, God's Spirit will then release your giftedness. When you start to live out your giftedness by God's empowering, you will be amazed by how God pours His love out to the world through your life.

Beth comes from a Catholic background. I come from a Luthern background and was trained in a conservative evangelical seminary. I longed to daily experience more of the power and presence of God in my life.

A year after Beth and I were married, she wanted to attend a conference on holiness in Alberta, Canada. Prior to this, I had only experienced traditional worship. The worship leader invited the Holy Spirit to be present before we started to worship—all he said was, "Come Holy Spirit, Come." It was the first time in my life that I could sense the literal presence of the holiness of the living God in such a tangible way. It was an Isaiah 6 experience:

*In the year of King Uzziah's death I saw the Lord sitting
on a throne, lofty and exalted, with the train of His
robe filling the temple. Seraphim stood above Him, each
having six wings: with two he covered his face, and with
two he covered his feet, and with two he flew.*

*And one called out to another and said,
"Holy, Holy, Holy, is the LORD of hosts,
The whole earth is full of His glory."*

*And the foundations of the thresholds trembled at the
voice of him who called out, while the temple was filling
with smoke.*

*Then I said,
**"Woe is me, for I am ruined!
Because I am a man of unclean lips,
And I live among a people of unclean lips;
For my eyes have seen the King, the** LORD **of
hosts."***

*Then one of the seraphim flew to me with a burning
coal in his hand, which he had taken from the altar with
tongs.*

*He touched my mouth with it and said, **"Behold, this
has touched your lips; and your iniquity is taken
away and your sin is forgiven."** Then I heard the voice
of the Lord, saying, "Whom shall I send, and who will go
for Us?" Then I said, "Here am I. Send me!"*
(Isaiah 6:1-8, NASB, emphasis added)

I cried throughout the entire worship time—a man who rarely
ever cried and certainly not in public. That experience awakened
my awe of the Holy Spirit. The presence of the living God was
very real and personal. I was awakened to see that the power of
the Kingdom of God was here, now, in the twenty-first century.

Open to God in New Ways

God greatly empowered me for ministry during that five-day conference. The next week astonished me in my private practice as a licensed psychologist. God gave me insight beyond my human wisdom. In one case, I perceived that a new client was having an affair. In our first session, I asked her husband to leave the room momentarily, and I asked her if she was having an affair. She turned ghost white and said, "Yes." I was stunned that God had given me this insight on her behalf. Instead of the client hiding in fear and shame for months (or perhaps never sharing the truth), she accepted gracious confrontation, ended her affair, and began to genuinely work on her marriage. The couple's therapy could have gone on indefinitely without this issue exposed and addressed so quickly. Their marriage came through the process well. They experienced the freedom, healing, restoration, and transformation that they needed to walk through their crisis and go to their core root issues.

My understanding and belief in deeper deliverance, healing, restoration, and transformation was changed by that experience. As you daily look beyond yourself to the Creator, the Giver of gifts, He will empower you to do the work of the Kingdom. However, focusing on spiritual gifts can also trap you in spiritual narcissism—self-centeredness. The apostle Paul gives perspective in valuing all spiritual gifts:

> Now **about spiritual gifts,** brothers, **I do not want you to be ignorant.** You know that when you were pagans, somehow or other you were influenced and led astray to mute idols. Therefore I tell you that no one who is speaking by the Spirit of God says, "Jesus be cursed," and **no one can say, "Jesus is Lord,"** except by the Holy Spirit. There are **different kinds of gifts,** but the same Spirit. There are different kinds of **service,** but the same Lord. There are different kinds of **working, but the same God works all of them in all men.**

Now **to each one the manifestation of the Spirit is given for the common good.** *To one there is given through the Spirit the message of* **wisdom,** *to another the message of* **knowledge** *by means of the same Spirit, to another* **faith** *by the same Spirit, to another* **gifts of healing** *by that one Spirit, to another* **miraculous powers,** *to another* **prophecy,** *to another* **distinguishing between spirits,** *to another* **speaking in different kinds of tongues,** *and to still another the* **interpretation of tongues.** **All these are the work of one and the same Spirit, and he gives them to each one, just as he determines.***

The body is a unit, though it is made up of many parts; and though all its parts are many, they form one body. So it is with Christ. For we were all baptized by one Spirit into one body—whether Jews or Greeks, slave or free—and we were all given the one Spirit to drink.

Now **the body is not made up of one part but of many.** *If the foot should say, "Because I am not a hand, I do not belong to the body," it would not for that reason cease to be part of the body. And if the ear should say, "Because I am not an eye, I do not belong to the body," it would not for that reason cease to be part of the body. If the whole body were an eye, where would the sense of hearing be? If the whole body were an ear, where would the sense of smell be? But in fact God has arranged the parts in the body, every one of them, just as he wanted them to be. If they were all one part, where would the body be? As it is,* **there are many parts, but one body.**

The eye cannot say to the hand, "I don't need you!" And the head cannot say to the feet, "I don't need you!" On the contrary, those parts of the body that seem to be weaker are indispensable, and the parts that we think are less honorable we treat with special honor.

*And the parts that are unpresentable are treated with
special modesty, while our presentable parts need no
special treatment. But God has combined the members
of the body and has given greater honor to the parts
that lacked it, so that **there should be no division in
the body,** but that its parts should have equal concern
for each other. If one part suffers, every part suffers
with it; if one part is honored, every part rejoices with
it.*

*Now **you are the body of Christ, and each one of you
is a part of it.** And in the church God has appointed
first of all **apostles,** second **prophets,** third **teachers,**
then **workers of miracles,** also those having **gifts of
healing,** those able to **help** others, those with gifts of
administration, and those speaking in different kinds
of **tongues.** Are all apostles? Are all prophets? Are all
teachers? Do all work miracles? Do all have gifts of
healing? Do all speak in tongues? Do all interpret?
But **eagerly desire the greater gifts.***

*And now I will show you **the most excellent way...***
(1 Corinthians 12:1-31, NIV, emphasis added)

Paul emphasizes that the body of Christ is made up of people
who are gifted in all sorts of ways that benefit each other. But
better than the gifts is "the most excellent way": Love is the most
excellent way. Faith and hope are pivotal for our Christian life,
now and for all eternity, but love is even more important. Love
is what enables us to live now, putting into perspective just how
small are the concerns that most offend our pride or consume our
attentions or would distract us from what really matters. Paul
describes the supreme nature of love:

*If I speak in the tongues of men and of angels, but have
not love, I am only a resounding gong or a clanging
cymbal. If I have the gift of prophecy and can fathom
all mysteries and all knowledge, and **if** I have a*

*faith that can move mountains, but **have not love,***
***I am nothing.** If I give all I possess to the poor and*
surrender my body to the flames, but have not love, I
gain nothing....

                      (1 Corinthians 13:1-3, NIV, emphasis added)

Spiritual gifts are powerful tools that God intends us to use for His glory and for the good of the Kingdom. But it is possible to do more harm than good with our gifts. For without love, the gifts are worthless. Tongues, prophecy, faith, helping the poor—any gift is worthless without love. Is it hard to fathom that? A context in which helping the poor is worthless? We are accustomed to attributing value to deeds, to "doing," not to the heart, to "being." Any gift can be misused. Without your gift being used to love, it is like a lot of worthless noise.

Yet, with love, the gifts are important! God does not give us unimportant things. The gifts are tools with which to love others, ourselves, and God. After Paul describes how worthless the gifts are without love, then he launches into what love looks like in daily life. This is a favorite passage of Christians and non-Christians alike. We are compelled toward love. Don't we all wish to experience love like this from others? Don't we all wish to live this kind of love ourselves?

> *...Love is patient, love is kind. It does not envy, it does not boast, it is not proud. It is not rude, it is not self-seeking, it is not easily angered, it keeps no record of wrongs. Love does not delight in evil but rejoices with the truth. It always protects, always trusts, always hopes, always perseveres.*

> ***Love never fails.** But where there are prophecies, they will cease; where there are tongues, they will be stilled; where there is knowledge, it will pass away. For we know in part and we prophesy in part, but when perfection comes, the imperfect disappears. When I was a child, I talked like a child, I thought like a child,*

I reasoned like a child. When I became a man, I put childish ways behind me. Now we see but a poor reflection as in a mirror; then we shall see face to face. Now I know in part; then I shall know fully, even as I am fully known.

*And now **these three remain: faith, hope and love. But the greatest of these is love.***
(1 Corinthians 13:4-13, NIV, emphasis added)

Love will endure when all of the gifts have faded and passed away. This passage suggests it is childish to focus on what is passing and temporary, but a mature man or woman puts away childish things. The mature person focuses on what is lasting and primary: faith, hope, and love. But the greatest of these is love.

Friend, my point is that as you continue in your spiritual homecoming, look to the Giver of the gifts, the Holy Spirit. In the process, the deep gifts that God has placed within you will be released in His timing for His glory. When God releases your giftedness, His goal is that you become a person who loves. Your gifts are tools for carrying out your purpose of loving God, yourself, and others well. And **growth as a Christian means increasing more and more in love.**

Releasing Your Purpose

How does God release your purpose? This is the conclusion from the wisest man in history, King Solomon:

The conclusion, when all has been heard, is: fear God and keep His commandments, because this applies to every person.
(Ecclesiastes 12:13, NASB)

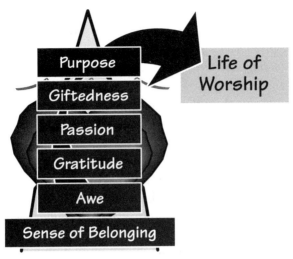

What is the greatest commandment? The Pharisees asked this of Jesus.

> *One of the scribes came and heard them arguing, and recognizing that He had answered them well, asked Him, "What commandment is the foremost of all?"*
>
> *Jesus answered, "The foremost is, 'HEAR, O ISRAEL! THE LORD OUR GOD IS ONE LORD; AND YOU SHALL LOVE THE LORD YOUR GOD WITH ALL YOUR HEART, AND WITH ALL YOUR SOUL, AND WITH ALL YOUR MIND, AND WITH ALL YOUR STRENGTH.' "The second is this, 'YOU SHALL LOVE YOUR NEIGHBOR AS YOURSELF.' There is no other commandment greater than these."*
>
> *The scribe said to Him, "Right, Teacher; You have truly stated that HE IS ONE, AND THERE IS NO ONE ELSE BESIDES HIM; AND TO LOVE HIM WITH ALL THE HEART AND WITH ALL THE UNDERSTANDING AND WITH ALL THE*

STRENGTH, AND TO LOVE ONE'S NEIGHBOR AS HIMSELF, is much more than all burnt offerings and sacrifices."

When Jesus saw that he had answered intelligently, He said to him, "You are not far from the kingdom of God." After that, no one would venture to ask Him any more questions.

(Mark 12:28-34, NASB)

Why is love the greatest commandment? The opposite of betrayal is love. The opposite of the four journey betrayals—betrayals of you, your betrayals of others, your betrayals of yourself, and your betrayals of God—is to love the Lord your God and to love others. This is the whole point of life on earth. When you fear (reverence) God and love Him, through that submission, He releases you to fulfill your purpose. **Your purpose is to glorify Him.**

The enemy of love is self-centeredness, or narcissism, which shows itself at your core in rebellion against the living God. For many of us, that knowledge will not necessarily cause us to change. It often takes a medical crisis, the death of a loved one, or other tragedy for us to acknowledge our human finiteness.

Moments before I went into surgery at the Mayo Clinic for prostate cancer at age 44, the brevity of life became real to me. As I lay there on the gurney, there was only one place to look, and that was up. I was being "stripped" of my health, perhaps stripped of my very life. If I died I would be stripped of being a husband to the woman of my dreams, stripped of being a father to five very young children. The ache I felt within was the grief that life was not as stable and secure as I had believed.

I wish I could say I responded to medical crisis with the maturity of faith and trust. I did just the opposite. I struggled with the immaturity of fear and uncertainty about the outcome of my life, marriage, family, private practice, and ministry. But Christ was a steady presence within me, and He surrounded me beyond the swirling chaos of going under the knife.

287

The stripping of all my props in life leveled my arrogance and pride. The helplessness of leaving my fate in the hands of others and, ultimately, God, was humbling. It brought me into a deeper reality, that of eternal life—life after death. It was a process of losing myself in the Spirit of God in order to be found in the Spirit of God; a process of accepting the stripping that left me naked in order to be clothed in the Spirit of God. His covering brought me into a deeper security and faith than I had ever known.

Sacred Intimacy

There is a sacred intimacy that God wants to give to His people:

- The love of God—to be in awe and gratitude that God is embracing me.
- The strength of God—to turn from rebellion to listening and obeying God.
- The fire of God—to burn up the bondage and strongholds of Baal worship or idolatry in my life.
- The water of God—to be washed in forgiveness and cleansing every day.
- The oil of God—to be healed and anointed to love God and others every day.

You see, before you can love the Lord your God with all of your heart, mind, and strength, you have to first receive His love. As the cup of your spirit is filled with the tenderness of love from the Lord God Almighty, then you can love God and others.

So, each day, as the candle is lit and a worship song plays, I hold a small crucifix in my hand and simply receive the love of God by declaring, "Abba, I belong to You. I ask You this day for my daily bread of belonging and being."

As I embrace the presence of God, He fills me with His strength of love to listen and to obey Him as I prepare to enter into listening prayer and listening obedience. I know today that my flesh is weak and that it is only in my weakness that His strength is made perfect.

Because of the surpassing greatness of the revelations,
*for this reason, **to keep me from exalting myself,***

there was given me a thorn in the flesh, a messenger
of Satan to torment me—to keep me from exalting
myself! Concerning this I implored the Lord three
times that it might leave me. And He has said to
me, "My grace is sufficient for you, for power
is perfected in weakness." Most gladly, therefore,
I will rather boast about my weaknesses, so that the
power of Christ may dwell in me. Therefore I am well
content with weaknesses, with insults, with distresses,
with persecutions, with difficulties, for Christ's sake;
for when I am weak, then I am strong.

(2 Corinthians 12:7-10, NASB, emphasis added)

Since my battle with cancer, I try to live each day with the hunger and thirst to have the power of the Holy Spirit guide the rest of this journey. As you can see, **the word "perfected" implies process.** Each day as you bring your earthly weakness to the Cross, the Lord Jesus will pour out His grace to you as you cry out to Him.

To daily die and daily rise with Christ, I need His holy fire to burn up the bondage and strongholds of Baal in my life that I have allowed in the last twenty-four hours. Human nature pulls us toward false gods. When I pray for the fire of God to fill me and empower me, I hold the candle of worship to represent this, and the Holy Spirit ministers to me.

As I daily release to the Cross my sin and pain, the effects the world has had upon me, and the impact of spiritual warfare in my life, then I receive God's forgiveness, cleansing, and gifts of His Spirit. I use holy water that I have blessed in prayer to make the sign of the Cross on my forehead to represent the cleansing of my spirit, soul, and body.

Finally, I use anointing oil to also make the sign of the Cross on my forehead to represent the healing and anointing with which the Holy Spirit wants to empower me each day.

To experience lasting change on this spiritual journey, you have to be filled with the love of God. You will need to choose daily deliverance and daily repentance. Daily deliverance—represented by God's fire, water, and oil—will bring you into a passionate release of freedom. However, it is daily repentance that will bring you into a deep inner healing of spirit, soul, and body.

To be blunt, most people are interested in the healing and restoration but not in the repentance. I hope it does not take a medical crisis or a death of a loved one for you to repent of your rebellion and idolatry. Repentance is what brings the awe and gratitude of worship that is the essence of your life now and your life forevermore.

As I quoted C. S. Lewis in Stage Six, God used pain as a megaphone to get my attention. He has my attention today! However, I had to be stripped of myself in the process. He used my pain to expose my rebellion.

> *You shall remember all the way which the LORD your God has **led you in the wilderness** these forty years, **that He might humble you, testing you, to know what was in your heart, whether you would keep His commandments or not.** He humbled you and let you be hungry, and fed you with manna which you did not know, nor did your fathers know, that He might make you understand that **man does not live by bread alone, but man lives by everything that proceeds out of the mouth of the LORD.***
> *(Deuteronomy 8:2, 3, NASB, emphasis added)*

As a good Father, God also uses pain to train us and build our character: He leads us, He humbles us, He tests us, He makes us hungry, and He feeds us.

*One thing God has spoken, two things that I have heard: that you, O God, are **STRONG,** and that you, O Lord, are **LOVING.***
                    (Psalm 62:11-12, NIV, emphasis added)

As you make your lifetime spiritual journey, allow God to lead you. Many times of humbling will come to draw you away from rebellion and back into awe and gratitude. The Lord God will test the true convictions of your heart. He will lovingly show you the hunger and thirst in your spirit. As He fills and empowers you with His love and strength, your passion, giftedness, and purpose will be released for His glory!

Jesus will feed your hunger and will draw a cold cup of living water from the well to quench your thirst. Nothing matters more on this journey, and the journey to come, than allowing Jesus to minister to you and for you to love God and love others in response. That is life.

Personal Journaling and Small Group Questions
Spiritual Homecoming Assignment Eleven

Personal Journaling Questions

1. Each day in the next week, ask yourself these questions:
    *   What are the daily choices I make to rebel against God?
    *   What emptiness do I feel—have I experienced betrayals recently?

2. Spend time praying, releasing those betrayals at the Cross and receiving God's forgiveness, cleansing, and gifts of the Holy Spirit.

3. Write down what you will do today to listen to God and obey Him.

4. Practice sacred intimacy with God:
    In your journal, write tangible ways in which you will pursue sacred intimacy with God this month:
    *   The love of God—to be in awe and gratitude that God is embracing me.
    *   The strength of God—to turn from rebellion to listening and obeying God.
    *   The fire of God—to burn up the bondage and strongholds of idolatry in my life.
    *   The water of God—to be washed in forgiveness and cleansing every day.
    *   The oil of God—to be healed and anointed to love God and others every day.

5. Answer these questions through the month:
    *   What is my passion?
    *   What is my giftedness?
    *   What is my purpose?

Small Group Questions

1. What... are the key truths that stood out to you in this stage?
2. Why... do you need to know these truths?
3. How... do you apply these truths to your life?

4. Your pain... What pain does this stage reveal in your life?
5. Your sin... What are you doing with your pain?
6. Repentance... What do you need to do differently?
7. Prayer... What do you need to ask God for help with?

STAGE TWELVE: The Journey Together
Living in Authentic Intimacy with Others

God, grant me serenity to accept the things I cannot change, courage to change the things I can and wisdom to know the difference: living one day at a time, enjoying one moment at a time: accepting hardship as a pathway to peace: taking, as Jesus did, this sinful world as it is not as I would have it: trusting that You will make all things right if I surrender to Your will: so that I may be reasonably happy in this life and supremely happy with You forever in the next. Amen.[32]

(Original Serenity Prayer, 1892-1971)

The final stage of your spiritual homecoming is walking out this spiritual journey together in community. You cannot do this journey alone; you need the support and challenge of fellow believers.

The apostle Paul lived out his ministry from the depths of rest and then passion. You will notice in his model for ministry to the church of Thessalonica that he came to them as a man who humbly served them in three capacities: a spiritual mother, a spiritual father, and a spiritual brother.

Taking Time to be Filled with God's Love

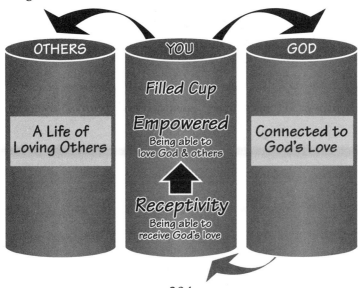

Paul came first with the tenderness of love to spiritually nurture the church. Then he graciously equipped them with a strength of love as a father would have for his children. However, he left them as a spiritual brother. They were brought up in the faith to a point of maturity that filled them with the peace of love that surpasses all understanding.

The Church: A Spiritual Mother

The apostle Paul is one of the most masculine men in the Bible. I believe his masculinity was exceptionally strong because he understood the wisdom of resting in his spirit with his God before passionately proclaiming the gospel through his life.

Modeling a Spiritual Mother

> *But we proved to be **gentle** among you, **as a nursing mother tenderly cares for her own children**. Having so fond an affection for you, we were well-pleased to impart to you not only the gospel of God but also our own lives, because you had become very dear to us.*
>
> (*1 Thessalonians 2:7-8, NASB, emphasis added*)

He came to the church with a relational sensitivity to the children of God who needed the milk of the Word of God. Paul took the time to receive the love of God first in his own life. (I guess a bolt of lightning from the heavens would put anyone's priorities in order!)

If we are going to shift to being a church that rests in the Spirit first, before doing, we will become a church of receptivity. As we choose to be healed of our pain regarding sense of belonging and sense of being, our rebellion will be disrupted in the process. We repent of our rebellion—repent of our restlessness and filling our lives with "doing"—by deliberately choosing to enter into rest.

Restoring Your Foundation: Sense of Belonging and Being

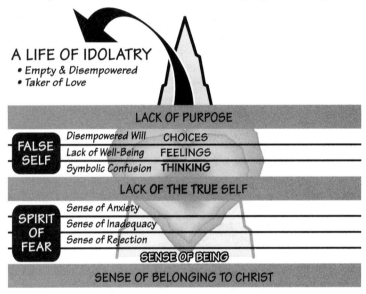

When you are in awe of God, you will start to see the mother heart of God that wants to tenderly care for the Church like a nursing mother tenderly cares for her own children.

> *O Jerusalem, Jerusalem, the city that kills the prophets*
> *and stones those sent to her! How often I wanted to*
> *gather your children together, just as a hen gathers her*
> *brood under her wings, and you would not have it!*
> *(Luke 13:34, NASB)*

296

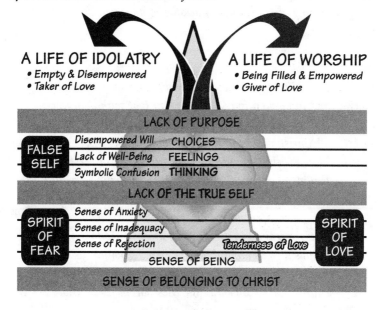

This is a picture of the mother heart of the Lord God—a hen with tenderness of love in longing to brood over her chicks. There has been such contempt for the feminine—misogyny—in the Church that we have historically rejected the "spiritual nursing" of spiritual growth and formation. We have a lot of spiritually stunted and malnourished adults trying to lead the Church through daily spiritual warfare.

Reflect on the prayer below that includes two prayers that Paul prayed for the "Church at large." Paul is asking God to fill His people with tenderness of love. As leaders in the Church, we need to take time before worship, during worship, and at the end of worship, to invite the presence of God to fill the people of God with tenderness of love:

Sense of Belonging and Being Prayers

> *Dear God,*
> *Would you fill your daughters and sons with your*
> *deep tenderness of love? God, would You start to fill*

and empower Your children with Your love for inner healing of their sense of belonging and their sense of being?

We ask:
That Christ will live in you as you open the door and invite him in. And I ask him that with both feet planted firmly on love, you'll be able to take in with all Christians the extravagant dimensions of Christ's love. Reach out and experience the breadth! Test its length! Plumb the depths! Rise to the heights! Live full lives, full in the fullness of God. God can do anything, you know—far more than you could ever imagine or guess or request in your wildest dreams! He does it not by pushing us around but by working within us, his Spirit deeply and gently within us. Glory to God in the church! Glory to God in the Messiah, in Jesus! Glory down all the generations! Glory through all millennia! Oh, yes!

(Ephesians 3:17-21, MSG)

Receive now the tenderness of God's love filling your spirit, soul, and body.

In the precious name of Jesus,
Amen!

Men, I learned the art of receptivity from a woman. Women naturally teach relational rest more effectively than men, according to Stasi Eldredge in her book *Captivating*.[33] I encourage men of the Church to learn from the women of the Church. God has gifted us differently; we need to learn from each other in order to be the Church that God desires us to be. We need to release each other to minister as the Lord releases giftedness in each of us. It is the Lord's ministry and the gifts of the Holy Spirit, not our ministry and not our gifts. Let us not, in any way, be obstacles to what the Holy Spirit wants to do through the entire Church.

> *"Then I passed by you and saw you, and behold, you
> were at the time for love; so I spread My skirt over
> you and covered your nakedness. I also swore to you
> and entered into a covenant with you so that you
> became Mine," declares the Lord GOD. "Then I bathed
> you with water, washed off your blood from you and
> anointed you with oil."*
>
> *(Ezekiel 16:8-9, NASB)*

The Lord is calling us back into the awe of seeing the beauty and strength of God. The Lord God is rebuilding the foundation of the Church. A foundational sense of being comes in part from embracing the daily presence of Christ. This will bring men and women into incredible rest. Listening prayer and listening obedience will not only fill us with the love of God but will also strengthen our intimacy with God.

As the Church chooses to enter into deeper levels of sacred intimacy, the fire of the Spirit will bring great deliverance to the Church. The water of the Spirit will continue to bring deep forgiveness and cleansing to the Church. The oil of the Spirit will bring transformational healing and anointing in the Church.

A sense of being in the spirit will steer the Church onto a path of becoming that will impact the world. As we choose to rest in God's mercy, we will receive the intimacy of relationship that we all desperately crave. Only the true God of the universe can fill us. This position of restful, relational receptivity will greatly empower the Church with magnificent gratitude and love for God and others!

The Church: A Spiritual Father
As a spiritual father, the apostle Paul had a great strength of love for his spiritual children as a spiritual father. He knew foundational sense of being and had a passion to release the power of the Holy Spirit to build up the Church.

Life of Ministry

Spiritual Father
(Strength of Love)

Spiritual Mother
(Tendernes of Love)

Sense of Belonging

*Having so fond an affection for you, we were well-pleased to impart to you not only the gospel of God but also our own lives, because you had become very dear to us. For you recall, brethren, our labor and hardship, how working night and day so as not to be a burden to any of you, we proclaimed to you the gospel of God. You are witnesses, and so is God, how devoutly and uprightly and blamelessly we behaved toward you believers; just as you know how we were **exhorting and encouraging and imploring each one of you as a father would his own children,** so that you would walk in a manner worthy of the God who calls you into His own kingdom and glory. For this reason we also constantly thank God that when you received the word of God which you heard from us, you accepted it not as the word of men, but for what it really is, the word of God, which also performs its work in you who believe.*

(1 Thessalonians 2:8-13, NASB, emphasis added)

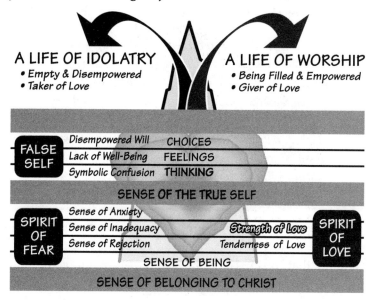

As the Church deepens in rest, the passion to move in the power of the Holy Spirit will explode like the days of Pentecost. I believe that God is about to release signs and wonders that will bring both those who know Him and those who do not into the wondrous mystery of the Father, the Son, and the Holy Spirit!

> *So he got up and came to his father. But while he was still a long way off, his **father saw him and felt compassion for him,** and ran and embraced him and kissed him.*
> *(Luke 15:20, NASB, emphasis added)*

This story in Luke illustrates the father-heart of God. God is a father with the passion to move toward His child. His love is tender and yet has a relentless strength; a love that is filled with compassion and longing to embrace. God is a father to the fatherless generation. He longs to adopt you as His son or daughter. When this happens, you will be filled with the spirit of adoption. The spirit of adoption is how the Lord fills us with His love and how we experience our spiritual homecoming. It is the opposite of the spirit of fear. It gives us a new identity

301

and yearning for our Heavenly Father—it puts a cry of "Abba" (Daddy) into our hearts for the Father God of the universe.

> For **you have not received a spirit of slavery leading to fear** again, **but you have received a spirit of adoption** as sons by which we cry out, "Abba! Father!" The Spirit Himself testifies with our spirit that we are children of God, and if children, heirs also, heirs of God and fellow heirs with Christ, if indeed we suffer with Him so that we may also be glorified with Him.
>
> (Romans 8:15-17, NASB, emphasis added)

One of the most amazing things that will occur when you are filled and empowered by the Holy Spirit is that the Spirit of God will testify that you are His child and He is now your Father. Your spirit will naturally cry out, "Abba!"

The Coming Battle

When we are sealed by the spirit of adoption, we are warriors of our Father, engaged in battles that are not against flesh and blood but against principalities and powers. The holy fire of God is coming to tear up the strongholds of Baal that have been erected in every culture. The Holy Fire will bring tremendous power to set the captives free of generational strongholds and bring great freedom to all who will bend their knees to the Almighty God of the universe.

The time is coming to call rebellion what it is. As mentioned earlier, we are being devoured by personal disasters, man-made disasters and natural disasters. The Lord God is roaring as the Lion of Judah saying, "Enough is enough!" God is crying out to all of humanity. Hear the cry of the Father that sees death knocking at the door of His beloved children.

> [If] My people who are called by My name humble themselves and pray and seek My face and turn from their wicked ways, then I will hear from heaven, will forgive their sin and will heal their land.
>
> (2 Chronicles 7:14, NASB)

God is calling us to:
- Humble ourselves
- Pray to Him
- Seek His face
- Turn from our wicked ways

The glorious coming of our King is on the horizon, and we are preparing as the Church to become the Bride of Christ. It is critical that we renew our spiritual vows every day. As Church leaders personally take up their crosses daily and follow Christ, the rest of the body of Christ will follow with new courage and humility.

> *"The Son of Man must suffer many things and be rejected by the elders and chief priests and scribes, and be killed and be raised up on the third day." And He was saying to them all, **"If anyone wishes to come after Me, he must deny himself, and take up his cross daily and follow Me.** For whoever wishes to save his life will lose it, but whoever loses his life for My sake, he is the one who will save it. For what is a man profited if he gains the whole world, and loses or forfeits himself? For whoever is ashamed of Me and My words, the Son of Man will be ashamed of him when He comes in His glory, and the glory of the Father and of the holy angels. But I say to you truthfully, there are some of those standing here who will not taste death until they see the kingdom of God."*
> —Jesus (Luke 9:22-27, NASB, emphasis added)

As followers of Christ, we need to first personally live out daily dying and daily rising with Him. Baal worship is destroying the spirits of all people. As we mature spiritually, with receptivity to the love of the Lord, we will grow in the strength of the Lord. We are living in dangerous times where we need the Holy Spirit to fill and empower us each step of the way.

Let's reflect again on the prayers of empowerment from the apostle Paul.

> *For this reason I too, having heard of the faith in the Lord Jesus which exists among you and your love for all the saints, do not cease giving thanks for you, while making mention of you in my prayers; that the God of our Lord Jesus Christ, the Father of glory, may give to you **a spirit of wisdom and of revelation** in the knowledge of Him. I pray that the **eyes of your heart may be enlightened, so that you will know what is the hope of His calling...***
> (Ephesians 1:15-18, NASB, emphasis added)

The apostle Paul prays that the Church will be filled with the spirit of wisdom and the spirit of revelation because he knows that as the Church is filled with wisdom and revelation, our eyes will open to the satanic deception that has darkened the hearts of humankind. Paul knew that as people are filled with wisdom and revelation right from the very heart of God, they would receive and experience the surpassing greatness of God's power in their lives.

> *Dear God,*
> *Please fill your daughters and sons with your deep strength of love? God, let your love start to fill and empower your children with a passion to live with deep purpose in becoming a people of the Cross of Christ?*
>
> *Father, impassion us to fight as the army of Christ in representing Christ well to the nation and to the nations.*
>
> *Lord Jesus, we hear the shout from the heavens. We are prepared for the blast of the trumpets. Come Holy Spirit, come!*

We ask:

*For this reason I bow my knees before the Father, from whom every family in heaven and on earth derives its name, that He would grant you, according to the riches of His glory, **to be strengthened with power through His Spirit in the inner man.***

(Ephesians 3:14-16, NASB, *emphasis added*)

***I pray that the eyes of your heart may be enlightened,** so that you will know what is the hope of His calling, what are the riches of the glory of His inheritance in the saints, and what is the surpassing greatness of His power toward us who believe. These are in accordance with the working of the strength of His might which He brought about in Christ, when He raised Him from the dead and seated Him at His right hand in the heavenly places, far above all rule and authority and power and dominion, and every name that is named, not only in this age but also in the one to come. And He put all things in subjection under His feet, and gave Him as head over all things to the church, which is His body, the fullness of Him who fills all in all.*

(Ephesians 1:18-23, NASB, *emphasis added*)

In the mighty name of the Lord Jesus Christ, Amen!

The Church: A Spiritual Brother

The apostle Paul wanted to empower believers as his equals. He started out by relating to them with the tender love of a spiritual mother. He then guided them with the strength of a spiritual father. Finally, he left them with the peaceful love of a spiritual brother.

For you, **brethren,** became imitators of the churches of God in Christ Jesus that are in Judea, for you also endured the same sufferings at the hands of your own countrymen, even as they did from the Jews, who both killed the Lord Jesus and the prophets, and drove us out. They are not pleasing to God, but hostile to all men, hindering us from speaking to the Gentiles so that they may be saved; with the result that they always fill up the measure of their sins. But wrath has come upon them to the utmost. But we, **brethren,** having been taken away from you for a short while—in person, not in spirit—were all the more eager with great desire to see your face. For we wanted to come to you—I, Paul, more than once—and yet Satan hindered us. For **who is our hope or joy or crown of exultation? Is it not even you,** in the presence of our Lord Jesus at His coming? For **you are our glory and joy.**

(1 Thessalonians 2:14-20, NASB, emphasis added)

306

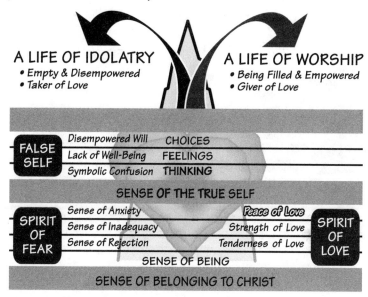

A LIFE OF IDOLATRY
- Empty & Disempowered
- Taker of Love

A LIFE OF WORSHIP
- Being Filled & Empowered
- Giver of Love

FALSE SELF	Disempowered Will	CHOICES
	Lack of Well-Being	FEELINGS
	Symbolic Confusion	THINKING

SENSE OF THE TRUE SELF

SPIRIT OF FEAR	Sense of Anxiety		Peace of Love	SPIRIT OF LOVE
	Sense of Inadequacy		Strength of Love	
	Sense of Rejection		Tenderness of Love	

SENSE OF BEING

SENSE OF BELONGING TO CHRIST

God's design is that we follow Him together. You can't follow Christ without the support of the Body of Christ. We each need people around us who will challenge us about our pain and about our sin. We need others around us who are also looking to the Cross, so we can look to the Cross to receive forgiveness, cleansing, and the gifts of the Spirit. The life of a Christian happens in relationships.

A Cross-Centered Small Group
Focus on the Cross

As you form small groups, don't focus on your addictions and co-addictions as the foundation of your time together. I encourage you to mature in your faith and serve one another as brothers and sisters in Christ by a Cross-centered small group format.

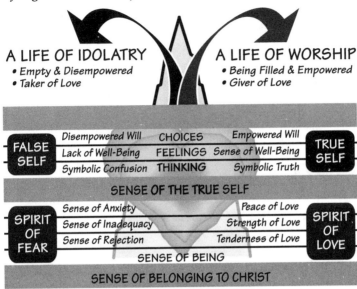

A LIFE OF IDOLATRY		A LIFE OF WORSHIP	
• Empty & Disempowered		• Being Filled & Empowered	
• Taker of Love		• Giver of Love	

FALSE SELF	Disempowered Will	CHOICES	Empowered Will	TRUE SELF
	Lack of Well-Being	FEELINGS	Sense of Well-Being	
	Symbolic Confusion	THINKING	Symbolic Truth	

SENSE OF THE TRUE SELF

SPIRIT OF FEAR	Sense of Anxiety		Peace of Love	SPIRIT OF LOVE
	Sense of Inadequacy		Strength of Love	
	Sense of Rejection		Tenderness of Love	

SENSE OF BEING

SENSE OF BELONGING TO CHRIST

When you gather as a small group and open with worship, designate someone to lift a small wooden cross or crucifix up high as you begin. Designate another person to invite the presence of the Trinity—the Father, the Son, and the Holy Spirit—into your meeting. As you gather around the Cross for worship, have some people pray the prayers of receptivity. Have others pray the prayers of empowerment. Consider closing your worship time with the Lord's Prayer.

> *Pray, then, in this way: "Our Father who is in heaven, Hallowed be Your name. Your kingdom come. Your will be done, on earth as it is in heaven. Give us this day our daily bread. And forgive us our debts, as we also have forgiven our debtors. And do not lead us into temptation, but deliver us from evil. [For Yours is the kingdom and the power and the glory forever. Amen.]"*
>
> *(Matthew 6:9-13, NASB)*

Boldly proclaim the name of Jesus in your worship and look to Him as the one who will fill you and empower you for the rest of the journey.

Accountability at the Cross

When you gather as a small group, do not simply talk about your struggles. Many times, that will reinforce introspection—immersion in thinking about yourself and your problems. I encourage you instead to ask one another if you are being faithful to:

- Embrace the presence of God.
- Spend time in listening prayer (and listening obedience).
- Renew your spiritual vows.

That is the type of spiritual accountability you need in order to disrupt the clinical problems with which you and the group struggle. That accountability will fill you with the love of God and empower you with the strength of God to experience long-term change.

Dialogue at the Cross

After everyone has shared in spiritual accountability, spend some time sharing what you have been hearing in your private time of listening prayer, and share whether you are responding with listening obedience or rebellion toward God. This is the incarnational dialogue that will bring deep deliverance and healing to your small group community and church.

Ministry of Confession

I also encourage you to have accountability partners in the group to offer the ministry of confession. This is someone with whom you can share your personal struggles. However, in order to keep the emphasis on sharing your listening prayer and listening obedience, I recommend that each person keep a written accountability log and simply give it to his or her accountability partner at the end of your time together.

Personal Prayer

It is good for the group to end with each person praying with his or her accountability partner. Invite each other to release his or her sin and pain up, out, and onto the Cross. Proclaim the forgiveness of the Lord Jesus Christ in your partner's life, and if you have holy water, make the sign of the Cross on each other's forehead to represent this. Also pray for God's hand of healing and anointing in his or her life, and anoint the person with oil if you have it.

As you serve one another in this way and walk together as brothers and sisters in the Lord, you will become a people of the Cross of Christ, a powerful force for Him that influences others in your culture and beyond, until all tribes have heard of the Lord Jesus Christ!

I pray that the Lord Jesus Christ will fill you and your community with the peace of love that surpasses all understanding.

> *So when it was evening on that day, the first day of the week, and when the doors were shut where the disciples were, for fear of the Jews, Jesus came and stood in their midst and said to them, "Peace be with you." And when He had said this, He showed them both His hands and His side. The disciples then rejoiced when they saw the Lord.*
>
> *So Jesus said to them again, **"Peace be with you; as the Father has sent Me, I also send you."** And when He had said this, He breathed on them and said to them, **"Receive the Holy Spirit. If you forgive the sins of any, their sins have been forgiven them; if you retain the sins of any, they have been retained."** But Thomas, one of the twelve, called Didymus, was not with them when Jesus came. So the other disciples were saying to him, "We have seen the Lord!" But he said to them, "Unless I see in His hands the imprint of the nails, and put my finger into the place of the nails, and put my hand into His side, I will not believe."*
>
> *After eight days His disciples were again inside, and Thomas with them. Jesus came, the doors having been shut, and stood in their midst and said, **"Peace be with you."** Then He said to Thomas, "Reach here*

with your finger, and see My hands; and reach here your hand and put it into My side; and do not be unbelieving, but believing."

Thomas answered and said to Him, "My Lord and my God!"

Jesus said to him, "Because you have seen Me, have you believed? **Blessed are they who did not see, and yet believed."** *Therefore many other signs Jesus also performed in the presence of the disciples, which are not written in this book; but* **these have been written so that you may believe that Jesus is the Christ, the Son of God; and that believing you may have life in His name.**

(John 20:19-31, NASB, emphasis added)

The Lord your God is in your midst. As you go to the Cross, the Holy Spirit within you—the Comforter—will give you everything you need. Memorize the sacred words that Jesus said to His disciples about the Comforter, the one who would see each one through his own spiritual homecoming journey.

"Do not let your heart be troubled; believe in God, believe also in Me. In My Father's house are many dwelling places; if it were not so, I would have told you; for I go to prepare a place for you. If I go and prepare a place for you, **I will come again and receive you to Myself, that where I am, there you may be also.** *And you know the way where I am going." Thomas said to Him, "Lord, we do not know where You are going, how do we know the way?" Jesus said to him,* **"I am the way, and the truth, and the life; no one comes to the Father but through Me.** *If you had known Me, you would have known My Father also; from now on you know Him, and have seen Him." Philip said to Him, "Lord, show us the Father, and it is enough for us." Jesus said to him, "Have I been so long with you, and*

yet you have not come to know Me, Philip? He who has seen Me has seen the Father; how can you say, 'Show us the Father'? Do you not believe that **I am in the Father, and the Father is in Me?** *The words that I say to you I do not speak on My own initiative, but the Father abiding in Me does His works. Believe Me that I am in the Father and the Father is in Me; otherwise believe because of the works themselves. Truly, truly, I say to you, he who believes in Me, the works that I do, he will do also; and greater works than these he will do; because I go to the Father.* **Whatever you ask in My name, that will I do, so that the Father may be glorified in the Son.** *If you ask Me anything in My name, I will do it.* **If you love Me, you will keep My commandments.** *I will ask the Father, and He will give you another* **Helper, that He may be with you forever;** *that is* **the Spirit of truth,** *whom the world cannot receive, because it does not see Him or know Him, but you know Him because* **He abides with you and will be in you.** *I will not leave you as orphans; I will come to you. After a little while the world will no longer see Me, but you will see Me; because I live, you will live also. In that day you will know that* **I am in My Father, and you in Me, and I in you.** *He who has My commandments and keeps them is the one who loves Me; and he who loves Me will be loved by My Father, and I will love him and will disclose Myself to him." Judas (not Iscariot) said to Him, "Lord, what then has happened that You are going to disclose Yourself to us and not to the world?" Jesus answered and said to him,* **"If anyone loves Me, he will keep My word; and My Father will love him, and We will come to him and make Our abode with him.** *He who does not love Me does not keep My words; and the word which you hear is not Mine, but the Father's who sent Me. These things I have spoken to you while abiding with you. But* **the Helper, the Holy Spirit,** *whom the Father will send in My name,* **He will teach you all** *things, and bring to your remembrance all that I said to you. Peace I leave with you; My peace I give to you; not as the world gives do I give to you. Do not let your heart be troubled, nor let it be fearful. You heard that I said to you, 'I go away, and I will come to you.' If you loved Me, you would have rejoiced because I go to the Father, for the Father is greater than I. Now I have told you before it happens, so that when it happens, you may believe. I will not speak much more with you, for the ruler of the world is coming, and he has nothing in Me; but **so that the world may know that I love the Father, I do exactly as the Father commanded Me.** Get up, let us go from here."*

(John 14:1-31, NASB, emphasis added)

Shifting to Your True Purpose

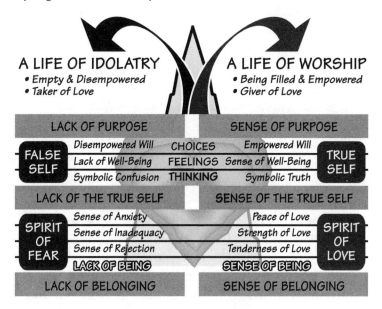

To love Jesus is to obey Jesus. Men and women of the Lord, rise up for the cause of Christ. He will be with you to the end, and He is the beginning of your life to come! Welcome to the spiritual homecoming party!

Personal Journaling and Small Group Questions
Spiritual Homecoming Assignment Twelve

Personal Journaling Questions
1. How did Paul minister as a spiritual mother?
2. How does honoring the feminine in the church restore receptivity?
3. How did Paul minister as a spiritual father?
4. How does honoring the masculine in the church restore empowerment?
5. How did Paul minister as a spiritual brother?
6. Spend time in your small group community discussing each aspect of a Cross-centered small group from Stage Twelve. Discuss how you would like your group to function in light of each of the five Cross-centered characteristics.

Small Group Questions
1. What... are the key truths that stood out to you in this stage?
2. Why... do you need to know these truths?
3. How... do you apply these truths to your life?
4. Your pain... What pain does this stage reveal in your life?
5. Your sin... What are you doing with your pain?
6. Repentance... What do you need to do differently?
7. Prayer... What do you need to ask God for help with?

If you are not in a small group, consider talking to several close friends about your spiritual homecoming journey and asking them if they would be interested in spending time together, encouraging and supporting one another in your spiritual journeys.

Postlude to a Journey
Living out Your Spiritual Homecoming

As I close, I would like to end this book on a personal note about my own spiritual homecoming. C. S. Lewis states that God uses pain as a megaphone to get our attention. Like many, I too lived in the trance of the walking dead. With physical death, our human spirit is separated from our human body. However, with spiritual death, our human spirit is separated from God's Spirit eternally. My medical crisis with cancer was part of the wake-up call that saved my life both physically and spiritually. Cancer became a gift to me and was actually one of the best things that ever happened to me.

As you may recall, in listening prayer one day I sensed the Lord directing me to go and see a urologist. The urologist I saw in Minneapolis was very kind, gentle, and competent. He said, "Paul, do you realize your PSA results have been misinterpreted by your clinic for four years and there is a high probability you have prostate cancer?" That morning, I was filled with fear, and death became a reality that I did not think I would have to think about until I was old.

My oldest brother, Dr. Errol Singh, happens to be a urological surgeon. I was very frustrated with the medical community about misinterpreting my PSA blood work for four years, so I asked my brother, whom I trusted, if he would do my biopsy. After he received the results, he flew from Columbus, Ohio, to Minneapolis, Minnesota, to tell Beth and me the news that I did have prostate cancer.

At age 44, and with no family history of cancer, I was already in stage three of the cancer and had a grade four tumor. A grade one cancer tumor is like a baby kitten, and grade five is like an aggressive lion ready to eat you alive. I was shocked and terrified to realize how advanced my cancer was. A grade four could spread to the rest of my body like wildfire. At that moment, I was desperate for hope.

315

Hope
by Janelle Jakubowski

Scared and trembling, I walk down these halls
Waiting for my name to be called.
As my heart starts to race, I wonder what I might hear;
Will these words give me hope or will they bring despair?

Won't you bring hope, can I have life?
Lord, I'm not ready for this.
Won't you bring hope, I want to have life;
Lord, won't you let me live?
Lord, let me live.

I don't understand how this could be;
I've watched others suffer, now it's me.
I want to run, I want to hide, I can't seem to shake this fear;
How will I ever make it through, Oh Jesus, tell me you are here.

Won't you bring hope, can I have life?
Lord, I'm not ready for this.
Won't you bring hope, I want to have life;
Lord, won't you let me live?
Lord, let me live.

My eyes are clouded by fear, I cannot see you;
My mind keeps struggling with, is this really true?
My will to live is so strong, but what can I do;
Oh Jesus, tell me that you are...
Holding me....

Won't you bring hope, can I have life?
Lord guide me through this;
Won't you bring hope, I want to have life;
Lord, won't you let me live?
Lord, let me live.[34]

Beth and I wept that evening, uncertain what would become of my life. Prior to this diagnosis, I had been in excellent health. Now my wife was faced with the possibility of raising five young children by herself. I struggled between denial and anger that this was happening to me. These are the moments we are desperate to hear God's voice. Had God been speaking to me about my health for years and I refused to listen? I wondered and tried to understand it all.

My first task was to tell my five young children. My oldest son was thirteen at the time, and my youngest daughter was just five. I decided to tell my two girls that Sunday morning at the zoo, and I would tell my three boys that evening. However, as the girls and I left for the day, the boys immediately went to Beth and demanded to know what was going on with me. Beth said that they should directly ask me when I came home. However, my sons, persisted with Beth and finally figured it out, so she immediately called me. Life seemed to be going so fast!

When you start to awaken from the robotic trance we so easily fall into, you realize how powerless and helpless you are with the chaos and brokenness of this world. As you start to see your smallness within suffering, you finally get your first glimpse of God's greatness within the universe. Why does suffering and pain finally break the trance? The gift to go from spiritual blindness to spiritual sight brings gratefulness. However, in our human arrogance, sometimes it takes suffering to realize that there is a living, eternal God, whether we can see Him or not.

The girls and I had a wonderful day at Como Zoo in St. Paul. It was a beautiful, sunny August day. My daughters and I were having a blast on our father-daughter date. How could I spoil such a great time together by breaking this painful news to them? I realized this could be our last season together. The possibility that I might not live to be a long-term father, that I might not walk my girls down the aisle one day, that I might not be there in the hospital when they gave birth to their own children was the hardest for me to bear. The fragility of humanity seemed more

317

evident the further I went on this journey of cancer, which I never signed up for. I had an internal scream...WHY is this happening to me GOD?! Where are you? Did I move away from you? This all seemed so maddening.

After the zoo, I took the girls out to lunch. Juliana, only five years old, looked at me without batting an eye and said, "Dad, do you have cancer?" I was stunned that what was so difficult for me to express, she simply and easily asked. I said yes and assured the girls I would be okay just like their cousin, Drew. Drew had also battled cancer and had successfully come through it the year before. I think our children are the ones who keep our hearts tender in times of tragedy. They can be filled with God's peace when we offer them God's tenderness and strength within the broken pieces of our lives.

When the surgery was over, my Mayo Clinic physician said, "Paul, it is a miracle you had a biopsy at such a young age and without any history of cancer in your family. However, had you waited, you would have died in six to twelve months." I had mixed feelings at that moment. I was grateful to an awesome God who rescued me from death. I was also mad and disappointed about life. Is anything stable and secure on this planet? What's next? The bird flu, terrorist attacks, a nuclear explosion? After surgery, I was in awe of the mercy of the living God and incredibly grateful that God had saved my life! However, recovery was painful and humiliating. I couldn't take care of myself in basic ways. Once, I had been a strong provider and protector of my family. Now, Beth and the children helped me to change the catheter bag that I wore for nineteen days. I could not bend over due to the incision across my entire stomach. Beth was my night nurse in addition to her day job, with no breaks from this routine for months. Furthermore, we had to wait three months before we would even know whether the surgery had been successful. The best outcome would be if my PSA count was zero.

Those were the three longest months of my entire life and marriage. With all that God had done for me, you would have thought that I would have become a great man of faith. But the opposite happened. I entered into the most hellacious months of my spiritual journey. In this place, where death could be imminent, I couldn't seem to find my way to God. The fear of cancer returning consumed me every hour of every day, and it undermined all of my certainty about life after death. All of the guilt and shame of my life seemed to erupt at that time, and I felt so alone in the valley of the shadow of death. I pored over Psalm 23. Though I walk through the valley of death, I shall fear no evil. However, I was overcome by fear. All my Christian maturity seemed to evaporate, and I was angry that this had happened to me. I was also angry that my faith seemed immature and weak in crisis.

As I lived in the valley of the shadow of death, fears haunted me. What if they did not get all the cancer cells and just one remaining cell could spread like wildfire throughout the rest of my mortal body? I sunk into a spiritual depression. Where was this living God in my greatest time of need and fear? Why could I not find and experience the hand of God that had been with me in the foundational times of my faith? Even though God's Spirit had alerted me to the cancer, not everyone is healed of cancer. In fact, many cancer patients die. The uncertainty seemed to be killing me as the cancer had attempted to do. Even with all of my training as a psychologist and a pastor, I could not pull myself out of the valley of the shadow of death. I did not know about spiritual depression until Valerie McIntyre helped me to identify it. I knew as a psychologist that to work through an issue, you first had to identify it. At that moment, there was hope in working through with God what had seemed vague and ambiguous.

When I had struggled as a college student, doubting my security in Christ, 1 John 5:11-12 had ministered to me, and it did again in my battle with cancer.

> *And the testimony is this, that God has given us eternal life, and this life is in His Son. **He who has the Son has the life;** he who does not have the Son of God does not have the life.*
>
> *(1 John 5:11-12, NASB, emphasis added)*

319

I knew I had accepted the Son of God into my life. He who has the Son has life. I opened the door of my heart and invited Jesus in during my college years. Now, at age 44, I had to cling to that truth, and it started me back on the road to my Abba Father. I knew Jesus would bring me to the Father, and the Father would eventually release the gifts of the Holy Spirit back into my life. I really longed to have the gift of peace that only God could offer me.

After three months, my PSA report was zero. The surgery had been a success. Yet, in spite of this jubilant news, I continued to struggle with spiritual depression. It lasted for about two years. It was a painfully slow recovery both physically and spiritually. But I was making my way back to my Abba God. By daily talking with Him about the issues behind my guilt and shame, incident by incident, I began to reconnect with Him. He displaced the fear in my heart with His love. It was a long and difficult process. "Lordship" took on a brand-new meaning for me. Louis Palau says that when God's will intersects your will and you die to your will and surrender to God's will you are taking up your Cross daily. During these two years of spiritual depression, I had to choose to die to fear and to surrender to faith in God. Many days, I struggled very poorly. I wondered if this gospel was really true. I knew in my head the gospel was true, but my heart was paralyzed with fear.

In my season of spiritual depression, I had a few friends who faithfully listened to me and allowed me to cry like a baby before them as my life seemed to be unraveling before their eyes. These were friends who loved me without any judgments of how poorly I was fighting or how much I was struggling. They would lay hands on me and pray for Beth, the children, and me. My community of faith helped to disrupt the intensity of fear in my human spirit, confirming to me that we were not designed to walk this journey alone.

My two mentors, Dr. Richard Averbeck and Dr. John Mackett, sacrificially stood with me during the times that my faith seemed to be unraveling. They listened, counseled, and prayed for me. As

I lived in uncertainty of the outcome of my life, my community gently lived out the certainty of God's love for me. This was the vital bridge back to Jesus that I needed. At those moments, Jesus brought me back to my Abba Father. Those were also the moments that the Father sent His Holy Spirit to comfort me. Taking life one day at a time, with a few who loved me, brought me back to the Father's love for me. Little did I know at the time that my faith was not unraveling during this time but growing stronger through a new life of brokenness.

I remember waking up one morning two years later and feeling good for the first time in a long time. That was the first day I thought that maybe the depression had begun to lift. On my way to the office, I went to a drive-through for a salad and a baked potato. An elderly grandmother delivered it to my car. She looked at me in my jeans and T-shirt and said, "Kid, I made that salad fresh—just for you!"

It was the first time in a long time that I had been called "kid." I just smiled from ear to ear and realized I was starting to feel like my old self again. I noticed what a clear blue, beautiful, sunny day it was. I felt normal for the first time as a cancer survivor. In fact, I did not feel like a cancer survivor that day. I felt the goodness of the Lord in the land of the living. My spirit was filled with awe and gratitude to God. The spiritual depression has not returned since then.

Reflecting on my struggle with spiritual depression, I realize that I had thought I loved God with all of my heart, strength, soul, and mind prior to cancer. But, I really did not. The truth is that I had found "life" in the earthly pursuits of my marriage, my children, my clinical work, and my ministry. Unknowingly, I had been in the quicksand of idolatry, finding the passion of my life primarily in relationships and activities other than God.

I realize now that God had used cancer as a lifeline to pull me out of that quicksand of idolatry. I saw that everything I valued in life might be lost in a heartbeat. The cancer ripped away the idols in

321

my life. I remember lying on the gurney prior to surgery knowing that everything that gave me life could be stripped away. At that moment, the only direction I could look was up. The One who could give me life was inviting me to life again. In that way, the cancer was God's severe mercy in stripping me of my pride and arrogance. I believe that He allowed it in order to save me from deadness of passion—from walking through life without life in me.

Nothing in this world is secure or stable. The only thing stable and secure is inviting Jesus, the Son of God, into your heart. Whatever happens to us in this lifetime, Jesus securely escorts us to the Father. The Father pours into us the Holy Spirit, who seals us for all eternity, and He can daily fill and empower us for this life. We will never escape the pain of life, but we can live through it with Him and escape the pain of eternal death by eternal life with Him.

There is a day when Jesus, the Son of God, will come back to earth. This will be your defining moment on the journey. Look at how the story will play out:

> *Immediately after the distress of those days, "the sun will be darkened, and the moon will not give its light; the stars will fall from the sky, and the heavenly bodies will be shaken." At that time the sign of the Son of Man will appear in the sky, and all the nations of the earth will mourn. They will see the Son of Man coming on the clouds of the sky, with power and great glory. And he will send his angels with a loud trumpet call, and they will gather his elect from the four winds, from one end of the heavens to the other.*
> *(Matthew 24:29-31, NIV)*

I have already started to prepare for this day because the suffering of cancer can either cause you to become bitter or resilient, preparing for the unknown. We do not know when Jesus is coming back; we just know that He is coming back. The passage continues:

322

*As it was in the days of Noah, so it will be at the coming of the Son of Man. For in the days before the flood, people were eating and drinking, marrying and giving in marriage, up to the day Noah entered the ark; and **they knew nothing about what would happen** until the flood came and took them all away. **That is how it will be at the coming of the Son of Man.** Two men will be in the field; one will be taken and the other left. Two women will be grinding with a hand mill; one will be taken and the other left. Therefore **keep watch,** because **you do not know on what day your Lord will come.***

(Matthew 24:37-42, NIV, *emphasis added*)

A medical crisis can mature you very quickly. Beth and I have wept as we have watched little children dying of cancer. Many times, they have a maturity that surpasses even gray-haired adults. When they know they are going to die, they start to prepare for the next journey, regardless of how the adults in their world handle it. Matthew 24 is a picture of what will happen to all of us at some moment. Are you ready for that? It is worth thinking about now.

The gift of cancer forced me to be ready for my final day. It made me put my relationship with God before anything else, including my wife and kids. Now I passionately put my wife and children before my work and ministry because every day with them is a day I might not have had.

I now see the greatness of God and am growing in awe for who He is. I also now see what God has done for me and am developing a fuller sense of gratitude. I can love my family with a new surrender because I understand God's love more deeply. My previous demand to be loved is transforming into a desire to love others. Each day of my spiritual homecoming, I long to receive God's tenderness of love, strength of love, and peace of love. Each day I get to live, I want to offer that tenderness, strength, and peace to them.

323

It took cancer to get me off the treadmill of "doing" in life. Today, I realize that it is a gift to be a husband and to be a father.

God offers to fill you with His tenderness, strength, and peace. However, you need to lay down your idols and seek His face. This passage in Ephesians tells us what the living God wants to fill us with:

> For this reason I kneel before the Father, from whom his whole family in heaven and on earth derives its name. I pray that out of his glorious riches he may **strengthen you with power** through his Spirit in your inner being, so that Christ may dwell in your hearts through faith. And I pray that you, being **rooted and established in love**, may have power, together with all the saints, to grasp how wide and long and high and deep is the love of Christ, and to know this love that surpasses knowledge—that you may be **filled to the measure of all the fullness of God.** Now to him who is able to do immeasurably more than all we ask or imagine, according to his power that is at work within us, to him be glory in the church and in Christ Jesus throughout all generations, for ever and ever! Amen.
>
> (Ephesians 3:14-21, NIV, emphasis added)

When you are filled with the tenderness of God's love, you become rooted and established in love with power to grasp the dimensions of the love of Christ. This brings together the head and heart of the believer to experience all the fullness of God's love, strength, and peace. This is how the miracle of restoring your sense of belonging and being occurs.

> But you will **receive power when the Holy Spirit comes on you;** and you will be my witnesses in Jerusalem, and in all Judea and Samaria, and to the ends of the earth.
>
> (Act 1:8, NIV, emphasis added)

After my battle with cancer, my fears were finally dispelled by experiencing the truth of God's love for me. Because I have the Son I have life. To give up my idolatry means to live a life of worshiping God. This is where the power of Acts 1:8 can transform the life of the new or old believer. But, you have to choose to turn from your idolatry (your addictions and co-addictions) and humbly turn to your Abba Daddy, who awaits you!

God can redeem your suffering in ways beyond belief and be your comfort in your suffering.

> Praise be to the God and Father of our Lord Jesus Christ, **the Father of compassion and the God of all comfort, who comforts us in all our troubles,** so that we can comfort those in any trouble with the comfort we ourselves have received from God.
> (2 Corinthians 1:3-4, NIV, emphasis added)

Then, He uses us in each other's lives to extend the same comfort from God that we have personally experienced. God takes what Satan means for evil and turns it into something miraculously good. We cannot control what happens to us. However, by the power of Christ living within us, we can control how we respond.

Cancer has rearranged my earthly priorities and sharpened my eternal sight. God not only exposed my idolatry and saved me from it, but He reminded me that His greater mercy toward me is that He saved me from Hell.

A spiritual homecoming is about a sense of eternal belonging to our Abba Father and a sense of eternal being. The final homecoming will be a celebratory wedding party, worshiping the King of the universe, with the finest food and drink available, uniting family and friends in perfect love. The spectacular music of the universe and the passionate dance of togetherness will hold us in God's eternal embrace of tenderness, strength, and peace.

We do not know the day or the hour in which we will face God. Make sure you are ready now. The abundant life of a follower of Christ does not start in the next life—it starts now! We live now with a foretaste of the greater celebration to come. A foretaste of the inconceivable joy and fulfillment that will be our spiritual homecoming banquet, our wedding to the Son, our eternity in Heaven, adoring the King of Kings and Lord of Lords.

I pray you have chosen to embark on your spiritual homecoming even in the midst of suffering, betrayals, or uncertainties of your life. This journey is not a quick fix. It may take several years of surrendering at the Cross to finally experience real freedom, healing, restoration, and transformation in your life. Your Abba Father will give you strength to persevere toward Him in those years. But greater than this portion of your journey is your lifetime journey toward the freedom, joy, and awe that you will know in the life to come.

> *But there's far more to life for us. We're citizens of high heaven! We're waiting the arrival of the Savior, the Master, Jesus Christ, who will transform our earthy bodies into glorious bodies like his own.* **He'll make us beautiful and whole** *with the same powerful skill by which he is putting everything as it should be, under and around him.*
>
> *(Philippians 3:20-21, MSG, emphasis added)*

Hear this awesome description of the return of Christ from the book of Revelation:

> *Then the angel showed me the river of the water of life, as clear as crystal, flowing from the throne of God and of the Lamb down the middle of the great street of the city. On each side of the river stood the tree of life, bearing twelve crops of fruit, yielding its fruit every month. And the leaves of the tree are for the healing of the nations. No longer will there be any curse. The throne of God and of the Lamb will be in the city, and*

his servants will serve him. They will see his face, and his name will be on their foreheads. There will be no more night. They will not need the light of a lamp or the light of the sun, for the Lord God will give them light. And they will reign for ever and ever. The angel said to me, **"These words are trustworthy and true.** *The Lord, the God of the spirits of the prophets, sent his angel to show his servants the things that must soon take place."*

"Behold, I am coming soon! *Blessed is he who keeps the words of the prophecy in this book."*

I, John, am the one who heard and saw these things. And when I had heard and seen them, I fell down to worship at the feet of the angel who had been showing them to me. But he said to me, "Do not do it! I am a fellow servant with you and with your brothers the prophets and of all who keep the words of this book. **Worship God!"**

Then he told me, "Do not seal up the words of the prophecy of this book, because the time is near. Let him who does wrong continue to do wrong; let him who is vile continue to be vile; let him who does right continue to do right; and let him who is holy continue to be holy."

"Behold, I am coming soon! My reward is with me, and I will give to everyone according to what he has done. *I am the Alpha and the Omega, the First and the Last, the Beginning and the End."*

Blessed are those who wash their robes, that they may have the right to the tree of life *and may go through the gates into the city. Outside are the dogs, those who practice magic arts, the sexually immoral, the murderers, the idolaters and everyone who loves and practices falsehood.*

"I, Jesus, have sent my angel to give you this testimony for the churches. I am the Root and the Offspring of David, and the bright Morning Star."

The Spirit and the bride say, "Come!" And let him who hears say, "Come!" **Whoever is thirsty, let him come; and whoever wishes, let him take the free gift of the water of life.**

I warn everyone who hears the words of the prophecy of this book: If anyone adds anything to them, God will add to him the plagues described in this book. And if anyone takes words away from this book of prophecy, God will take away from him his share in the tree of life and in the holy city, which are described in this book.

He who testifies to these things says, **"Yes, I am coming soon."**

Amen. Come, Lord Jesus.

The grace of the Lord Jesus be with God's people. Amen.

                    (Revelation 22, NIV, emphasis added)

Does your heart soar with joy at the prospect of the Son of God's return? Or, does it stir up fear? Or, are you indifferent? Whoever is thirsty, let him come; and whoever wishes, let him take the free gift of the water of life. I pray that you will not be indifferent, that you will not be immobilized by fear, but that you will make your spiritual homecoming journey to your Abba Father.

The invitation is open to you right now. When you accept Jesus Christ as your Lord, your Abba Father places within your spirit a Spirit of adoption, adoption for this life and for the life to come. Remember the verse from Stage Five that paints a picture of how you can receive your sense of belonging and being:

Here I am! I stand at the door and knock. If anyone **hears** *my voice and* **opens** *the door,* **I will come in** *and eat with him, and he with me.*

(Revelation 3:20, NIV, emphasis added)

If you have never opened the door of your life to Jesus Christ, the Son of God, you can do it now by a very simple prayer.

Jesus, I am a sinner who has betrayed You and others. Today, Jesus, I choose to follow you as my Lord and Savior. Please come into my heart today. Fill me now with the power of the Holy Spirit so that I can listen and obey you for the rest of my journey. Abba Father, I long to live a new life in the Holy Spirit. Thank you for your love, strength, and peace. Enable me to worship You all the days of my life until you take me into eternal life.
Amen.

If you have ever said a prayer like this, you have been spiritually adopted as a son or daughter of God—your Abba Daddy. In this life, His adoption means living with a sense of belonging and being; living in the true self, not the false self; living a life of passion, giftedness, and purpose today. Living in intimacy with your Abba Father. In the life to come, His adoption means coming home to a reunion celebration like no other—the wedding supper of the Lord Jesus Christ. A wedding in which we, the followers of Jesus Christ, are the bride.

If you have been a believer for years but are tired and exhausted from a life of "doing," may you learn to simply rest in your Abba Daddy. May He refill you with a deeper sense of belonging and being than you have ever known and empower you to go forth "doing" in His name with great passion, giftedness, and purpose for His glory! May you know the God of the universe as your intimate Father and may He rekindle your spirit with His love, strength, and peace for the rest of your journey.

329

Worship is the key to deliverance, healing, and restoration. One of my favorite worship songs is "Make Me Holy."

Make Me Holy
by Janelle Jakubowski

Lift my face to your Holy gaze
Place in me a hunger and thirst for your ways
Jesus you are the prince of peace, the Holy One,
God's own son
You are Holy, make me holy
You are Holy, make me holy

Draw my heart close to you
Help me move in the ways that you do
Jesus you are the prince of peace, the Holy one
God's own son
You are Holy, make me holy
You are Holy, make me holy[35]

I pray that He will draw you to Himself and quench your spiritual thirst with His water. I pray that you will lay down your life of idolatry for a life of awe and gratitude—of worship. Friend, a life of worship is a life transformed. May you be transformed.

Presenting the God of Love and Strength

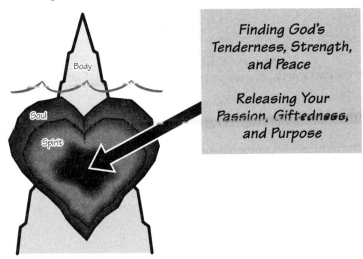

Body

Soul

Spirit

Finding God's
Tenderness, Strength,
and Peace

Releasing Your
Passion, Giftedness,
and Purpose

One thing God has spoken,
two things have I heard:
*that you, O God, are **STRONG**,*
*and that you, O Lord, are **LOVING**.*
Surely you will reward each person
according to what he has done.
                    (Psalm 62:11-12, NIV, emphasis added)

This is the God of love and strength. This is the God who restored my sense of belonging and being. This is the God who fills me with awe and gratitude. This is the God who I want my children and their next generations to know and experience. This is the God of life everlasting. This is the God that invites you back home into His arms of love and strength.

I commend to you my life verse as you make your spiritual homecoming:

So do not fear, for I am with you;
Do not be dismayed, for I am your God.
*I will **strengthen** you and **help** you;*
*I will **uphold** you with my righteous right hand.*
                    (Isaiah 41:10, NIV, emphasis added)

On this journey with you,

Paul Singh

Acknowledgments

The person who has theologically and clinically influenced me the most, this side of heaven, is my mentor and friend, Richard E. Averbeck, PhD, LPC. If you ever have the privilege of meeting Dr. Averbeck, you will encounter a humble and wise man who has been filled and empowered by God's love and strength and authentically loves God and people through a daily life of worship.

Dick, it has been an honor to have you as a spiritual father throughout the last twenty years. Thank you for being there during my struggles with cancer. Thank you for how you and Melinda have demonstrated your love for Beth, my five children, and me with a tenderness and strength of love that has blessed our marriage, family, and ministry. If you had not sacrificially imparted the gospel to me through your very life, meeting weekly with me for the last twenty years, this book would not have been birthed. In many ways, the readers are hearing your heart through my heart. Your passion to be impressed by the living God is contagious, and your commitment to the lordship of Christ has been disruptive but gracious! Thank you for showing me the love of our Abba Daddy through friendship. Melinda Averbeck, Beth and I really love you and are grateful for how you created time for Dick to mentor me within the fullness of your lives. Thank you! May the Holy Spirit continue to bless you both, your marriage, your family, and your generations to come!

Dr. Larry Crabb has also influenced my spiritual model for how to professionally care for people. I did my clinical training in graduate school under Dr. Larry Crabb at Grace Theological Seminary in Indiana. Larry taught me that the core issue in the journey is to love. The greatest commandment is to love God and love your neighbor as yourself. Larry has a deep heart to equip people in living out the greatest commandment. Thank you, Larry, for imparting this vision to me.

Dr. Dan Allender also oversaw the graduate program when I was at Grace. Much of my understanding of betrayal, false relational styles, the impact of sexual abuse in our lives, holy sexuality, and intimate worship stem from Dan's training. Thank you, Dan, for conveying the biblical foundation and a passionate heart for awe and gratitude toward a powerful and living, loving God.

Leanne Payne has also influenced my work. I initially met Leanne at one of her Pastoral Care Ministries conferences. This was by far the best Christian conference I had ever attended. Leanne skillfully takes people directly to the Cross to release their sin and pain. In return they receive God's forgiveness, cleansing, and the gifts of the Holy Spirit. Leanne also taught me much about embracing God's presence, listening prayer, and daily renewing my baptism. Thank you, Leanne, for teaching me how to find my way to the Cross to experience the magnificent and sacrificial love of Christ.

Thank you to Valerie McIntyre with Leanne Payne's Pastoral Care Ministry. Val, your life is marked by deep, biblical reality and conviction. The transparency of your life is a breath of fresh air to the culture and the Church. Your healing gifts have personally blessed me and shaped my ministry. Blessings to you, Mark, and your daughter.

Dr. John Mackett has been a great friend and faithful, healing, prayer partner for many years. His sacrificial heart for God has strength of tenderness that draws many into the living grace of God. John, thank you for the years you have weekly prayed for me and for the times you stood with me during my struggles with cancer. John, you have humbly modeled the profound and yet simple reality of how the presence of Christ living within us can bring the believer into deliverance, healing, restoration, and transformation. May God continue to refresh you, Betsy, and your boys in spirit, soul, and body.

I came to Christ through the Navigators in 1979 at the University of Minnesota. The ministry of The Navigators is to know Christ and to make Him known. Since its inception, certain worldwide values have characterized the Navigator ministry:

- the passion to know and love Christ;
- the essential place of the Holy Spirit and prayer in our lives and ministry;
- the Scripture as foundational to life and ministry;
- the worth, dignity, and potential of all persons;
- authentic, grace-based relationships rooted in love for one another;
- personal transformation to Christ-likeness;
- spiritual generations of laborers living out Christ among the lost; and
- the place of families and relational networks in discipling the nations.

I am very grateful that this organization found me as a college student at the University of Minnesota. Thank you to Jerry Zeidler who led me to Christ and lives out the gospel through a life of love and friendship. Thank you to Tom and Jenny Board who equipped me in the discipleship ministry. In many ways, the conviction for this book was birthed in 1979, when I responded to Matthew 28:19-20: *"Go therefore and make disciples of all the nations, baptizing them in the name of the Father and the Son and the Holy Spirit, teaching them to observe all that I commanded you; and lo, I am with you always, even to the end of the age."*

Thank you to Sally Figini, my first biblical counselor who helped me to boldly face the depths of the pain and sin in my heart with incredible truth and grace. Sally, your life modeled to me the tenderness and strength of the gospel in ways that brought me to experiencing grace at the foot of the Cross. Thank you for your wisdom, patience, and prayers. May you, Steve, and your boys continue to know and experience the extravagant love and power of Christ within the journey this side of heaven!

Thank you to Dr. Carla Waterman for teaching me the reality of renewing my baptism. Carla, your heart of biblical competency and joyful compassion is a refreshing blend in teaching and ministry. You have tenderness of strength in your character and are an excellent biblical lecturer and role model to the women of this culture and the "Church at large." Blessings to you, Wyatt, and your son.

Thank you to Marsha Stoltzmann, the conference director of "Rekindling Your Spirit" ministries. Marsha, your vision for the body of Christ to work and live in unity has been a gift that you have imparted to our ministry team and conferences. You have extremely high personal integrity and passion that are off the charts for God and His people. You and Bill are dear friends. May God continue to bless your health, family, and ministry.

Thank you to Janelle Jakubowski, the worship leader for "Rekindling Your Spirit" ministries. Janelle, you and Greg have been a Holy Spirit blessing to the conferences. Your personal integrity of worship is reflected in how you bring many into holy, intimate worship of our King. Thank you for how you and Greg co-labor with Beth and me in this inner healing ministry. May God richly bless your first worship CD, *In the Light of You*. May the Holy Spirit continue to fill and empower you, Greg, and your children with faith, hope, and love.

Thank you to Doug and Peggy Lang for your faithful friendship and co-laboring with Beth and me in ministry. May your latter years be your best years! Blessings to you both as grandparents and blessings to your children and your grandbabies! Have fun!

Thank you to the "Rekindling Your Spirit" ministry team for your kind friendship and sacrificial service to our King! I could not want a better community to do ordinary life in than our "work hard-play hard" community. Your friendships mean a lot to Beth and me. May the Holy Spirit continue to fill and empower each one of you, your spouses, and families with His extravagant love and holy power!

Thank you to Scott Straw for faithfully creating my PowerPoint slides for the last decade of conferences. Scott, your integrity and creativity is refreshing. God has truly given you a great gift in expressing His truth and life in the Spirit through the art of illustration. Deep blessings to you, Kathy, and the boys!

Thank you to Heather and Douglas Dart for helping me wordsmith and order the slides. You both have given sacrificially to this project amidst a growing family. Heather, thank you for your contribution to the sexuality stage. You have a brilliant mind and a compassionate heart. Blessings to you both and your girls!

Thank you to Guy Mahmarian with Vision Van Gogh, and to his graphic arts designer, Lisa Lundquist, for the years of marketing design they have done for "Rekindling Your Spirit" ministries. Guy and Lisa, you both have an amazing mark of excellence within the artistry of your passion and giftedness! Your work invites people to look at the beauty and strength of the gospel. May the Lord God continue to bless the work of your hands in bringing greater glory to the Cross!

Thank you to my sister-in-law, Cheryl Smith, for designing the illustrator slides and putting this entire book together. Cheryl, thank you for your sacrificial passion and giftedness to help advance the cause of Christ! May God continue to bless you, Joseph, and your four children!

Thank you to Kraig Skistad for walking the journey with me these last ten years! Kraig, you are a very competent and gifted, Christ-centered therapist. I have appreciated your friendship and your passion for the glory of God to be revealed in the land. Kraig, your heart has brought many into the Kingdom through your biblical counseling. May you enjoy living out your passion, giftedness, and purpose on behalf of our King! You and Sara are friends. Blessings to you two and your children.

Thank you to Marilyn Gnekow, with the Navigators, for your biblical consultations and editing giftedness throughout this book project. Marilyn, you also live with a tenderness of strength that has brought much fruit to the kingdom of God. Your life and ministry reveal the faithfulness of God to this generation. You are a dear friend to Beth and me. May God continue to bless your health and life, granting you the desires of your heart!

Thank you to Lisa Harrell for your biblical and clinical bantering about various topics throughout the book. Lisa, you will be an excellent Christian therapist and spiritual director. May the journey bring you the deepest longings of your heart.

Thank you to Connie Bendickson, author of *The Healthy Moms Healthy Families Handbook*. Your passion for healthy food has inspired and challenged me post-cancer to move toward a plant-based diet. Tofu, anyone? Connie, may the Lord bless you, Rich, and your two children with health and a lot of fun together as a family!

Thank you to Gail Lossing for doing the first edit. Gail, you are a very patient and talented editor. Thank you for your grace as we started to craft this project. You are extremely gifted and also have a brilliant mind. May God continue to bless you, Craig, and your children.

Thank you to Patsy Brekke for believing in this project and sacrificially editing, time and again. Patsy, your heart of compassion for the Lord and His people is evident as you paint God's glory into this broken culture with your passion and giftedness. May the Holy Spirit continue to fill and empower you and your family! May God also abundantly bless you and your children with His extravagant love, strength, and peace!

Thank you to Terry McDowell for sacrificially taking on the final copy editing. Terry, you have a brilliant mind and excellent editorial giftings. I pray that you will experience many times of refreshment in the Spirit as you take time to relax at the North Shore.

Thank you to Sheree Meader for doing the final edit of this book. Your Christ-centered passion and vision to walk in step with the Spirit is refreshing! Your work flows from the very life of God that dwells within your spirit. Sheree, thank you! May you, John, Krista, and your older children experience the abundance of God's goodness beyond what you could ask or imagine.

Thank you, Susan Brill, my senior editor, for your editorial competence and biblical depth in helping me to weave this book into its final form. Susan, throughout this book project, it has been clear to me that as you edit, you are very sensitive to the leading of the Holy Spirit. Your editorial work is authentically seasoned with grace and truth. This book was brought into form and life by your intercessory heart, your passion for excellence, and your commitment to Christ-centered integrity. May God continue to release your passion, giftedness, and purpose into the culture and the body of Christ!

Finally, thank you to my mother and father for showing me God's love and strength in so many ways. Dad, thank you for your strength of vision to bring our family to the United States. You sacrificed much to bless us with your heart of protection and provision. Mom, your tender relationship with Christ has shaped the inner, healing heart of my ministry with the mercy and compassion of God. In your seventies, you are radically living out the gospel on the mission field! Mom and Dad, may your latter years be your best years! I love you both so much!

Endnotes:

#	Pg #	Reference
1	5	Adapted from graduate school teaching of Dr. Richard Averbeck.
2	12	Adapted from graduate school teaching of Dr. Dan B. Allender. See also his book, *The Wounded Heart* (Colorado Springs, CO: NavPress, 1990).
3	27	Craig R. Lockwood, *Falling Forward: The Pursuit of Sexual Purity* (Kansas City, MO: Desert Stream Press, 2000), 134.
4	31	Craig R. Lockwood, *Falling Forward: The Pursuit of Sexual Purity* (Kansas City, MO: Desert Stream Press, 2000), 145.
5	33	Dr. Dan B. Allender, *The Wounded Heart* (Colorado Springs, CO: NavPress, 1990), 79.
6	66	This section is adapted from the teaching of Dr. Richard Averbeck.
7	78	Psalm 139:23-24, MSG.
8	78	Jeremiah 33:3, NASB.
9	95	Dr. D. James Kennedy, Evangelism Explosion International, a Lay-witnessing Training Program (1962).
10	98	Dr. D. James Kennedy, Evangelism Explosion International, a Lay-witnessing Training Program (1962).
11	109	*The Breastplate of St. Patrick*, http://leannepayne.com/home/stpatrickmenu.php?view=hymn
12	129	Adapted from graduate school teaching of Dr. Dan B. Allender. See also his book, *The Wounded Heart* (Colorado Springs, CO: NavPress, 1990).
13	153	John-Paul Singh, at age 10, desired to help me finish writing the book.
14	153	Adapted from graduate school teaching of Dr. Larry Crabb. See also his book, *Inside Out* (Colorado Springs, CO: NavPress, 1998).

#	Pg #	Reference
15	155	This section is adapted from a message (*Elijah: A Man Like Us* — James 5:16-18), given by Dave Johnson, Senior Pastor, Church of the Open Door, Maple Grove, MN.
16	178	This is part of a prayer that Leanne Payne uses during her ministry and an explanation of what some expect.
17	193	Dr. Dan B. Allender and Tremper Longman, *Intimate Allies* (Wheaton, IL: Tyndale House Publishers, Inc., 1995), 100.
18	195	Dr. Dan B. Allender and Tremper Longman, *Intimate Allies* (Wheaton, IL: Tyndale House Publishers, Inc., 1995), 98.
19	199	Adapted from graduate school teaching of Dr. Richard Averbeck.
20	207	Dr. Dan B. Allender and Tremper Longman, *Intimate Allies* (Wheaton, IL: Tyndale House Publishers, Inc., 1995), 309.
21	208	Dr. Dan B. Allender and Tremper Longman, *Intimate Allies* (Wheaton, IL: Tyndale House Publishers, Inc., 1995), 276 {Footnote}.
22	217	Dr. Dan B. Allender and Tremper Longman, *Intimate Allies* (Wheaton, IL: Tyndale House Publishers, Inc., 1995), 22.
23	221	Dr. Dan B. Allender and Tremper Longman, *Intimate Allies* (Wheaton, IL: Tyndale House Publishers, Inc., 1995), 347.
24	230	Taken from my graduate notes of Dr. Dan B. Allender's lectures.
25	232	Dr. Dan B. Allender and Tremper Longman, *Intimate Allies* (Wheaton, IL: Tyndale House Publishers, Inc., 1995), 154.
26	238	Taken from my graduate notes of Dr. Dan B. Allender's lectures.
27	238	Taken from my graduate notes of Dr. Dan B. Allender's lectures.

#	Pg #	Reference
28	243	Taken from my graduate notes of Dr. Dan B. Allender's lectures.
29	257	Bill Hybels, *Too Busy Not to Pray* (Downer's Grove, IL: InterVarsity Press, 1998), 44.
30	259	*Webster's Revised Unabridged Dictionary*, © 1913.
31	260	http://www.infoplease.com/ipa/A0922052.html
32	294	*Serenity Prayer*, attributed to Reinhold Niebuhr (1892-1971).
33	298	John and Stasi Eldredge, *Captivating: Unveiling the Mystery of a Woman's Soul* (Nashville, TN: Thomas Nelson, Inc., 2005).
34	317	Janelle Jakubowski, *Hope*, Janellesings, Remnant Music/ASCAP (2006).
35	330	Janelle Jakubowski, *Make Me Holy* on *In the Light of You* {CD}. Janellesings, Remnant Music/ASCAP (2006).